The Right Balance for Banks

Theory and Evidence on Optimal Capital Requirements

POLICY ANALYSES IN INTERNATIONAL ECONOMICS 107

The Right Balance for Banks

Theory and Evidence on Optimal Capital Requirements

POLICY ANALYSES IN INTERNATIONAL ECONOMICS 107

William R. Cline

PETERSON INSTITUTE FOR
INTERNATIONAL ECONOMICS

Washington, DC
June 2017

William R. Cline has been a senior fellow at the Peterson Institute for International Economics since 1981. During 1996–2001 while on leave from the Institute, he was deputy managing director and chief economist of the Institute of International Finance (IIF) in Washington, DC. From 2002 through 2011 he held a joint appointment with the Peterson Institute and the Center for Global Development, where he is currently senior fellow emeritus. Before joining the Peterson Institute, he was senior fellow, the Brookings Institution (1973–81); deputy director of development and trade research, office of the assistant secretary for international affairs, US Treasury Department (1971–73); Ford Foundation visiting professor in Brazil (1970–71); and lecturer and assistant professor of economics at Princeton University (1967–70). He is the author of several books, including *Managing the Euro Area Debt Crisis* (2014) and *Financial Globalization, Economic Growth, and the Crisis of 2007–09* (2010).

PETERSON INSTITUTE FOR INTERNATIONAL ECONOMICS
1750 Massachusetts Avenue, NW
Washington, DC 20036-1903
(202) 328-9000   FAX: (202) 328-5432
www.piie.com

Adam S. Posen, *President*
Steven R. Weisman, *Vice President for Publications and Communications*

Cover Design by Fletcher Design, Inc.—
Washington, DC
Cover Photo by ©vasilypetkov/Thinkstock
Printing by Versa Press

Printed in the United States of America
19   18   17   5   4   3   2   1

Library of Congress Cataloging-in-Publication Data
Names: Cline, William R., author. Title: The right balance for banks : theory and evidence on optimal capital requirements / William R. Cline. Description: Washington, DC : Peterson Institute for International Economics, [2017] | Includes bibliographical references. Identifiers: LCCN 2016035251 (print) | LCCN 2016048685 (ebook) | ISBN 9780881327212 | ISBN 9780881327229 Subjects: LCSH: Bank capital. | Asset requirements. | Banks and banking. | Bank failures—Prevention. | Financial crises—Prevention. Classification: LCC HG1616.C34 C55 2017 (print) | LCC HG1616.C34 (ebook) | DDC 332.1—dc23 LC record available at https://lccn.loc.gov/2016035251

This publication has been subjected to a prepublication peer review intended to ensure analytical quality. The views expressed are those of the author. This publication is part of the overall program of the Peterson Institute for International Economics, as endorsed by its Board of Directors, but it does not necessarily reflect the views of individual members of the Board or of the Institute's staff or management.
The Peterson Institute for International Economics is a private nonpartisan, nonprofit institution for rigorous, intellectually open, and indepth study and discussion of international economic policy. Its purpose is to identify and analyze important issues to make globalization beneficial and sustainable for the people of the United States and the world, and then to develop and communicate practical new approaches for dealing with them.
Its work is funded by a highly diverse group of philanthropic foundations, private corporations, and interested individuals, as well as income on its capital fund. About 35 percent of the Institute's resources in its latest fiscal year were provided by contributors from outside the United States. A list of all financial supporters is posted at https://piie.com/sites/default/files/supporters.pdf.

Contents

Preface

In the aftermath of the Great Recession and the financial crisis that caused it, we need to construct the right regulatory framework for US and international banks. The crisis revealed woefully inadequate bank capital reserves for dealing with shocks, especially in the less regulated and supervised investment banking sector, and rectifying this weakness has been central to international reform efforts. Basel III, adopted in 2010, has substantially increased the amount of equity capital banks must hold, especially banks large enough to qualify as global systemically important banks (G-SIBs). In this book, Senior Fellow William Cline asks whether this aspect of reform has gone far enough. Cline works from first principles to identify the optimal level of equity capital for banks, given the real world trade-off between greater safety and sacrifice of potential output (because higher lending costs could curb new investment). He concludes that the Basel III capital requirements are insufficient and should be increased by about one-third to arrive at this optimal level—which he argues is the right balance for banks and the economy.

Some other leading experts insist that the new capital requirements for banks should be increased by several-fold rather than by a substantial but limited fraction. In part, they base their recommendation on a theoretical argument by Nobel economists Franco Modigliani and Merton Miller, who suggest that increasing capital has little or no cost. The Modigliani-Miller (M&M) theorem says raising the proportion of a company's financing from expensive equity capital, and reducing the proportion from cheaper debt, will not affect the company's average cost of capital: Modigliani-Miller asserts investors will reward the firm with a lower unit cost of equity due to a reduction in risk from lower leverage. If this theorem breaks down in practice, however, requiring banks to hold far higher equity capital would push up their average cost of capital and consequently their lending rates. The result would be to reduce new investment by firms and thereby reduce the future stock of capital and output capacity of the economy. In chapter 3, Cline tests the Modigliani-Miller theorem for US banks and finds that only about one-half of the M&M offset attains in practice, so additional equity capital is not costless to the banks or the economy.

In chapter 4, Cline goes on to examine the costs and benefits of additional bank capital given the practical limits of Modigliani-Miller. He first calculates damages from past banking crises to estimate the economy-wide benefits from reducing the chances of a crisis. He estimates that the typical total cost of a banking crisis, including long-term effects, amounts to about two-thirds of one year's GDP. He similarly estimates that in the past three decades the risk of occurrence of a banking crisis in the advanced industrial economies has been about 2½ percent annually. He then uses estimates compiled by international regulators to measure the responsiveness of this crisis probability to the level of bank capital.

On the cost side, with his estimate of the M&M offset in hand, Cline calculates the additional cost to banks, and thus to corporate borrowers, that are imposed by successively higher levels of bank equity capital. He estimates that an increase in equity capital of 1 percent of total bank assets reduces the long-term level of GDP by 0.15 percent. In his analysis, the optimal capital ratio occurs where the marginal benefits to the economy from crisis avoidance are just equal to the marginal cost to the economy from output sacrificed because of lesser capital stock formation. His calculations place the optimal ratio at 7 to 8 percent of total assets, corresponding to 12 to 14 percent of risk-weighted assets. Cline's theoretically grounded findings turn out by independent means to be at the same levels as the median results for 16 other leading studies. Basel III capital requirements for the large banks, however, are slightly less than 10 percent of risk-weighted assets, so still too low.

The Institute has a long history of undertaking relevant policy studies on bank regulation as well as on financial stability more broadly. These studies include Cline's own books, *International Debt: Systemic Risk and Policy Response* (1984), *International Debt Reexamined* (1995), and *Financial Globalization, Economic Growth, and the Crisis of 2007-09* (2010); and Morris Goldstein's 1997 book *The Case for an International Banking Standard*, 1998 book *The Asian Financial Crisis: Causes, Cures, and Systemic Implications*, and 2017 book *Banking's Final Exam: Stress Testing and Bank-Capital Reform*. Other recent works include *Responding to Financial Crisis: Lessons from Asia Then, the*

United States and Europe Now (2013) edited by Adam Posen and Changyong Rhee, *From Stress to Growth: Strengthening Asia's Financial Systems in a Post-Crisis World* (2015) edited by Marcus Noland and Donghyun Park, and a number of shorter studies by Anna Gelpern, Simon Johnson, Adam Posen, Edwin Truman, and Nicolas Véron on financial stability and bank reform in the European Union and the United States.

The Peterson Institute for International Economics is a private nonpartisan, nonprofit institution for rigorous, intellectually open, and in-depth study and discussion of international economic policy. Its purpose is to identify and analyze important issues to making globalization beneficial and sustainable for the people of the United States and the world, and then to develop and communicate practical new approaches for dealing with them.

The Institute's work is funded by a highly diverse group of philanthropic foundations, private corporations, public institutions, and interested individuals, as well as by income on its capital fund. About 35 percent of the Institute's resources in our latest fiscal year were provided by contributors from outside the United States. A list of all our financial supporters for the preceding year is posted at http://piie.com/institute/supporters.pdf.

The Executive Committee of the Institute's Board of Directors bears overall responsibility for the Institute's direction, gives general guidance and approval to its research program, and evaluates its performance in pursuit of its mission. The Institute's President is responsible for the identification of topics that are likely to become important over the medium term (one to three years) that should be addressed by Institute scholars. This rolling agenda is set in close consultation with the Institute's research staff, Board of Directors, and other stakeholders.

The President makes the final decision to publish any individual Institute study, following independent internal and external review of the work. Interested readers may access the data and computations underlying the Institute publications for research and replication by searching titles at www.piie.com.

The Institute hopes that its research and other activities will contribute to building a stronger foundation for international economic policy around the world. We invite readers of these publications to let us know how they think we can best accomplish this objective.

ADAM S. POSEN
President
April 2017

Acknowledgments

For comments in peer reviews of the penultimate manuscript, I thank without implicating Tamim Bayoumi, Hans-Helmut Kotz, and Philip Turner. For comments on earlier drafts or portions of this study, I thank without implicating Olivier Blanchard, Barry Bosworth, José de Gregorio, Giovanni Dell'Ariccia, Joseph Gagnon, Morris Goldstein, Simon Johnson, Robert Lawrence, Paolo Mauro, Marcus Noland, Tomihiro Sugo, Edwin Truman, Ángel Ubide, Nicolas Verón, Lawrence White, and participants in a study group held on July 25, 2016. For excellent research assistance, I thank Fredrick Toohey and Abir Varma.

1

Overview

A financial sector crisis was at the heart of the 2007–09 Great Recession in the United States and most other industrial economies.[1] Since the crisis, policymakers have pursued regulatory reforms designed to strengthen the banking sector, in order to reduce the chances of repeating that economic disaster.

These reforms have focused on increasing the required level of equity capital of banks. For the largest banks, deemed "global systemically important banks" (G-SIBs), major economies have also agreed to require an additional layer of protection in the form of "total loss-absorbing capacity" (TLAC) that is approximately equal to the amount of equity capital required. The extra protection is in the form of subordinated debt and contingent convertible (CoCo) debt, which converts into equity if certain adverse thresholds are breached.

Apart from higher equity and other TLAC, the reforms have also included the introduction of yearly stress tests, in which bank supervisory agencies review whether banks could withstand adverse shocks to the economy. In the United States, reform has also included curtailment of proprietary trading (the "Volcker rule"), as well as the requirement that large banks develop "living wills" that permit orderly "resolution" (the managed winding-down of an effectively bankrupt bank) to avoid catastrophic collapses such as that of Lehman Brothers in 2008.

---

1. Among major high-income economies, only Australia, Canada, Finland, Japan, New Zealand, and Norway escaped a banking crisis in this period (although Japan experienced a crisis in the late 1990s). See table 4.1 in chapter 4.

Equity capital is important because it is the cushion of assets in excess of liabilities that can be drawn down before a bank hits the point of insolvency. Equity is obtained either by issuing new shares or retaining earnings (rather than paying them out in dividends). Since the Great Recession, banks have increased equity capital mainly through retained earnings rather than new issuance, which would dilute existing shareholders and, at least initially, would have been on relatively unfavorable terms given market conditions (see Cohen 2013).

In 1988 the Group of Ten advanced industrial countries adopted the first Basel Accord on minimum bank capital requirements, motivated in part by the need to create a level playing field among internationally active banks. The agreement set a minimum capital requirement of 8 percent of risk-weighted assets for bank "capital," generously defined to include intangible good will and certain subordinated debt.[2] A revised Basel II agreement in 2004 sought to refine the risk weighting of assets, including through the use of internal models of risk by (typically larger) banks themselves.

The Great Recession precipitated tougher rules. In late 2010 the Basel Committee on Banking Supervision issued the Basel III rules (BCBS 2010b). They effectively set a minimum of 7 percent of risk-weighted assets for most banks but use a much stricter definition of capital (tangible common equity) than Basel I and Basel II had. For G-SIBs the minimum was set at 9.5 percent.

In late 2015 the Basel III rules were extended to require TLAC amounting to 18 percent of risk-weighted assets for G-SIBs (FSB 2015c). New rules constraining the use of banks' internal models for estimating risk weights had been scheduled to be completed by the end of 2016. However, disagreement between European and US negotiators and uncertainties associated with the new administration in the United States left this important modification of the Basel rules still unfinished by April 2017.[3]

The purpose of this study is to quantify the costs and benefits to the economy from requiring additional bank capital in order to determine whether Basel III struck the right balance between increased financial system

---

2. However, core tier 1 capital excluding goodwill was to be at least 4 percent of risk-weighted assets. Tier 2 capital included hybrid instruments with equity-like characteristics as well as subordinated debt with maturity of at least five years. Risk weights were set at zero for sovereign debt of all OECD countries, and 50 percent for fully secured mortgage loans on residential property (BCBS 1988).

3. Bankers have called the prospective rules "Basel IV," implying a further increase in capital requirements. Regulators have resisted this sobriquet, arguing that the purpose of the revisions is to reduce disparities in risk-weight outcomes across banks' models, not to raise the overall average for capital ratios (Caroline Binham and Laura Noonan, "Basel Committee Fail to Sign off on Latest Bank Reform Measures," *Financial Times*, November 30, 2016). For further discussion, see chapter 7.

safety and potential costs to economic activity. In an early response, the Institute of International Finance (a leading global association of private financial firms) projected that the increase in borrowing costs imposed on economies by the new requirements would cause output in the main industrial countries to decline by about 3 percent from levels it would otherwise have reached by 2015 (IIF 2011, 55). At the opposite extreme, a study by two prominent academic experts argues that the new requirements are far too lenient. Admati and Hellwig (2013, 179) argue that banks should be required to hold 20 to 30 percent of their total assets as equity, which would amount to about 35 to 55 percent of risk-weighted assets for US and euro area banks.

There was thus nearly an order of magnitude difference between the implied optimal levels for equity capital in this technical dispute, an unusually wide divergence for a central variable of economic policy.[4] This gap cried out for further analysis.

Plan of the Study and Principal Findings

A core argument in the Admati-Hellwig view is that financial theory posits that there should be no cost at all from higher equity and less debt leverage because of the Modigliani-Miller (M&M) theorem whereby capital structure is "irrelevant" (Modigliani and Miller 1958). The proposition is that equity investors will be satisfied with a lower rate of return if the firm has more equity and less debt, because the riskiness of the firm will have declined, and that the resulting decline in the unit cost of equity investors demand will be just enough to offset the shift from low-cost debt to higher-cost equity. The first central question in this policy area, then, is whether this theorem is operationally reliable for banks or breaks down in practice.

Chapter 2 provides a critical review of the literature on capital requirements. Chapter 3 begins the quantitative analysis with an empirical test of the M&M theorem for US banks. With an estimate in hand for the effective degree of the M&M "offset" (extent to which higher quantity of equity is offset by lower unit cost), chapter 4 turns to quantification of benefits and costs of higher bank capital and identifies the optimal capital ratio. Chapter 5 addresses TLAC requirements, both surveying the literature and providing new evidence on the losses of the largest US banks in the Great Recession, to determine whether they had engaged in excessive risk taking as a result of too big to fail (TBTF) incentive distortions. Chapter 6 critiques the recent empirical literature maintaining that there is already too much

---

4. Using the 7 percent tangible common equity benchmark, the gap between Admati-Hellwig and Basel III was 5- to 8-fold in one direction, and there was a considerable gap between the IIF and Basel III in the opposite direction.

finance, based on statistical correlations of growth with indicators of financial depth. If it were the case that finance is excessive, the curbing of bank activity by higher capital requirements might bring a supplementary benefit by shrinking finance back to the optimal size, but the tests in chapter 6 do not support this implicit proposition. Chapter 7 summarizes the study's main findings.

The principal quantitative findings of this study are as follows:

- Only about 45 percent of the M&M risk offset attains in practice (chapter 3).

- Each percentage point increase in capital required relative to total assets (not risk-weighted assets) reduces the long-run level of GDP by 0.15 percentage points (chapter 4).

- A banking crisis imposes damage equal to about two-thirds of one year's GDP in present-value terms, including longer-term effects (chapter 4).

- The optimal level of tangible common equity is 7 to 8 percent of total assets, corresponding to 12 to 14 percent of risk-weighted assets (chapter 4).

- Correspondingly, the optimal capital ratio is about one-third larger than the target set in Basel III (13 percent of risk-weighted assets compared with 9.5 percent for tangible common equity for G-SIBs). In practice, however, US banks hold close to the optimal amount, because they maintain a cushion above the required minimum (chapter 4).

- In the Great Recession, the largest US banks did not experience losses that were proportionally significantly greater than those of medium-size banks, casting doubt on the proposition of excessive risk taking spurred by TBTF incentive distortions (chapter 5).

- New tests cast doubt on the too much finance literature (chapter 6).

Salient Themes in the Literature

Chapter 2 frames the issues and examines the state of analytical work in a critical review of the literature. It surveys four categories of studies: "heuristic seawall" studies, calibrated studies of transitional costs, calibrated long-term cost-benefit studies, and a variant of calibrated studies using dynamic stochastic general equilibrium models.[5]

The analysis of Admati and Hellwig (2013) is prominent in the first group. It is based on the observation of higher historical levels of bank capital;

---

5. Studies in a fifth category, on TLAC, are surveyed in chapter 5.

the argument that banking is no different from other corporate sectors, where much higher equity capital is common; a strong M&M assumption; and the argument that analysis should be based on social costs, correcting for the distortion of tax deductibility of debt interest but not equity earnings. I argue that banking is different, if only because more than half of its production activity is inherently financed by debt in the form of deposits and that it would not be optimal to apply social pricing to one sector while leaving the financing cost distortion unchanged in the rest of the economy.

An important study in the first group is an IMF-based analysis by Dagher et al. (2016). It uses a seawall approach to examine what levels of capital would have been required to cover 85 percent of bank losses in past banking crises based on nonperforming loan data and alternative assumptions about the loss incidence of nonperforming loans.

Two studies stand out in the second set of studies, on transitional effects. Based on a large number of macroeconomic models, the Macroeconomic Assessment Group (MAG 2010) estimates that the phase-in of Basel III requirements would temporarily reduce output by a maximum of about 0.25 percentage point from baseline after three years. As noted, the IIF (2011) instead estimated an output loss more than an order of magnitude larger. Writing in late 2014, Cecchetti (2014) pronounced that "the jury is in" and that the effects had been even milder than anticipated by the Macroeconomic Assessment Group. The exceptionally low interest rate environment in this period may cloud this diagnosis, however. Cohen (2013) provides support for the moderate or low-cost diagnosis. He finds that banks adjusted mainly by building up retained earnings, thereby avoiding the most severe adverse effects from either sharp reductions in outstanding claims or forced recourse to high-cost share issuance under adverse conditions.

In the third group of studies, the preeminent calibrated long-term study remains the Long-Term Economic Impact (LEI) analysis of the Basel Committee on Banking Supervision (BCBS 2010a). Placing the median long-term cost of a banking crisis at 63 percent of one year's GDP and considering the extent of reduction in probability of a crisis at successive levels of bank capital, the study shows a wide range over which higher tangible common equity capital would be socially beneficial, with the optimal level at 13 percent of risk-weighted assets.

An important study by Miles, Yang, and Marcheggiano (2012) places the desirable range at 16 to 20 percent of risk-weighted assets. The median estimate across 16 leading studies (including those in the seawall and dynamic stochastic general equilibrium groupings) places the optimal capital ratio at 13 percent for common equity tier 1 capital relative to risk-weighted assets (see table 2.1 in chapter 2).

My estimates (in chapter 4) are also at this level: 12 to 14 percent of risk-weighted assets (7 to 8 percent of total assets). This outcome is the same as that of the BCBS (2010a), even though I allow for a considerable (45 percent) M&M offset. The production function approach of Miles, Yang, and Marcheggiano (2012), which I use, generates a substantially larger adverse impact on output from a given rise in average borrowing cost than does the compilation of macroeconomic models. Those models may inappropriately incorporate monetary policy feedbacks and may not be designed to capture the effects of permanent long-term reductions in available capital stock as opposed to short-term fluctuations in demand.

The last group of studies, the dynamic stochastic general equilibrium models, provides methodologically elegant but ultimately less credible estimates of optimal capital requirements. One study concludes that capital requirements were already too high before the Great Recession. None of the main dynamic stochastic general equilibrium models incorporates the centerpieces of this issue: the response of the probability of a banking crisis to capital levels and the economic cost of a banking crisis. Instead, they are driven by such influences as an initial phase of benefit from reducing excessive risk taking as capital rises followed by a phase of cost to output from reduced capital stock.

Testing Modigliani-Miller for Banks

Chapter 3 uses data on 51 large US banks in 2001–13 to test the M&M theorem. With assets ranging from about $6 billion to $2.4 trillion, these banks accounted for about 75 percent of the total assets of US banks (including noncommercial bank subsidiaries of bank holding companies) in 2013.

The discussion begins with the question of whether the banking sector is special. The ratio of total assets to equity capital has typically been only about 3:1 for the nonfinancial sector but about 10:1 or higher for banking. In their analysis of equity returns, Fama and French (1992, 429) specifically excluded financial firms, because they judged that the high leverage normal for the sector did not have the same meaning of distress as in nonfinancial firms. The major product of banks—liquid deposit services to customers—constitutes debt, making them inherently different from nonbanks with respect to the ratio of debt to equity (Herring 2011, DeAngelo and Stulz 2013).

Those empirical tests of M&M for banking that have been conducted, moreover, have typically sought to identify the influence of the capital structure irrelevance theorem by calculating the relationship of bank "beta" coefficients to leverage ratios (capital relative to assets).[6] In the capital asset

---

6. Beta is a measure of relative volatility. It tells the percent by which the stock price rises when the overall market rises by one percent, or falls when the overall market falls by 1 percent.

pricing model (CAPM), the unit cost of equity equals the risk-free rate plus the firm's beta coefficient multiplied by the excess of the diversified market yield over the risk-free rate (equity premium). Although tests do tend to find that bank beta coefficients are related to leverage, the underlying CAPM framework is known to perform poorly in explaining cross-section stock returns (Fama and French 1992). In any event, the original model of Modigliani and Miller (1958) provides a much more direct estimating form, and the tests in chapter 3 apply this form.

In those tests the cost of equity capital is estimated as a linear function of the ratio of debt to equity. The constant in the resulting equation should be the return to capital in the banking sector. The coefficient on the ratio of debt to equity should be the difference between this return and the interest rate on debt.

The tests in chapter 3 apply two alternative measures of equity cost: the inverse of the price-to-earnings ratio and the ratio of net earnings to the book value of equity. For both the data are constrained to force the observed equity cost to no less than the risk-free rate plus 100 basis points, so that negative earnings instances (concentrated in 2007–10) do not give misleading signals of returns demanded by investors. Although about 8 percent of bank-year observations show negative earnings, only 1 percent of the sample had losses exceeding 3 percent of bank assets, suggesting a lower needed seawall than typically perceived.

The estimates show a statistically significant coefficient of equity cost on leverage for one of the specifications (net earnings relative to book value of equity). Using the average coefficients estimated for the two specifications, and considering the base levels of equity cost and likely levels for interest rates on debt, a 15 percentage point increase in the ratio of equity capital from an illustrative base level of 10 percent (as proposed by Admati and Hellwig 2013) would raise the average cost of capital to banks by a central estimate of 62 basis points. If there were no M&M effect at all, the corresponding increase would be 112 percent, so the estimated M&M offset amounts to 0.45. Slightly less than half of the cost impact of higher capital requirements would thus be offset by the lower unit cost of equity thanks to lower risk.

Calculating the Optimal Capital-to-Assets Ratio

Chapter 4 presents a model estimating the optimal capital-to-assets ratio, using as a key input the M&M offset coefficient estimated in chapter 3. The cost of a higher capital ratio to the economy stems from the increase in the unit cost of capital to borrowing firms and households, the consequential reduction in the economywide stock of capital, and hence the reduction of

future output from its baseline path. The benefit of higher capital requirements comes from the crisis damage avoided, equal to the reduction in the
probability of a banking crisis multiplied by the long-term cost of a banking
crisis.

The chapter first develops new estimates of damage from banking
crises. The analysis takes account of the fact that output may have been
above potential before the crisis. It also points out that even if output does
not return to its baseline trend for potential by the fifth year of the crisis,
the shortfall would not be perpetual, because the forgone capital stock sacrificed to the recession would not have had an infinite life. Based on past
banking crisis episodes, and allowing a 15-year capital life following the
recession to calculate lingering costs, I estimate that the typical long-term
cost of a banking crisis in an advanced industrial economy has been 64
percent of one year's GDP, almost identical to the median estimate in the
Basel Committee's Long-Term Economic Impact analysis (BCBS 2010a).

The next step is to identify the relationship between the probability of
crisis and the level of the capital ratio. I apply the schedule of this relationship reported by the Basel Committee (BCBS 2010a), which is based on
cross-country regression models and models of banking system contagion
from interbank exposures. There is a relatively rapid drop-off in the probability of crisis as the capital ratio increases. For tangible common equity,
an increase in the ratio of capital to risk-weighted assets from 7 to 8 percent
reduces the annual probability of crisis from 4.6 to 3.0 percent in the BCBS
schedule; the probability falls to 1 percent when the capital ratio reaches 11
percent, and it declines by only another 0.1 percent (from 0.4 to 0.3 percent)
when the increase is from 14 to 15 percent. I adopt this degree of curvature
but set the base probability at 2.6 percent rather than 4.6 percent (for 7
percent capital to risk-weighted assets), because I see the relevant period as
considerably longer (1977–2015) and hence the baseline annual frequency
of banking crises as lower (given the concentration of crises in 2007–08).
The overall result is a sharply concave curve relating benefits to higher
capital ratios (see figure 4.2 in chapter 4).

The analysis then incorporates the cost to the economy of higher capital
requirements. Using the same production function framework proposed by
Miles, Yang, and Marcheggiano (2012), I set the proportional output loss
equal to the proportional rise in the unit cost of capital multiplied by the
product of the elasticity of output with respect to capital and the elasticity
of substitution between capital and labor, all divided by unity minus the
elasticity of output with respect to capital. The derivative of this cost turns
out to be a constant that is influenced by the shares of bank and nonbank
finance, the gap between the unit cost of equity capital and the cost of debt
to banks, and the M&M offset coefficient. At the central values, this con-

stant turns out to be a loss of 0.15 percent of GDP for each percentage point increase in the required ratio of capital to total assets.

There is thus a straight-line upward-sloping cost curve for the capital requirement. The optimal level for the capital ratio will then be where the slope of the concave benefits curve is identical to the slope of the cost line. The central value for the M&M offset is set at 0.45, based on the results of chapter 3. Using low, central, and high variants for this parameter and six others (loss from crisis, unit cost of equity to banks, coefficient for spill-over to capital cost in nonbank lending, elasticity of output with respect to capital, elasticity of substitution between capital and labor, and crisis probability curve), the analysis generates 2,187 possible outcomes for the capital ratio at which marginal benefits equal marginal costs. The median outcome is 6.9 percent of total assets; the 75th percentile outcome is 7.9 percent. The main result is thus that the optimal capital ratio is 7 to 8 percent of total assets, corresponding to 12 to 14 percent of risk-weighted assets (using the ratio of risk-weighted assets to total assets in euro area and US banks).

Total Loss-Absorbing Capacity

Chapter 5 considers the role of TLAC—namely, CoCos, contingent write-down debt, and subordinated debt—as essentially buffers that are imperfect substitutes for equity but have a lower cost. The minimum requirement for the large G-SIB banks is 9.5 percent of risk-weighted assets for tier 1 common equity; their TLAC requirement is a minimum of 18 percent of risk-weighted assets.[7] In effect, the G-SIBs are required to arrive at total equity and quasi-equity that amounts to twice their tier 1 common equity.

A substantial body of literature applies to TLAC. Much of it concerns the disciplinary role of subordinated debt. There seems to be little recognition in the literature, however, that the mobilization of nonequity TLAC in a crisis could cause problems of its own. With respect to CoCos, the most likely holders are hedge funds, which would be fleet of foot in an incipient crisis, causing a plunge in CoCo prices as well as the stock prices of the banks in question (Persaud 2014). A taste of this phenomenon occurred in early 2016, when concerns arose that one of the largest European banks (Deutsche Bank) would be unable to make a coupon payment on contingent write-down debt because certain triggers appeared imminent (see appendix 5A). As for outright subordinated debt that is eligible to qualify as

---

7. This requirement is to be met by 2022. The target is to be firm specific. The average for eight US G-SIBs is 19.9 percent. The highest is for JPMorgan Chase, at 23.5 percent (Financial Stability Board press release, November 9, 2015, and Federal Reserve press release, October 30, 2015).

TLAC, virtually none of the literature seems to focus on the fact that the writing down of subordinated debt is equivalent to a haircut in a default. Yet the whole purpose of regulatory structure should be to avoid the bankruptcy of banks and hence any need for default and haircut. Once again the problem is a shock to confidence in the banking system if the point of bankruptcy is reached. Much of the political pressure for TLAC seems to turn on the desire to avoid taxpayer bailouts of banks, but countenancing bankruptcy of banks for this purpose instead of increasing equity and avoiding bankruptcy constitutes a risky strategy.

On the disciplining role of subordinated debt, Ashcraft (2008) finds such a role before the Basel accord but not thereafter. He attributes the change to the Basel requirement that tier 2 subordinated debt cannot include restrictive covenants. Evanoff, Jagtiani, and Nakata (2011) find that for banks, spreads on subordinated debt are indeed related to risk (as indicated by nonperforming loans and other measures) and argue that the stronger relationship found for the subsample of banks with recent issuance means that a mandatory requirement for subordinated debt should not be rejected because past signals have seemed too noisy to justify such a change. Calomiris and Herring (2013) state the case for CoCos in terms of imposing strong incentives on management to recapitalize rather than waiting too long.

In the area of TBTF, the literature has tended to use the "ratings uplift" difference between "support" and "stand-alone" ratings of banks by major rating agencies as a measure of the implicit TBTF subsidy. Marques, Correa, and Sapriza (2013) find that bank "z-scores" or distance to insolvency ratios (return on assets plus capital-to-assets ratio, normalized by standard deviation of return on assets), are negatively related to the TBTF subsidy as measured by the ratings uplift. Afonso, Santos, and Traina (2014) similarly find risk taking as measured by impaired loans or net charge-offs to be significantly related to the ratings uplift. An important caveat to this literature, however, is that some studies find that by 2013 the bond spread advantage of TBTF firms had swung to a disadvantage, suggesting that reforms such as living will resolution plans required of large banks in the United States and the prospect of new mandatory bail-ins in the euro area's banking union reforms may have already substantially reduced the TBTF subsidy.

On economies of scale, Wheelock and Wilson (2012) and Hughes and Mester (2013) find important economies of scale in banking. Davies and Tracey (2014) argue that these economies disappear if social pricing is applied to the costs of funds, but their result is subject to the well-known problem that estimation using a single parametric (translog) function rather than nonparametric techniques yields misleading results (McAllister and McManus 1993). Moreover, in their simulation reestimating returns to scale replacing large banks' actual cost rates with median rates for banks under $100 billion in assets, Hughes and Mester (2013) find little change in their returns to scale estimates—the opposite of the social pricing finding in Davies and Tracey (2014).

Chapter 5 closes with a test for the experience of US banks in the Great Recession. It examines the change in net earnings as a fraction of assets from 2006–07 to 2008–10 for 16 TBTF banks with assets of more than $100 billion and compares it to the change for the next 34 largest banks. If the largest banks had engaged in excessive risk taking as a consequence of the TBTF subsidy, one would have expected them to have incurred substantially larger losses than the next tier of banks. But a simple test for significant difference of means fails to show any difference between the two groups. The implication is that the portrait of excessive risk taking may have been overdone, and correspondingly that the largest banks may place a greater weight on "charter value" (emphasized in earlier literature) relative to TBTF profits than generally recognized.[8] It may also be appropriate to pay closer attention to economies of scale, another controversial aspect of the literature.

Too Much Finance?

Chapter 6 addresses the recent literature purporting to identify a negative influence of high levels of financial intermediation on growth. If one believes that the financial sector is already too large in the major economies and is suppressing potential growth, the appropriate measure of the benefits of higher capital requirements would need to incorporate an economic gain from the fact that they would tend to reduce the size of the financial sector. The issue is thus highly germane to the policy debate on capital requirements, although it is virtually absent from the capital requirements literature and has instead proceeded on a separate path in the cross-country growth literature.

However, the analysis of chapter 6 suggests that the too much finance studies may be mistaking correlation for causation. Across countries, the depth of financial intermediation increases as per capita income rises. But the rate of growth per capita tends to decline as per capita income rises, reflecting the process of convergence. One could mistakenly conclude as a result that "too many doctors" or "too many telephones" or "too much R&D" cause growth to decline, as rising levels of these variables per capita also tend to accompany higher per capita incomes. For the purposes of identifying optimal capital requirements for banks, evidence of too much finance is insufficiently robust to welcome shrinkage of financial intermediation as a side benefit of raising capital requirements further.

---

8. Charter value is the value of being able to continue doing business in the future.

Framing Issues

Several key contextual issues should be kept in mind in interpreting the results of this study.

Lender of Last Resort and Resolution of Large Banks after Dodd-Frank

The Dodd-Frank Act of 2010 imposed new constraints on the ability of the Federal Reserve to act as the lender of last resort. At the same time, it emphasized and created a special framework for the resolution (expedited bankruptcy workout) of large banks. It gives the Federal Deposit Insurance Corporation (FDIC) Orderly Liquidation Authority (OLA), which it implements through the Single Point of Entry (SPOE) approach. Under this approach bank holding companies would become effectively bankrupt even as their subsidiaries would be kept in regular operating condition. Because of the possibly narrower scope for crisis response than in the Great Recession, and in view of the possibility that resolution of the largest banks under the new arrangements could well be far less seamless and more traumatic to the system than assumed under OLA and SPOE, Dodd-Frank increases the importance of preventing crises through the adequate capitalization of banks.

Risk-Weighted versus Total Assets

Under the 1988 Basel I agreement, standardized risk weights were applied (to five different risk categories) to arrive at risk-weighted assets (RWA). Required capital was then set at 4 percent of risk-weighted assets for tier 1 capital (equity and retained earnings). An additional 4 percent was required in supplementary tier 2 capital (subordinated long-term debt, hybrid instruments, and general provisions).

In 1996 an amendment to the agreement provided for weights based on market risk to be applied to the securities held in banks' trading books (as opposed to the "banking" portfolio meant to be held to maturity). It also allowed the largest banks to determine their risk weights using their internal (typically value at risk) models (Neumann and Turner 2005). The final Basel II rules issued in 2004 provided for the use of internal models for credit risk as well as market risk. The shift to internal models was especially important for European banks that were moving from commercial to universal banking.[9]

In part because of the resulting incentive to apply less conservative in-

---

9. In addition to commercial lending, universal banks are active in investment banking, insurance, and other financial services such as wealth management and underwriting.

ternal models, the clear correlation between capital to risk-weighted assets and capital to total assets ratios that had existed across major European banks in 1996 became a random scatter by 2002 (Bayoumi forthcoming). By 2002 the two measures were still closely correlated for mainly commercial banks, but the universal banks had much lower ratios of equity to total assets and no clear correlation between the two concepts; by 2008 the positive relationship had broken down even for European commercial banks.

Hoenig (2013) argues that the low risk weights on AAA collateralized debt obligations (such as mortgage-backed securities) and the zero weights on sovereign debt induced banks to leverage these assets excessively onto their balance sheets even as the risks of these asset classes escalated. Using data for G-SIBs in 2012, he shows that the leverage ratio of tier 1 capital to total assets provides a relatively good statistical explanation of market expectations of default frequency and credit default swap spreads whereas the ratio of tier 1 capital to risk-weighted assets does not.

Similarly, Goldstein (2017) is acerbic in his critique of risk-weighted assets. He strongly favors capital requirements based on total rather than risk-weighted assets.

The divergence between the two capital measures was most pronounced for investment banks, in part reflecting the fact that in the United States they were regulated by the Securities and Exchange Commission (SEC) rather than the Federal Reserve (which regulates the largest banks) or the Comptroller of the Currency (which regulates other banks). US commercial banks have been subject to prompt corrective action triggered by a leverage ratio of 5 percent for high-quality capital relative to total assets, whereas investment banks (and investment bank subsidiaries of the largest bank holding companies) have not. Thus whereas the largely commercial bank Wells Fargo reported risk-weighted assets equal to 84 percent of total assets in 2008, universal bank JPMorgan Chase reported this ratio at 57 percent and investment bank Morgan Stanley reported it at 42 percent, according to SEC 10-K reports. The potential for a distorted picture from the risk-weighted ratio is highlighted by the fact that in mid-2007 the reported tier 1 capital ratio was actually higher for ill-fated Lehman Brothers (11 percent of risk-weighted assets) than for Wells Fargo (8.5 percent) (Kato, Kobayashi, and Saita 2010). In Europe universal banks with large investment bank operations tended to have much lower risk weighting than standard commercial banks. Thus by 2008 the ratio of risk-weighted to total assets at Deutsche Bank was only about 1.7 percent whereas the same ratio for Italian bank Intesa Sanpaolo was about 8 percent (Bayoumi forthcoming).

In the United States, the minimum leverage ratio for a bank holding company with more than $500 million in assets is 3 percent for "strong" bank holding companies and 4 percent for all others. Bank holding companies with weaknesses or in the process of rapid expansion are expected to hold capital "well above" these levels (FDIC 2015). For a bank to be considered well capitalized, it must pass a leverage ratio threshold of 5 percent (a buffer of 2 percent above the Basel III minimum). Below this threshold, "prompt corrective action" can involve restrictions on dividends, buybacks, and discretionary bonus payments. In 2014 US regulators increased this threshold to 6 percent for insured depository bank subsidiaries of the largest bank holding companies (institutions with $700 billion or more in assets) and set the leverage ratio at 5 percent for these institutions (including their nonbank subsidiaries) as a whole (Comptroller 2014). These "supplementary" leverage ratios use the Basel III definition of exposure for the base; they thus include not only balance sheet assets but also off-balance-sheet assets, such as derivatives and repo-style transactions (Davis Polk 2014). The enhanced supplementary leverage ratio of 6 percent for US G-SIBs thus adds a buffer of 3 percentage points to the Basel III requirement of 3 percent.

The main analysis of this study is conducted using the metric of tangible common equity capital relative to total assets, a "leverage" capital ratio. However, the comparisons frequently translate this measure into what would be the corresponding average ratio of the same capital concept to risk-weighted assets, as the Basel III requirements are stated principally against risk-weighted assets.[10] The average relationship used in chapter 4 is that a given ratio of capital to risk-weighted assets will be 1.78 times the corresponding leverage ratio of capital to total assets (based on BCBS 2010a estimates for US and euro area banks). In principle, it would be desirable to have reliable risk weightings. In practice, there seems to have been sufficient distortion in understatement of risk, especially in investment bank operations, particularly after the shift to internal models in Europe by 2005, that there is much to be said for giving at least equal attention to the capital to total assets ("leverage") ratio as to the capital to risk-weighted assets ratio.

Goldstein (2017) makes a strong case that risk weighting and the use of internal models have caused risk-weighted assets to be much less reliable than total assets as the basis for determining capital needs. He argues that risk-based capital ratios were less successful in predicting bank failures in the 2007–10 crisis than simple leverage ratios. He notes that for 17 major international banks, the risk-weighted assets/total assets ratio fell from 70 percent in 1993 to 40 percent in 2011, without any evidence of an accompanying shift toward safer banking practices. He notes the critique in the Liikanen Report (2012) that the banks with the lowest risk-weighted assets/total assets ratios are those with the largest share of trading assets in total

---

10. In contrast, the Basel III leverage ratio is relatively low and typically not a binding constraint.

assets. He cites the observation by Hoenig (2013) that the very low 7 percent risk weighting on AAA collateralized debt obligations induced excessive investment in these instruments before the crisis.

One approach to imposing more discipline on risk weightings would be to place a floor on the admissible ratio of risk-weighted to total assets. On average, US and European banks have had a risk-weighted assets/total assets ratio of about 55 percent (see chapter 4). Regulators could impose a minimum of, say, 45 percent of total assets as the regulatory measure of risk-weighted assets in cases where banks' internal models indicated a lower ratio. An alternative approach would be to specify that for regulatory purposes, the risk-weighted assets/total assets ratio for a particular asset category can be no lower than a specified percentage point shortfall from the standard risk weighting for that category for banks not using internal models (say, 10 percentage points).

The "Basel IV" revisions for risk weighting take the latter approach. They would include an "output floor" below which internal models would not be allowed to reduce the risk weight for the asset category in question; discussions among regulators reportedly involve a floor range of 60 to 90 percent of the standard weight. Although regulators have stated that the revisions should not "significantly raise overall capital requirements," some estimates find that for global banks outside the United States, the consequence could be an increase in measured risk-weighted assets of 18 to 30 percent. European banks in particular have opposed this approach, in part because the standardized risk weight for residential mortgages (35 percent) is far above internal model weights in major European countries where defaults have been rare.[11] In contrast, US regulators favor relatively high output floors, partly because the Collins Amendment of the Dodd-Frank Act requires that risk weights be no lower than the "generally applicable risk-based capital requirements" specified by federal banking agencies (Tahyar 2010).

Basel III falls farther below the optimal capital ratio identified in this study using the leverage ratio than using the ratio of capital to risk-weighted assets. Thus the optimal requirement identified in chapter 4 is 7 to 8 percent for tangible common equity relative to total assets and 12 to 14 percent for the average ratio of capital to risk-weighted assets. In comparison, Basel III sets the minimum leverage target at 3 percent of "exposure," including securities financing transactions and off-balance-sheet assets.[12]

---

11. "Basel Bust-Up," *Economist*, November 26, 2016, 67.

12. The shortfall from the optimal level is greater in the leverage target even after taking account of the fact that the denominator in the Basel III leverage ratio uses a wider definition of exposure than total assets. As a consequence, its 3 percent target corresponds to a somewhat higher capital to total assets ratio, especially for US banks.

A complication for risk weighting may have been created by the advent of quantitative easing, which caused massive amounts of excess bank reserves to build up at the Federal Reserve. In October 2008 the Federal Reserve began paying interest on excess reserves, which rose from about $2 billion in 2007 to $2.5 trillion in 2014. This structural change helps explain why there was no explosion in prices despite a large increase in the money base. Instead, there was a collapse in the money multiplier from the base to broad money. In contrast, there was only a modest decline in velocity (the ratio of GDP to broad money) (Cline 2015b). It is unclear that increased bank reserves came from corresponding reductions in bank holdings of government securities and other safe assets. If they did not, then the ratio of safe to total assets rose, arguably justifying a lower leverage ratio.

In August 2016 the Bank of England recognized the incongruity posed by much higher excess reserves when it decided to exclude reserves held at the central bank from the calculation of banks' leverage ratios. Although adopted in response to recession fears following the referendum to exit the European Union (Brexit), the decision makes this exclusion permanent.[13]

European versus US Banks

In addition to the flexibility in the application of internal risk-weight models, at least three other differences between European and US banks warrant mention for purposes of placing bank capital reform into context. The first is that banks are considerably more important to finance in Europe, whereas there is a much greater reliance on the corporate bond market and other nonbank sources of finance in the United States. Merler and Véron (2015) estimate that in 2014, in the euro area bank loans accounted for 88 percent of financing to nonfinancial corporations and debt securities only 12 percent, whereas in the United States the share of loans was only 30 percent and that of debt securities 70 percent. By implication, the stakes in ensuring the safety of the banking system are even higher in Europe than in the United States. Moreover, Europe would likely benefit from greater diversification away from banks toward capital markets. For the United States, a corresponding implication is that policymakers must pay special attention to the spillover effects of bank regulatory reform onto the nonbank (or shadow banking) financial sector.

A second difference is in the emerging approaches to resolution of large failing banks. Chapter 5 discusses this issue in the US context. In the euro area,

---

13. Huw Jones, "Bank of England Eases Banks' Capital Leverage Rule to Help Support Economy," Reuters, August 4, 2016.

resolution is to take place through the Single Resolution Mechanism within the EU Bank Recovery and Resolution Directive.[14] The Single Supervisory Mechanism, comprising the European Central Bank and national supervisory authorities, determines when a failing bank needs to be resolved. The Single Resolution Board (comprising representatives from the national authorities involved, the Single Resolution Mechanism, and the European Commission) decides whether and when to place the bank in resolution. If it determines that resolution is needed, the bank is either sold or divided into a new bridge "good bank" and a "bad bank," where shareholders and creditors cover losses on bad assets. Under conditions of systemic stress, the Single Resolution Mechanism can provide state assistance to recapitalize the bank, but only after shareholders and creditors (excluding insured depositors) first take a "bail-in" loss amounting to 8 percent of the bank's liabilities. After that threshold is reached, the system's Single Resolution Fund can contribute up to 5 percent of the bank's liabilities; still larger losses would require an additional round of creditor bail-in losses. Each member state is to set up financing arrangements funded by contributions from banks and investment firms, to reach a cumulative target of at least 1 percent of deposits over 10 years and merged into the Single Resolution Fund.[15] The more rigid bail-in requirements of the Bank Recovery and Resolution Directive may play a role in the lower ratios of share prices to book values observed in Europe than in the United States as of late 2016 (see appendix 5A).

In the United States, the FDIC has long experience in implementing resolutions of failing banks. In contrast, the Single Resolution Mechanism remains untested. The potential for friction between national authorities seeking greater flexibility to avoid politically unpopular bail-in of smaller creditors and the Single Supervisory Mechanism became evident in early 2016 in Italy.[16] In part because of such potential tensions, the scope for the mechanism to deliver "immaculate bankruptcy" for large banks seems unlikely to be much greater than that of the US mechanism resulting from Dodd-Frank.

---

14. See European Commission, *EU Bank Recovery and Resolution Directive (BRRD): Frequently Asked Questions*, Memo/14/297, 2014.

15. Gros and De Groen calculate that this magnitude should be broadly consistent with state funding that would be needed even under a scenario as severe as the Great Recession, thanks to the structure requiring bail-in (Daniel Gros and Willem Pieter De Groen, "The Single Resolution Fund: How Much Is Needed?" VoxEU, December 2015, http://voxeu.org/article/size-single-resolution-fund).

16. See Nicolas Véron, "Italy's Banking Problem Is Serious but Not Intractable," RealTime Economic Issues Watch, July 14, 2016, Peterson Institute for International Economics, https://piie.com/blogs/realtime-economic-issues-watch/italys-banking-problem-serious-not-intractable.

A third notable difference between European and US banks concerns accounting. European banks use International Financial Reporting Standards (IFRS); US banks use Generally Accepted Accounting Principles (GAAP). Primarily because IFRS does not permit the netting out of derivatives, the reported assets of European banks tend to be larger than would be reported under GAAP. Hoenig (2013) estimates that for the eight US G-SIBs, total assets in 2012 stood at $10.2 trillion under GAAP but would have been reported as $15.9 trillion under IFRS.

As it turns out, this divergence is not as problematic for capital requirements as might be feared. For risk-weighted assets, the risk-weighting process (rather than IFRS or GAAP) determines the outcome, so comparison of the risk-weighted assets denominator for European and US banks is not necessarily distorted. Although in principle the potential for distortion could be greater for the leverage ratio of capital to total assets, the Basel III leverage requirement to be introduced by 2017 pays explicit attention to the treatment of derivatives in a fashion that is comparable for European and US banks.[17] The principal caveat regarding accounting is thus that caution should be used when comparing European to US banks using publicly reported assets.

Stress Tests and Liquidity Requirements

Higher capital requirements are only part of the reform of banking systems in response to the financial crisis. Basel III also provides for higher liquidity standards. The liquidity coverage ratio requires that high-quality liquid assets must equal or exceed expected net cash outflows over a 30-day period under a stress scenario (BCBS 2013). The net stable funding ratio requires that over a longer period of one year, the available amount of stable funding equal or exceed the required amount of stable funding (BCBS 2014b).[18]

For their part, stress tests simulating the impact on banks from severe downturns in the economy have become a salient supervisory instrument

---

17. Bilateral netting of derivatives is allowed under the Basel III leverage requirement, but treatment of securities financing transaction exposures is stricter than under either IFRS or GAAP (BCBS 2014a).

18. Five "available stable funding" categories have "factors" that range from 100 percent for regulatory capital and liabilities with more than a one-year term to 50 percent for funding with residual maturity of less than one year from nonfinancial corporate customers or with maturities of 6 to 12 months from others and zero for lending not enumerated in higher-factor categories. Eight "required stable funding" categories have corresponding factors, such as zero for central bank reserves, 50 percent for high-quality liquid assets encumbered for 6 to 12 months and loans to financial institutions with residual maturities of 6 to 12 months, 65 percent for residual maturity of one year and risk weight of 35 percent or less (for example), and 100 percent for all assets encumbered for one year or more.

(see Goldstein 2017 for an extensive assessment). They played a key role in restoring confidence in US banks in 2009. Stress test results have determined whether banks are allowed to increase dividends and carry out buybacks, providing a strong incentive to meet capital levels and operational practices likely to pass the tests.[19]

Conclusion

The Basel III reforms requiring stronger capitalization of banks have not gone far enough: The additional gains from reducing crisis risk would outweigh the additional costs of more capital. The equity capital target for large banks needs to be set about a third higher than in Basel III to reach the point at which marginal costs equal marginal benefits. Tangible common equity needs to reach 7 to 8 percent of total assets (12 to 14 percent of risk-weighted assets) rather than the Basel III target of 9.5 percent of risk-weighted assets for the largest banks. A level of 13 percent of risk-weighted assets also seems to be emerging as a central estimate among a number of studies adopting alternative approaches (see table 2.1).

At the same time, the shortfall from optimal capitalization is far smaller than some critics have argued. Moreover, in practice the large US banks appear to be holding capital relatively close to the optimal level, reflecting a behavioral cushion. It would seem more prudent, however, to set the target as a requirement than to count on this voluntary behavior.

A natural question is why the TLAC target of 18 percent of risk-weighted assets would not effectively meet or even exceed the optimal capitalization level. The problem with this approach is that CoCos and subordinated debt raise the risk of panic dynamics and (in the case of subordinated debt) contagion associated with the bankruptcy implications of imposing debt haircuts. The principal role of the extra TLAC remains one of assuring taxpayers rather than ensuring systemic stability. By implication policymakers would do well to increase the equity component of the TLAC requirement, providing a larger buffer against potential bankruptcy while leaving some role for the disciplinary influence of nonequity TLAC.

---

19. In 2014, for example, Citigroup failed the stress test; its request to increase dividends and carry out buybacks was denied. Bank of America passed the stress test; it received approval for its first dividend increase since the financial crisis (Michael J. Moore and Elizabeth Dexheimer, "Citigroup Fails Fed Stress Test as BofA Gets Dividend Boost," Bloomberg, March 27, 2014).

A Survey of Literature on Optimal Capital Requirements for Banks

Economic studies of the costs and benefits of capital requirements for banks may usefully be divided into five categories. The first includes what might be called heuristic seawall studies. These more informal approaches (hence "heuristic") often appeal to the general proposition of Modigliani and Miller (1958) that equity can replace debt with no adverse profit implications for the firm, such that the very notion of an optimal capital ratio would be flawed. They tend instead to consider capital ratios in earlier historical periods, magnitudes of losses by banks in the Great Recession, and cursory calculations of enormous output losses in banking crises.

Studies in this category tend to generate what may be called a "seawall" estimate of how high the capital levee needs to be to protect the economic coastline from the infrequent severe storm. Such estimates calculate the amount of losses banks would experience in a crisis and then add that amount to a core amount of capital that the authors believe banks should retain even at the depth of a banking crisis in order to estimate the total capital banks should hold in normal times.

A second category involves transient analyses. These studies focus on possible costs and benefits in the period in which banks adjust to higher capital requirements. The central message of these studies is that if banks were required to reach sharply higher capital standards overnight, their equity prices would fall as a result of the flood of new issuances, with possible adverse effects for the economy as they scaled back activities. The policy implication of these studies tends to focus on phasing in higher capital requirements over time.

The third category is more formal modeling of banking crisis costs in comparison with the long-term economic costs of higher capital requirements. The analysis of chapter 4 is in this category. This category represents calibrated optimization based on the measurement of the marginal benefits and cost of additional bank capital.

A fourth category includes dynamic stochastic general equilibrium (DSGE) models. These models examine such effects as overinvestment in risky projects by banks in response to the subsidy provided by deposit guarantees, compared to eventual scarcity of capital formation if capital requirements are raised too high.

A fifth category concerns extension of bank regulatory requirements to include assessment of total loss-absorbing capacity (TLAC). It represents a variant of the seawall approach that focuses on ensuring that taxpayers do not foot the bill in banking crises, that banks instead go bankrupt if necessary, with the costs borne only by their shareholders and creditors. This approach tends to be premised on the proposition that banks engage in risk shifting spurred by subsidized deposit guarantees.

This chapter examines the literature on the two approaches most germane to the main calculations of this study: the seawall and calibrated optimization approaches. Appendix 2A surveys the literature on transient effects and DSGE model estimates. Chapter 5 examines the literature on TLAC and the analytical issues it involves, including economies of scale in banking and panic dynamics for the quasi-equity securities involved (contingent-convertible [CoCo] debt, contingent write-down debt, and subordinated debt).

Heuristic and Seawall Studies

The prominent analysis of Admati and Hellwig (2013) calls for exceptionally high capital requirements, although the authors do not attempt to calculate an optimal capital ratio. They rely heavily on the Modigliani-Miller (M&M) theorem to argue that higher equity capital would not increase costs. They state that the minimum equity capital for banks should be 20 to 30 percent of total assets (p. 179), which would correspond to 36 to 53 percent of risk-weighted assets. This range is based not on a comparison of marginal benefits against marginal costs but on a general appeal to typical equity ratios in the nonbank corporate sector and evidence on historical capital ratios for banks (pp. 30–31). The authors argue that nonbank firms maintain a minimum equity of 30 percent of assets and that banks are no different from other corporations. However, because banks are in the business of taking deposits, their main business line inherently involves much more debt (to depositors) than is typical of other sectors.

Admati and Hellwig give a potentially misleading impression of the time trend of the equity ratios when they state that equity was 25 percent of assets "early in the 20th century" but declined to 6 to 8 percent "by the early 1990s" (p. 31). Hoenig (2013, chart 5) shows that this decline had already occurred by 1945, and that equity ratios changed little between then and the early 1990s. In most areas of economic policy, norms that prevailed in the prewar period are considered less relevant than those of the postwar period. Calomiris (2013, 19) observes more specifically that the evidence from the early 20th century is misleading because after the 1930s asset risk declined substantially as a consequence of the very large increase in bank holdings of cash. Moreover, elimination of restrictions on inter-state banking in the United States in the early 1990s (see chapter 5) would seem to constitute an important reason why lower equity ratios would have been needed than in earlier periods, when domination by "political elites at the state level . . . [led to] a fragmented system of tiny banks that were highly vulnerable to local downturns and subject to frequent panics."[1]

Hanson, Kashyap, and Stein (2010) make a brief estimate of the "seawall-type. They argue that "the regulatory minimum in good times must substantially exceed the market-imposed standard in bad times." They observe that in the first quarter of 2010, the four largest US banks held 8 percent of risk-weighted assets, considerably above the 6 percent level that was the precrisis regulatory standard for "well-capitalized" banks. They note that the IMF (2010) estimated cumulative credit losses at US banks from 2007 to 2010 at 7 percent of assets. On this basis, they suggest, "one could argue for a good-times regulatory minimum ratio of equity-to-assets of 15 percent" (p. 8).

A problem with this back-of-the-envelope estimate is that it mixes risk-weighted asset apples with total asset oranges. In the first quarter of 2010, the four banks noted by the authors had total assets of $7.70 trillion versus risk-weighted assets of $4.68 trillion.[2] So although common equity tier 1 was 8.2 percent of risk-weighted assets for the four banks combined, it represented just 5.0 percent of total assets.

Moreover, the 7 percent loss figure appears to be overstated. A more recent study of the capital needs of global systemically important bank (G-SIBs) by the Financial Stability Board (FSB 2015a) examines losses by large international banks in the Great Recession and the Japanese banking

---

1. Liaquat Ahamed, "How Banks Fail" (book review of *Fragile by Design: The Political Origins of Banking Crises and Scarce Credit*, by Charles W. Calomiris and Stephen H. Haber), *New York Times*, April 11, 2014.

2. This estimate is based on data from Hanson, Kashyap, and Stein (p. 34) and the author's compilation from 10-Q and 10-K reports to the Securities and Exchange Commission.

crisis of the 1990s. It finds that "total losses have been up to almost 5 percent of total assets (Merrill Lynch, Wachovia), with half of the banks in a 2–4 percent range" (p. 6). Even the upper end of the loss range might thus more appropriately be set at 5 percent of total assets. On this basis, a restatement of the Hanson-Kashyap-Stein approach could reasonably set a target of common equity of 10 percent of total assets rather than 15 percent.

But a more basic question is why fully 5 percent of capital should be left in a crisis if there is an effective lender of last resort. At the extreme, the lender of last resort would provide support even if the bank were marginally solvent, with capital of zero. The optimal capital range identified in chapter 4 (7 to 8 percent of total assets) would be consistent in the seawall approach with a 5 percent loss that left a solvency cushion of 2.5 percent of total assets.

Goldstein (2017) uses a heuristic seawall approach to arrive at a range of 10 to 18 percent of total assets as the optimal ratio for bank capital requirements, with smaller US banks at the low end of this range and the largest G-SIBs at the upper end. By implication, he seeks a range of 18 to 32 percent for capital relative to risk-weighted assets.[3] For the G-SIBs, the target would thus be about three times as large as the equity capital target in Basel III. It would be nearly twice as large even if one were to attribute complete equity equivalence to the TLAC requirement of 18 percent of risk-weighted assets.

Goldstein identifies 600 basis points as the needed increase in the capital-to-assets ratio, on a weighted-average basis. He estimates that such an increase would boost bank lending rates by 15 basis points. He invokes a rule of thumb that macro models show that an increase in the federal funds rate of 100 basis points reduces output by 100 basis points two years later. Illustratively positing that an increase in bank lending rates translates to only a third as large an impact as a comparable increase in the federal funds rate, he implies that a 15-basis-point increase in bank lending rates would reduce output by only 5 basis points.

In contrast, in the model in chapter 4 a 600 basis point increase in the ratio of capital to total assets would raise the bank lending rate by 25 basis points.[4] But a more important difference is my use of an aggregate production function, in which the long-term output effect of an increase of 100 basis points in the unit cost of capital to the economy is far greater

---

3. Applying the ratio of 1.78 for total assets relative to risk-weighted assets in BCBS (2010a).

4. With the base case equity capital cost at 10 percent and the bank borrowing cost at 2.5 percent, the direct effect of shifting 8 percent of bank funding sources from borrowing to equity would amount to 45 basis points (600 × [0.10 – 0.025]). Allowing 45 percent for the M&M offset, the bank lending rate would rise by 25 basis points.

than the 100-basis-point reduction Goldstein cites from macro models.[5] One reason the macro-model example may understate growth impacts is that the change in the discount rate tends to be considerably greater than the change in the long-term interest rate, but the latter is what matters for investment, so a 100 basis point rise in the relevant long-term rate would imply a considerably larger rise in the federal funds rate.

More fundamentally, Goldstein's two-year horizon is far too short to evaluate the cumulative long-term impact on the stock of capital (considering that depreciation is on a time scale more like 15 years). Overall, I find that a 100-basis-point increase in the capital-to-assets ratio would reduce long-term output by 15 basis points, so Goldstein's 600-basis-point increment would cut long-term production by 90 basis points, not his 5 basis points.[6]

Goldstein's target for capital loosely follows the seawall approach of Hanson, Kashyap, and Stein, amplified in a judgment call taking many factors into account. Citing the International Monetary Fund (IMF 2010), he states that US banks lost 7 percent of assets in credit write-downs in the 2007–09 crisis and indicates that the eight US G-SIBs had a leverage ratio of 8 percent in 2012. He therefore posits that the target ratio for capital relative to total assets should be 15 percent (8 percent plus another 7 percent against the next Great Recession).

The 7 percent write-down cited for the United States by both Hanson-Kashyap-Stein and Goldstein constitutes an estimated $885 billion in write-downs for 2007–10, of which about $200 billion was in mortgages, $400 billion in other loans, and $300 billion in securities, of which about two-thirds were residential mortgage securities (IMF 2010, 12). But over this four-year period, the 54 large US banks examined in chapter 3 reported cumulative positive net income of $177 billion (calculated from the Securities and Exchange Commission's 10-K dataset, discussed in chapter 3). Together they show a loss in only one year—2008 (when there was an aggregate $10 billion loss, the largest loss being the $27 billion by Citigroup). This dataset excludes Lehman Brothers, but if one applies the midpoint of the $100 billion to $200 billion hole in Lehman's balance

---

5. I estimate the base value of the real unit cost of capital, sourced equally from banks, non-bank finance, and firms' internal funds, at 460 basis points. An increase of 100 basis points would be a 21.7 percent proportionate rise in the unit cost of capital to the economy. Applying a capital share of 40 percent and an elasticity of substitution between labor and capital of 0.5, the corresponding output effect would be a decline of 720 basis points in long-term output, not 100 basis points (see equation 4.13 in chapter 4).

6. The parameter relating output cost to change in the capital-to-assets ratio is $\psi = 0.15$ (see equation 4.14 in chapter 4).

sheet at the time of its bankruptcy (estimated in Cline and Gagnon 2013), adding Lehman would still leave the large bank net income slightly positive for 2007–10.

Use of gross write-downs as the metric for bank stress thus gives a misleading picture by failing to consider that the banks had other profits that more than offset specific write-downs over this four-year period. Correspondingly, use of the 7 percent figure to calibrate the needed height of the seawall is a major overstatement. Moreover, it is not clear why the appropriate target for capital left after an extreme disaster should be as high as 8 percent of assets. A more moderate but still significant net capital position of, say, 3 percent would seem to be a more reasonable immediate postcrisis target. The banks would still be solvent, because assets would exceed liabilities.

Goldstein argues that bank losses in the Great Recession are actually too small to serve as the proper size of the seawall, because the losses would have been much greater if governments had not taken extraordinary interventions to strengthen economies. This argument seems to explain why he does not take account of other bank profits that more than offset the credit write-downs. But this view seems to throw out the widely accepted principle that providing liquidity to solvent financial institutions is precisely what the central bank is supposed to do in a crisis. The extraordinary interventions in the Great Recession, such as Federal Deposit Insurance Corporation (FDIC) guarantees of new bank debt and guarantees for money market funds, amounted to massive lender-of-last-resort liquidity to the system precisely when such support was the appropriate policy response. Arguing that the proper metric for counterfactual bank losses in the Great Recession should add what banks' incremental losses would have been in the absence of such measures discards proper lender-of-last-resort policy. Goldstein implicitly assumes that the United States has tied its hands politically and would be unable to take such lender-of-last-resort measures in the next Great Recession. But suppressing potential output over the next several decades because of the assumption that it would be politically impossible to take the right action in the next 100-year flood seems misguided.

A recent study by researchers at the International Monetary Fund (Dagher et al. 2016) also applies a seawall framework to determine desirable capital requirements for banks. The authors use the same banking crisis database used in chapter 4 of the present study but focus on the observed levels of nonperforming loans (NPLs) recorded in that database. They then calculate what percent of loan losses bank capital would have covered if capital had been at alternative levels relative to risk-weighted assets. They assume either a central estimate of 50 percent loss given default on NPLs or a conservative estimate of 75 percent. They show a sharply nonlinear curve: Initially, additional capital covers large portions of losses, but as capital is raised still higher, additional loss coverage turns modest (similar to the benefits curve in figure 4.2 of chapter 4). For advanced economies, covering 85 percent of bank losses in banking crisis episodes would have required broadly defined capital ratios of 15 percent of risk-weighted assets in the case of 50 percent loss given default and 23 percent in the case of 75 percent loss given default. Stripping out intangible equity, subordinated debt, and cyclical peak additional capital, this range corresponds to 9 to 17 percent of risk-weighted assets (5 to 10 percent of total assets).[7]

Dagher et al. note that the top rate of the Basel III capital requirements schedule (for G-SIBs) plus a countercyclical buffer reaches 15.5 percent broadly defined capital relative to risk-weighted assets.[8] Considering further that banks tend to hold more than the legally required minimum capital, they interpret their findings as being consistent with Basel III requirements for G-SIBs, as well as with the Financial Stability Board recommendations for TLAC. After adjusting for the different capital concepts, their 15 to 23 percent range is relatively close to the 12 to 14 percent range for tangible common equity relative to risk-weighted assets identified in this study.

King (2010) estimates the impact of higher capital requirements on lending rates. Using data for nearly 7,000 banks from 13 countries in the Organization for Economic Cooperation and Development (OECD) for the period 1993–2007, he identifies key profiles relevant to the lending cost impact. He finds that loans represented about half of total assets, investments and securities 1/6th, interbank claims 1/8th, and trading assets 1/10th. Deposits represented 44 percent of assets, trading-related liabilities 15 percent, wholesale funding 14 percent, and interbank funding 13 percent. Total shareholders' equity was 5.3 percent of assets, and risk-weighted assets represented 53 percent of total assets. The return on equity was 15.5 percent.

King estimates average spreads on loans for the period at 275 basis points for US banks and 256 basis points for euro area banks. He estimates that the rates at which banks borrow average 100 basis points above the deposit rate for short-term debt and 200 basis points for debt with maturity of more than one year.

He assumes that higher capital requirements would necessitate the replacement of term debt by higher-cost equity. For a representative bank, an increase of 15 basis points in the lending spread would be necessary

---

7. The deductions are 1.5 percent for intangible equity, 2.0 percent for subordinated debt, and 2.5 percent for the buffer imposed only at cyclical peaks.

8. This amount corresponds to 9.5 percent of risk-weighted assets for tangible common equity for G-SIBs, excluding the cyclical peak amount.

to offset an increase in the (risk-weighted) capital ratio by 1 percentage point.[9] The calculation assumes no M&M offset in the reduction of the unit cost of equity. This estimate is almost the same as the estimates in BCBS (2010a) and Slovik and Cournède (2011) but somewhat higher than the 10 basis point median estimate across 10 studies in a recent BCBS (2016a) survey. The study estimates the corresponding impact on lending spreads from Basel III liquidity requirements (the net stable funding ratio) at 12 basis points.

Although the study does not recommend a particular level of bank capitalization, it provides relevant estimates on the cost side as well as a useful financial profile of OECD banks in the precrisis period. In this regard, it warrants remark that the study finds that on average, deposits were less than half of liabilities. There is much emphasis in the literature on distortions from subsidized funding through government deposit guarantees. However, with deposits less than half of liabilities, and with a considerable portion of deposits too large to be included under guarantee ceilings (e.g., corporate deposits), the influence of the guarantee subsidy would seem to be much more modest than the literature might imply.

Calibrated Optimization

Perhaps the most important study of optimal capital requirements remains that prepared by the Basel Committee's Long-Term Economic Impact (LEI) working group (BCBS 2010a). Based on a review of 19 studies of historical banking crisis episodes, the study places the median estimate of losses from a crisis at 19 percent of one year's GDP if there are no permanent effects, 158 percent of GDP if there are permanent effects, and 63 percent as the median for all studies (p. 35). Based on the compilations of banking crisis episodes in Reinhart and Rogoff (2008) and Laeven and Valencia (2008), it places the frequency of banking crises in 1985–2009 at 4.1 to 5.2 percent for G-10 countries (p. 39). However, as discussed in chapter 4, expanding the horizon to 1977–2015 reduces this incidence to only 2.6 percent.

To arrive at a mapping from bank capital to incidence of banking crises, the LEI working group considered the results of reduced-form econometric studies (including Barrell et al. 2010 and Kato, Kobayashi, and Saita 2010). It also incorporated findings of models treating the banking system as a portfolio of securities and examining the link between capital and default (as in Elsinger, Lehar, and Summer 2006). The resulting curve for all models shows the probability of a banking crisis falling from 4.6

---

9. The corresponding lending rate impact in the analysis of chapter 4 is only 4 basis points, reflecting a lower estimate of unit equity cost and an M&M offset of 45 percent.

percent at a capital requirement of 7 percent for tangible common equity relative to risk-weighted assets to a probability of 3 percent at a capital requirement of 8 percent, 1.9 percent at a requirement of 9 percent, and 0.3 percent at a requirement of 15 percent (see table 4.2).

On the cost side, the LEI study examined funding costs based on data for 6,600 banks in 13 countries during 1993–2007 to estimate that cost of equity. It reports an average return on equity of 14.8 percent and the cost of debt of 100 basis points above the deposit rate for short-term debt and 200 basis points for long-term debt. Higher capital requirements impose a cost, reflecting the differential between the return on equity and the rate on long-term debt as equity is increased relative to debt. Banks are assumed to pass on fully the higher cost in lending spreads, which are calculated to rise by 13 basis points for a 1 percent increase in the ratio of capital to risk-weighted assets. The LEI considers the impact near an upper bound, in part because it makes no allowance for any M&M offset.

The study then uses a set of existing models—including dynamic stochastic general equilibrium models, semistructural forecasting models, and reduced-form models, such as vector error correction models—to translate the impact of higher lending rates to changes in steady-state output. The output effect is found to be largely linear. An increase of 1 percent in the capital requirement reduces long-term output by 0.09 percent. Meeting the net stable funding ratio reduces output by an additional 0.08 percent. Overall the net benefits of higher capital ratios rise to a peak of about 1.9 percent of output as the ratio of tangible common equity to risk-weighted assets rises from 8 to 12 percent; they plateau at that level as the capital ratio is increased further to 16 percent.

A subsequent survey of the literature by the Basel Committee (BCBS 2016a) interprets the LEI findings as placing the optimum at a capital requirement of 13 percent of risk-weighted assets, well above the 9.5 percent level for large banks in Basel III (7 percent plus 2.5 percent for G-SIBs). The 13 percent optimum is at the center of the 12 to 14 percent range identified in chapter 4. This similarity reflects my use of the LEI quantification of the response of the probability of crisis to the capital ratio as well as the virtually identical central estimates of crisis damage (63 percent of one year's GDP in the LEI, 64 percent in chapter 4). Key differences tend to be in offsetting directions.[10]

---

10. The LEI study uses a higher unit cost of equity capital but makes no allowance for the M&M offset. Moreover, the macro models' typical response of output to higher borrowing costs in the LEI would appear to be substantially below the impact derived from the production function approach of Miles, Yang, and Marcheggiano (2012), applied in chapter 4. See the discussion of Tsatsaronis et al. (2015) in chapter 6.

An important early study of optimal capital requirements is by Barrell et al. (2009). The authors first estimate a logit function explaining the incidence of banking crises in OECD countries as a function of bank capital, the liquidity ratio, and the rate of increase in housing prices. The function shows a 22 percent probability of crisis in the United Kingdom in 2007, which could have been cut to 7 percent by a 3 percentage point increase in the ratio of capital to total assets (pp. 14–15).[11] They place the cost of crises at up to 80 percent of GDP and suggest a long-term scarring effect boosting risk premiums and hence the cost of capital. They argue that higher bank capital has economic costs, judging that M&M effects are incomplete not only because of tax incentives but also because of bankruptcy costs from fire sales under asymmetric information about fundamental values (p. 8).

Barrell et al. adopt a production function approach to calculate the long-term output impact of higher lending costs stemming from higher capital requirements. Applying the National Institute Global Econometric Model (NiGEM), they estimate that a 1 percentage point increase in the capital adequacy target would reduce output by 0.08 percent in the long term.

A problematic issue is that they treat the ratio of capital to risk-weighted assets as virtually identical to the ratio to total assets, based on data for UK banks (pp. 25–26), yet for US and euro area banks risk-weighted assets represent only slightly more than half of total assets. Their central estimate places the optimal increase in the capital ratio at 3 percentage points (p. 42). This increase would be to about the same level as the optimal range estimated in chapter 4 if the increment is measured in capital relative to total assets.[12]

Miles, Yang, and Marcheggiano (2012) provide an approach to optimal capital requirements that is similar to that in BCBS (2010a), in underlying concepts but different in arriving at the calibrated parameters. On the cost side, the driving force is once again an increase in the lending rate imposed as a consequence of the required shift away from cheaper debt finance to more expensive equity finance. The authors first examine the M&M offset by estimating the equity market beta coefficient for seven large UK banks using daily stock prices for 1992–2010. In their main variant, only 45 percent of the M&M offset is obtained. Based on equity unit cost of 15 percent and debt cost of 5 percent, they estimate that halving the leverage of banks from a debt to equity ratio of 30 to a ratio of 15 would boost the weighted-average cost of capital to banks by 33 basis points excluding any

---

11. The authors identify 14 systemic and 14 nonsystemic crises in the OECD in 1980–2007.

12. As set forth in chapter 4, the point of departure before Basel III is a ratio of 3.9 percent for tangible common equity relative to total assets.

M&M offset but by 18 basis points after allowing for the 45 percent offset (p. 13).

They then translate higher lending costs to output effects using a production function approach in which the stock of capital declines in response to a higher price of capital, after taking account of the factor share of capital and the degree of substitutability between capital and labor. Their output equation is far more transparent than the output component of such studies as BCBS (2010a). After considering that bank finance represents only one-third of corporate funding, the authors estimate that halving the debt leverage of banks would reduce long-term output by 0.15 percent. This impact corresponds to an output loss of 0.05 percent for each percentage point increase in the capital required relative to total assets.[13]

On the benefit side, the authors place the present value of output loss in a banking crisis at 140 percent of base GDP (p. 25), well above the BCBS (2010a) median figure of 63 percent. They use an unusual method for calibrating the response of crisis probability to bank capital. They assume that the proportionate decline in risk-weighted assets in a financial crisis is equal to the proportionate decline in GDP. They examine the frequency distribution of declines in GDP over the past 200 years for 31 countries, and find a higher incidence of extreme declines than would be expected. Declines of more than 15 percent occurred 1.2 percent of the time, implying that a capital ratio of 15 percent of risk-weighted assets would be insufficient to avoid banking crisis 1.2 percent of the time.

On the basis of such frequencies the authors compare marginal benefits with marginal costs. Their marginal benefits curve (p. 26) is not monotonic; it surges once again when capital ratios reach extremely high levels (40 percent), corresponding to the tail of extreme declines in GDP (e.g., war experiences). This aspect is troublesome, because in principle the gains from additional capital ought to take account of the probability of such instances already in the lower range of capital ratios. The authors do not present a single equation for benefits, or for marginal benefits, ruling out identification of a unique capital ratio at which marginal benefits begin to fall below marginal costs. In their policy recommendation, they instead emphasize that even if the upper extreme is ignored completely, the range for optimal capital requirements is 16 to 20 percent of risk-weighted assets, corresponding to 7 to 9 percent of total assets (p. 29).

---

13. Reducing the leverage ratio from 30:1 to 15:1 boosts the ratio of capital to assets from 1/31 to 1/16, or by 6.2 − 3.2 = 3.0 percentage points, translating the output loss of 0.15 to 0.05 percent per percentage point in the ratio of capital to total assets. For a comparison with the cost estimates of this study, see the discussion in chapter 4.

Kato, Kobayashi, and Saita (2010) estimate a probit model of the probability of a banking crisis, using the episodes identified by Laeven and Valencia (2008) for 13 industrial countries. Their approach emphasizes the interaction between liquidity and capital. Their independent variables are the ratio of capital to total assets, the ratio of liquid to total assets and the corresponding liquidity ratio for liabilities, the rate of real estate inflation, and the current account balance as a percent of GDP. Their tests include the capital ratio interacted with the liquidity ratios on both the asset and liability sides. Pointing out that the US investment banks in which the government intervened had higher capital-to-assets ratios than other banks (p. 5), they stress that the Lehman shock was triggered not by undercapitalization but by liquidity stress and the inability to roll over short-term funding, especially in the repo market (p. 19).[14] They place the cost of a banking crisis at 10 percent of GDP, far lower than the model median 63 percent reported in BCBS (2010a).

For the cost of additional capital, the authors apply the formula proposed by Van den Heuvel (2008): $\Delta C = D \times (R^e - R^d) \times (\Delta k / [1 - k])$, where Δ indicates change, C consumption (or GDP), D deposits, R the rate of return, e equity, d debt, and k the ratio of capital to total assets.[15] For Japan they place deposits at 250 percent of consumption, R^e at 3.75 percent, and R^d at zero.[16] By implication, and with an illustrative value of $k = 0.1$, an increase in the capital ratio by 1 percentage point would reduce consumption by 0.09 percent ($0.01 \times 250 \times 0.0375 = 0.094$).[17] The welfare cost of additional liquidity in assets is based on the difference between average bank lending rates and the yield on liquid assets.

On the liability side, the cost of raising the liquidity ratio depends on the excess of the cost of retail liabilities (e.g., deposits) over wholesale liabilities (e.g., repos). At intermediate asset- and liability-side liquidity ratios, the authors arrive at a range of 6 to 8 for the optimal ratio of capital to total assets across three states of the business cycle (p. 32). These ratios are

---

14. Higher capital ratios for the investment banks however, apparently reflected heavy reliance on optimistic risk weighting. Based on simple ratios of equity to total assets, the large investment banks were instead much more highly leveraged than the commercial banks (Cline 2010, 288). Moreover, Cline and Gagnon (2013) find that Lehman was a case of insolvency, not illiquidity.

15. Van den Heuvel (2008, 308) treats the spread $R^e - R^d$ as "the amount of consumption households are willing to forgo in order to enjoy the liquidity services of one additional unit of deposits."

16. This ratio is far higher than in the United States, where bank deposits at the end of 2015 amounted to 61 percent of GDP (Federal Reserve 2016a).

17. This impact is smaller but of the same order of magnitude as the corresponding estimate of 0.15 in chapter 4 (parameter ψ).

relatively high, especially considering that the benefit of avoiding a crisis is estimated at only 10 percent of GDP.

Researchers at the Bank of England (Schanz et al. 2011) use a method similar to that in chapter 4 to evaluate optimal capital ratios. They estimate that for UK banks, raising the capital ratio by 1 percent of risk-weighted assets would boost lending rates by 7.4 basis points, assuming no M&M offset. Applying a simple production function, assuming corporations have a cost of capital of 10 percent and, assuming that banks account for only one-third of financing of corporations, they estimate a reduction in output of 0.04 percent for each percentage point increase in the capital ratio. But in chapter 4 I suggest that the average corporate cost of capital is only 4.6 percent, so the proportionate increase in the cost of capital—and hence the output impact—would be about twice as high as calculated in the Bank of England study for a given increment in the average cost of capital.[18]

On the benefits side, Schanz et al. estimate the lost present value from a banking crisis at 140 percent of one year's GDP—on the high side compared with the benchmark BCBS (2010a) study. They use a Merton-style structural credit risk portfolio model to relate the probability of banking crisis to the capital to risk-weighted assets ratio, calibrated to identify a crisis when two of the United Kingdom's large banks default because their capital falls below 4 percent of risk-weighted assets. Their probability mapping (p. 77) starts out far higher than that in BCBS (2010a), with a 20 percent probability of a banking crisis versus 4.5 percent, at an 8 percent capital to risk-weighted assets ratio and 3 percent probability versus 1.4 percent at a 10 percent ratio (see table 4.2). They conclude that appropriate capital requirements are "somewhere between 10 percent and 15 percent of risk-weighted assets" (p. 73). This range is consistent with the optimal range calculated in chapter 4 (12 to 14 percent of risk-weighted assets), reflecting offsetting differences in the estimates for individual components in the two studies.

Gambacorta (2011) applies a vector error correction model to quarterly data for the US economy in 1994–2008 to examine the impact of changes in capital and liquidity requirements. He finds that the bank lending spread is a function of capital and liquidity requirements; the level

---

18. The 0.04 percent impact in Schanz et al. translates into 0.07 percent for a 1 percent increase in capital relative to total assets. The impact estimated in chapter 4 is $\psi = 0.15$ percent, about twice as high, reflecting the lower average cost of capital to nonfinancial firms in my estimates. Chapter 4 allows nearly half the M&M offset (tending to reduce rather than increase the impact) but uses a higher capital share (0.4 instead of 0.3, working in the opposite direction).

of output is a function of the real interest rate, the bank lending spread, and government spending; bank lending to the economy is a function of the level of GDP and the lending spread; and the return on bank equity is a function of lending relative to GDP and the lending spread.

One might wonder why this system would capture long-term effects accurately, with a lag structure of only three quarters, no equation directly relating output to capital and labor, no equations translating lending rates to capital stock, no explicit consideration of the share of bank lending in total finance to the economy, and no direct test of the M&M offset (although by implication it would show up in a muted influence of the capital requirement on output). Furthermore, no exogenous changes in required bank capital were imposed in this period, suggesting difficulties in attributing causality.

Nonetheless, Gambacorta's key results turn out to be relatively similar to those in the calibrated model developed in chapter 4. In particular, in the long-term equilibrium, an increase in the capital requirement (tangible common equity relative to risk-weighted assets) of 6 percentage points increases the bank lending spread by 15 basis points (p. 84). The corresponding impact in the model in chapter 4 would be 13.9 basis points.[19] In the Gambacorta results, an increase in the capital ratio of 1 percentage point reduces steady-state output by 0.1 percent. When this impact is translated into the corresponding metric for capital relative to total assets, the impact reaches a 0.178 percent decline in output for a 1 percentage point increase in the capital requirement, close to the parameter identified in chapter 4 ($\psi = 0.15$).

According to Gambacorta, with "moderate permanent effects" of crises, the gross benefits of crisis avoidance rise from 0.6 percent of GDP at a 7 percent risk-weighted capital ratio to 2.2 percent of GDP at 10 percent, 2.4 percent of GDP at 12 percent, and 2.6 percent at 15 percent. Costs rise linearly, from nearly zero at 7 to 0.7 percent of GDP at 15 percent. Marginal costs equal marginal benefits at a risk-weighted capital ratio of 12 percent (p. 87). Again this finding is almost the same as that in chapter 4.

Yan, Hall, and Turner (2011) estimate a model of optimal capital requirements for the UK economy. On the benefit side, they estimate a probit model relating the probability of a banking crisis to the ratio of tangible common equity to risk-weighted assets, interacted with liquidity (the net stable financing ratio). Their test also includes the rate of inflation in real

---

19. A 6 percent risk-weighted capital ratio corresponds to a 3.37 percent for the ratio of capital to total assets. Applying the base case parameters of tables 4.3 and 4.4 in chapter 4 (return on equity of 10 percent, bank debt cost of 2.5 percent, and M&M offset of 0.45) yields an increase in the lending rate of 13.9 basis points.

estate and the size of the current account deficit. A banking crisis is defined as occurring in the first quarter of 2008 through the second quarter of 2010. Data for the 12 largest banks provide the capital and liquidity information. Estimated using quarterly data beginning in 1997, the model would seem to be inherently limited, given its reliance on a single country. Its results seem exceedingly binary, indicating that, whereas a 7 percent capital ratio reduces the probability of a crisis by 3.2 percent and a ratio of 8 percent reduces it by 4.6 percent, higher levels of capital have almost no additional impact reducing crisis probability. This outcome is sharply at odds with the BCBS (2010a) survey, which shows considerable additional reductions as the capital ratio reaches higher levels (see table 4.2 in chapter 4).[20]

On the cost side, the study relies on a vector autoregression and vector error correction approach, which generates coefficients relating lending spreads to capital requirements and relating output to lending spreads. Curiously, this relationship is concave rather than the usual linear result.[21]

More fundamentally, it seems unlikely that a vector auto regression approach would be as reliable as a calibrated capital cost and production function approach, for several reasons. The lag structure, for example, is only three quarters, far too short to capture steady-state effects. The key output equation includes only the lending spread, the real interest rate, and the rate of return on equity as explanatory variables (p. 13). There is almost no variation in the capital ratio over the period 2000–08 (p. 32).[22] Although the optimal capital ratio identified by the study (10 percent of risk-weighted assets) is not implausible, the underpinnings of the estimate may not be robust.

Researchers at the Bank of England examined optimal systemic capital requirements in a framework representing "a panel of correlated Merton (1974) balance sheet models, jointly estimated using observed bank equity returns, and combined with a network of interbank exposures" (Webber and Willison 2011, 8). An iterative approach imposes contagious losses, with interbank exposures cleared using the algorithm of Eisenberg and Noe (2001). Under the assumption that M&M does not hold completely and thus that higher capital requirements impose costs on the economy, the authors minimize the total capital required for the system subject to a 5 percent target value at risk that system assets will fall below system

20. The model applies 210 percent of output as the permanent loss from a banking crisis—on the high side of most estimates.

21. At 7 percent, 1 additional percentage point in the capital ratio reduces output by 0.08 percent; at 10 percent the marginal impact is a .04 percent reduction in output.

22. The ratio falls from 7.8 percent in 1997–99 to 4.9 percent in 2000, moves back to 5.5 percent in 2001, and is flat (at 5.8 percent) thereafter (p. 32).

liabilities (p. 13). Their stepwise iterative procedure involves 50,000 simulations of a model calibrated to five major UK banks in 2004–09. They use observed equity prices to estimate the expected return on banks' assets and the variance-covariance structure between the banks' asset returns.

A distinctive feature of the model is that the cost-minimizing capital structure differentiates among banks, reflecting greater idiosyncratic risk at some banks than others as well as taking account of differing interbank exposure. Thus for 2008 the optimal systemic surcharge is set at 6 percent of assets for "bank 1" but only 0.8 percent for "bank 5" and an average of 2.4 percent for the five banks (p. 21). Experiments show a surprising insensitivity to further expansion of large-bank size (a doubling of bank 1's balance sheet increases its optimal capital surcharge only from 6 to 7 percent; p. 22).

In research at Norway's central bank, Kragh-Sørensen (2012) estimates optimal capital ratios in a framework similar to those applied by BCBS (2010a) and Miles, Yang, and Marcheggiano (2012). However, he develops an independent estimate of the relationship between the probability of a banking crisis and the capital ratio. This estimate is based on data on problem loans to households and corporations in Norway in 1990–2011. He applies an estimated distribution to simulate the stock of problem loans for the six largest Norwegian banks, with a banking crisis identified if two or more are found to have capital ratios below 4.5 percent.

It turns out that his results show much higher probabilities of banking crises at given capital ratios for Norway than in the broader BCBS (2010a) study. For example, an increase in the capital ratio from 9 to 13 percent of risk-weighted assets reduces the probability of a banking crisis from 7.0 to 1.7 percent in his estimates for Norway (p. 6), in contrast to a reduction from 2.6 to 0.5 percent in the broader BCBS (2010a) study.

Alternative estimates of the long-term output cost of higher capital requirements include one from the Norges Bank's Financial Stability Model indicating an output decline of 0.09 percent for an increase in the capital requirement of 1 percentage point at the high end and a model providing much lower cost (much higher M&M offset) at the low end. When banking crisis damage is set at a reasonable 60 percent of one year's GDP, the result is an average estimate of 19 percent for the optimal ratio of capital to risk-weighted assets across the variants, ranging from a low of 16 percent to a high of 23 percent (p. 11). The driving force behind this high range is the much higher path of the crisis probability curve than in other leading studies (BCBS 2010b, Miles, Yang, and Marcheggiano 2012). By implication, the most desirable policy would seem more likely to be to set an especially stringent capital requirement in Norway (and perhaps other countries sharing above-average fragility) rather than to place broader Basel capital targets as high as indicated in the Norway-specific study.

Researchers at the Financial Services Authority examined the costs and benefits of higher capital requirements for UK banks (de-Ramon et al. 2012). Like Barrell et al. (2009), they use a logit function to relate the incidence of banking crisis to capital requirements and apply the NiGEM model to calculate output effects. They extend the crisis function by adding the current account as an explanatory variable. They add considerable detail to modeling the dynamic profile of banks' adjustments to higher capital requirements, including special attention to the cutback of total assets and change in risk composition.[23] They also take into account an expected narrowing of banks' voluntary buffers as the capital requirement increases.

de-Ramon et al. estimate the long-term loss from a UK banking crisis at an ongoing 3 percent of annual GDP (implicitly equivalent to 120 percent of one year's GDP, or about twice the BCBS 2010a median, if discounted at 2.5 percent) (p. 51). They calculate that a 1 percent increase in the ratio of capital to risk-weighted assets imposes an increase of 9.4 basis points in the spread between bank deposit and lending rates (p. 31). The full Basel III package causes a short-term increase in bank lending rates of 126 basis points and a long-term increase of 67 basis points (p. 55). Higher lending rates cause lower output, working through the NiGEM model. The study's central estimate is that the Basel III regulatory reform produces an annual gross benefit to the United Kingdom of 1.29 percent of GDP at an output cost of 0.38 percent of GDP, yielding a net benefit of 0.92 percent of GDP (£11.9 billion at 2010 prices; p. 53).

de-Ramon et al. report that in their stochastic simulations the net benefits of the Basel III package could reach as high as 4.9 percent of GDP at the favorable 90th percentile (p. 61), but they do not report the assumptions that would raise the net benefits this high.[24] Despite this seemingly large upside potential, the authors imply that the optimal capital requirements are not much different from Basel III: "The costs of requiring higher

---

23. Starting from a base ratio of 14 percent for observed bank holdings of total regulatory capital (including their voluntary buffer above the minimum), by year 5 the effect of a 1 percent increase in the required ratio of capital to risk-weighted assets is to increase total regulatory capital by 3.6 percent (half the full 1 percent/14 percent = 7 percent), while reducing assets by 1.9 percent and reducing risk-weighted assets by 3.2 percent (p. 16).

24. Given the modest estimate on the cost side, the alternative gains would have to come mainly from still more frequent banking crisis and still higher damages in the absence of higher capital.

capital ratios beyond the [Basel III] policy package. . . rise faster than the benefits" (p. 54).

Their conclusion is somewhat misleading in this regard. It states that "prudential standards could be raised further by up to an additional 22 percentage points in terms of banks' aggregate risk-weighted capital ratio, and still be expected to produce overall positive net benefits in the long run" (p. 65). But this statement means that fairly close to the Basel III ratio additional capital would start to impose costs that would eat away at the net benefits achieved at the Basel III level and that after an additional 22 percentage points those gains would have all been lost. Their 22 percent additional capital would correspond to the point in figure 4.3 in chapter 4 at which the benefits curve crosses the cost curve (eliminating the net benefits indicated by the vertical difference between the two curves), a point that is far to the right of the optimal capital requirement, where the slopes of the two curves are equal.

Finally, a report issued in preliminary form by the Federal Reserve Bank of Minneapolis (Minneapolis Plan 2016) uses the Dagher et al. (2016) data on nonperforming loans in past crises together with simulations of the large macroeconomic model of the US Federal Reserve to estimate the optimal capital ratio, which it finds to be 23.5 percent. (Appendix 4A examines this study in detail). The study calls for a capital requirement of 38 percent of risk-weighted assets on G-SIBs in order to eliminate too big to fail (but this estimate is not obtained using optimization).

Overview

Table 2.1 summarizes the optimal capital ratios identified in the studies surveyed here (including several dynamic stochastic general equilibrium models, described in appendix 2A, and one vector error correction study). The ratios refer to common equity tier 1 relative to risk-weighted assets; in some cases the table entries are accordingly adjusted from the studies' main reported estimates (as indicated in the notes).[25] It is evident in the table that the study by Admati and Hellwig (2013) is an outlier, with an optimal range far higher than any other of the main estimates. As it turns out, my own estimates (presented in chapter 4) are centered at the median for the full set of estimates: an optimal ratio of 13 percent for common equity tier 1 relative to risk-weighted assets (corresponding to the 7 to 8 percent estimate in chapter 4 for the median and 75th percentile optimal ratios of common equity tier 1 to total assets).

---

25. The table applies the value 1.78 for the ratio of total assets to risk-weighted assets, based on data on the US and the euro area reported in BCBS (2010a) and as discussed in chapter 4.

Table 2.1   Literature estimates of optimal ratio of capital[a] to risk-weighted assets (percent)

Study	Method	Optimal ratio	Notes
Admati and Hellwig (2013)	Hist-MM	36–53	b
Hanson, Kashyap, and Stein (2010) (US)	SW	27	c
Goldstein (2017) (US)	SW	18–32	d
Dagher, Dell'Ariccia, Laeven, Ratnovski, and Tong (2016)	SW	9–17	e
Basel Committee on Banking Supervision (BCBS 2010a)	COM	13	f
Barrell, Davis, Fic, Holland, Kirby, and Liadze (2009) (UK)	COM	9	g
Miles, Yang, and Marcheggiano (2012)	CM	16–20	h
Kato, Kobayashi, and Saita (2010)	COM	11–14	i
Gambacorta (2011) (US)	VECM	12	j
Yan, Hall, and Turner (2011) (UK)	COM	10	k
Kragh-Sørensen (2012) (Norway)	COM	16–23	l
de-Ramon, Iscenko, Osborne, Straughan, and Andrews (2015) (UK)	COM	10	m
Van den Heuvel (2008)	DSGE	< 5	n
Clerc et al. (2015)	DSGE	10.5	o
Mendicino, Nikolov, Suarez, and Supera (2015) (euro area)	DSGE	10	p
Minneapolis Plan (2016) (US)	COM	23.5	q
This study	**COM**	**12–14**	r
Median		*13*	

Hist-MM = historical, strong Modigliani & Miller assumption; SW = seawall; COM = calibrated optimization model; CM = calibrated model; VECM: vector error correction method; DSGE = dynamic stochastic general equilibrium model

a. Common equity tier 1.
b. 20 to 30 percent of total assets.
c. 15 percent of total assets.
d. 10 to 18 percent of total assets.
e. 15 to 23 percent including intangible equity, subordinated debt, and cyclical peak buffer.
f. See BCBS (2016a) for identification of optimal 13 percent within BCBS (2010a) range.
g. 3 percentage points above 2007 actual level. Study treats risk-weighted and total assets as equivalent. Base for risk-weighted actual set at 5.7 percent (Cohen 2013).
h. Authors do not calculate optimal level but identify preferred range.
i. 6 to 8 percent of total assets.
j. Uses quarterly data for the United States.
k. UK basis.
l. Norway only.
m. Based on maximum net benefit at 4 percentage point increase in capital adequacy (p. 59), combined with 5.7 percent actual base in 2009 (Cohen 2013).
n. Study completed before the Great Recession.
o. Benefits from curbing excessive risk taking, eventually swamped by costs of reduced capital formation. No crisis costs incorporated.
p. Study finds 13.5 percent optimal but including 3.5 percent in capital other than tier 1 common equity.
q. For too big to fail G-SIBs: 38 percent, but not calculated using optimization.
r. 7 to 8 percent of total assets.

Although the studies are treated equally in arriving at the median estimate, the dynamic stochastic general equilibrium estimates are less satisfactory than most of the calibrated optimization models. (Indeed, one of these models completed shortly before the Great Recession concluded that bank capital requirements were already too high.) None of these studies contains an explicit modeling of the probability of a banking crisis or an estimation of the economic cost associated with such a crisis, although such impacts are at the heart of the policy debate about reforming the banking sector.

The median optimal capital ratio of 13 percent is substantially above the Basel III ratio of 7 percent (4.5 percent minimum common equity plus 2.5 percent capital conservation buffer); it is also well above the corresponding ratio for G-SIBs (which adds another 2.5 percent for a total of 9.5 percent). The broad implication is that the Basel III requirements fall short of the optimal levels for capital. The principal caveat is that Basel III also requires TLAC of 18 percent of risk-weighted assets for the largest banks, nearly doubling the cushion provided by common equity capital alone. If the securities included in TLAC (equity plus CoCos plus eligible subordinated debt) were all of equal quality for purposes of safety of the banking sector, one might conclude instead that Basel III had already gone more than far enough to ensure the stability of the system. However, the discussion in chapter 5 suggests that TLAC is not a fully adequate substitute for equity capital.

Appendix 2A

Literature on Transient and Dynamic Stochastic General Equilibrium (DSGE) Estimates

Transient Estimates

In 2010 the Macroeconomic Assessment Group (MAG 2010) of the Basel Committee on Banking Supervision estimated the prospective effects of the transition to higher capital requirements under Basel III. Drawing on nearly 100 model simulations from central banks and regulators of 17 countries, IMF country models, and European Central Bank and European Commission models for the euro area, the study estimated that "bringing the global common equity capital ratio to a level that would meet the agreed minimum and the capital conservation buffer would result in a maximum decline in GDP, relative to baseline forecasts, of 0.22 percent, which would occur after 35 quarters" (p. 2). Typically the models calculated the impact of a 1 percentage point increase in the capital ratio, phased in smoothly over eight years. Median estimates indicated a maximum decline of output (from baseline) of 0.15 percent in the 35th quarter, rebounding to 0.1 percent below baseline by the 48th quarter.

IMF estimates indicate that additional adverse spillover effects from simultaneous increases in capital requirements across countries would boost the maximum loss by an additional 0.02 percent by the 35th quarter. Among about 70 models based primarily on credit spread impacts, about half excluded induced monetary policy changes and found larger maximum losses (0.18 percent); the half that included endogenous monetary policy found smaller maximum losses (0.11 percent). By implication monetary policy was capable of offsetting about one-third of the transient impact.

Simulations indicate that if the full adjustment were compressed to a much shorter period of only two years, the maximum output loss per percentage point increase in capital ratio would be 0.22 percent from baseline before partial recovery rather than 0.17 percent (0.15 percent plus the 0.02 percent spillover; p. 9). This difference is somewhat smaller than might have been expected from the general perception of a need to phase in higher requirements gradually.

The estimates also imply a surprisingly small increase of only 1.3 percent in the capital ratio to get from actual practice in 2009 to the Basel III targets. Thus the study places the common equity tier 1 capital ratio of large internationally active banks at 5.7 percent of risk-weighted assets in December 2009. It estimates that reaching the new Basel III target of 7 percent (4.5 percent plus 2.5 percent capital conservation) would cause an increase of only 1.3 percentage points in the capital ratio from the "starting point" for large internationally active banks (p. 7).

A 2011 study by researchers at the OECD (Slovik and Cournède 2011) estimates the medium-term decline in growth associated with the increases in capital requirements under Basel III of 0.05 to 0.15 percentage points a year. They estimate that by 2019, banks in the United States, the euro area, and Japan would need to raise common equity relative to risk-weighted assets by an average of 3.7 percentage points (p. 6)—even though the result would be to boost the ratio in the United States (for example) from 10.5 percent in 2009 to 13.6 percent, far above the Basel III minimum of 9.5 percent even for G-SIBs. The authors assume that banks would maintain relatively high voluntary buffers above the minimum requirements. They estimate that a 1 percentage point increase in the capital ratio would raise bank lending spreads by 15 basis points. They use the OECD's New Global Model to place the semi-elasticity of long-term GDP with respect to bank lending rates at –1.45 percent of GDP per 100 basis points (p. 9). With full phase-in of Basel III boosting bank lending rates by 52 basis points, they calculate that the long-term impact on GDP (five years after implementation) would be a decline of 0.75 percent. They thus place the reduction in annual growth in the medium term at 0.05 to 0.15 percent, reflecting interim (2015) and full (2019) effects. They note that this range is about three times as large as the MAG (2010) estimate, a difference the authors attribute to their assumption that relatively large capital buffers above the Basel III minimums would be maintained. They also emphasize that monetary policy could be loosened to offset the slow-down in growth, implying a reduction in policy rates of 30 to 80 basis points from their levels otherwise. However, it is unclear that monetary easing would be the appropriate response in an environment in which output is being squeezed on the supply side from lower capital formation.

The parameters from the OECD study provide a useful comparison with those used in chapter 4. In Slovik and Cournède (2011), a 1 percentage point increase in the ratio of capital to risk-weighted assets has a long-term negative effect on GDP of 0.22 percent (15.2 basis points on the lending spread and 1.45 percent of GDP for 100 basis points on the bank lending rate ($0.152 \times 1.45 = 0.22$)). Considering the relationship of total assets to risk-weighted assets (set at 1.78 in chapter 4), the corresponding parameter would be a reduction of 0.39 percent in GDP for a 1 percentage point increase in the ratio of capital to total assets. This parameter is more than twice as large as that estimated in chapter 4 (0.15). However, much of this difference is explained by the fact that Slovik and Cournède make no allowance for an M&M offset, whereas I set the offset at 45 percent of the direct impact of increased capital requirements on lending spreads.

A key study by the leading global association of financial institutions, the Institute of International Finance (IIF 2011), examines the prospective impact of the set of regulatory reforms in Basel III, including especially the increased capital requirements for banks.[26] It estimates that the reforms would cause an average increase in bank lending rates to the private sector in the United States, the euro area, the United Kingdom, Switzerland, and Japan of 364 basis points in 2011–15 and 281 basis points in 2011–20 (p. 54). Based on application of the NiGEM, it projects that real GDP in 2015 would be 3.2 percent lower than it would have been in the absence of the new regulations (p. 55).

However, actual experience in 2011–15 was not kind to this projection. Average bank lending rates in the United States, France, and Germany fell rather than rose in this period (see figure 3C.1 in appendix 3C in chapter 3), and any increases in spreads above risk-free rates were far smaller than the IIF projected.

The report acknowledges the M&M theorem but states: "Most industry practitioners question the validity and applicability of the M&M theorem. This. . .[is] likely to reflect the outcome of experience. . . . in the short run, as ownership dilution concerns dominate. . .heavy required (and/or feared) equity issuance could depress bank equity prices, thus raising the short-run cost of equity finance" (p. 45). It describes official sector studies as "too sanguine about funding implications" (p. 16).

In its equation for the "return on equity," the study calculates the "shadow" cost of equity as equal to the target return on equity plus a coefficient of 0.5 multiplied by the excess in the growth of core tier 1 equity over the growth rate of nominal GDP. It allows an M&M offset of 0.25 times the excess of the core tier 1 capital ratio over 7 percent.[27] This formulation generates an increase in lending rates of 364 basis points over five years.

The overall thrust of the study is that the rising equity costs associated with dilution effects in the face of the relatively rapid phase-in of higher capital requirements would far outweigh M&M effects, so that the average cost of capital would rise not only as a result of the increase in the fraction of financing coming from equity but also because of an increase in the cost of equity capital itself. The report does not provide specifics on these funding shares or the pre- and postreform levels of equity capital costs. It

---

26. The author was deputy managing director and chief economist of the Institute of International Finance in 1996–2001, with supervisory responsibility for its analysis of emerging-market economies.

27. In addition, the equation includes the coefficient 0.5 times the excess of target return on equity minus realized return on equity.

does state that "everyone accepts that most of the costs will be borne in the near term, whereas the benefits will be longer term in accruing" (p. 11).

If this view is combined with the apparent outcome that effects in the near term have not been as severe as expected by the IIF, the broad implication would seem to be that the tradeoff was not as adverse as the IIF feared in 2011.

In contrast, this study focuses on the persistent rather than the short-term costs of higher equity requirements. It examines much larger capital increases than those agreed to in Basel III.

Roger and Vlček (2011) use a dynamic stochastic general equilibrium (DSGE) model to examine the transient costs of phasing in higher capital requirements. To the typical model structure of impatient and patient households, entrepreneurs, producers, government, and monetary authority, they add a banking sector that lends to households and the production sector. Banks face a quadratic penalty function for revenues when their capital ratio differs from the regulatory requirement. Increasing the capital requirement by 2 percentage points of risk-weighted assets over two years causes cumulative output losses over five years equivalent to 1 percent of one year's GDP if banks adjust mainly by cutting dividends and accepting lower return on equity, 2 percent if they mainly raise lending margins, and up to 4 percent if they adjust by cutting the volume of assets (these figures are averages for euro area and US banks). These costs are little affected by the speed of the phase-in.[28] The costs are about one-fourth higher if normal monetary policy response (the Taylor rule) is unavailable (e.g., because interest rates are already at a zero bound). Although the model focuses on a five-year horizon, its steady state finds that in the scenario with bank adjustment through increased lending spreads, the 2 percentage point increase in the risk-weighted capital-to-assets ratio boosts lending spreads by 15 to 20 basis points and leads to "slightly lower" steady-state output (p. 14).[29]

Roger and Vlček do not calculate the effects of equity issuance as the mode of bank response, because "the dynamic effects are essentially nonexistent with this model" (p. 11), a sharply different modeling approach from that of the IIF (2011). Even with adjustment limited to lending spreads, a

---

28. If the phase-in period is doubled to four years, cumulative costs fall from an average of 1.05 percent of one year's GDP to 0.65 percent at the low end and from 4.15 to 3.9 percent at the high end (p. 19).

29. Using the parameters of chapter 4, the corresponding estimate for the impact on bank lending spreads for a 2 percentage point increase in the risk-weighted capital ratio would be only 7.7 basis points. These figures are different from the estimates in Roger and Vlček (2011) because the authors make no allowance for an M&M offset and likely use a substantially higher unit cost of equity capital (such as 15 percent instead of the 10 percent base case in chapter 4).

longer (four-year) phase-in period, and allowance of monetary authority response, the costs are not trivial: The 2 percentage point increase in the capital ratio causes a cumulative loss of 2 percent of one year's output. This estimate serves as a caveat to the argument that active monetary policy could easily offset costs of higher capital requirements.

Estimates by the European Commission (2011) are close to those of the MAG (2010) and far from those of the IIF (2011). Using its QUEST model (a DSGE model incorporating a financial sector), it estimates that a 1 percentage point increase in the capital requirement would reduce output by 0.1 percent from baseline by year 4, 0.15 percent by year 8, and 0.36 percent in the long term. This estimate is far more optimistic than that of the IIF, which the European Commission interpreted as indicating a decline in output from baseline by 2.1 percent in year 4. Although its estimate for year 8 is virtually the same as the median-model estimate by the MAG (2010), its "long-term" estimate is much larger than implied by the MAG results (which show output returning partially to baseline after a maximum decline by the 35th quarter). In an attempt to consider the IIF argument regarding higher rather than lower required return on equity in the face of higher capital requirements, the European Commission calculated that an increase of 50 basis points in return on equity would boost the potential long-term loss from a 1 percent additional capital requirement from 0.36 to 0.58 percent (still considerably smaller than the IIF estimate).

Cohen (2013) provides an early review of the experience of banks in adjusting to the new capital requirements of Basel III. For 82 large global banks over the period 2009–12, he finds that retained earnings accounted for the bulk of the increase in risk-weighted capital ratios; reduction in risk weights played a smaller role. Lower dividend payouts and wider lending spreads contributed to retained earnings. Lending continued to expand, as banks from advanced economies increased their assets by 8 percent (European banks by less) and banks from emerging-market economies increased their assets by 47 percent. Banks that emerged from the crisis with relatively low levels of capital tended to have slower asset growth.[30] For the large global banks, the weighted average of capital ratios (common equity) rose from 5.7 percent of risk-weighted assets at the end of 2009 to 9 percent at the end of 2012.[31] Their common equity capital rose 34 percent. The denominator of the capital ratio (risk-weighted assets) rose 5 percent

---

30. A bank with a 1 percentage point higher capital ratio at end-2009 was likely to have a 3 percentage point higher rate of asset growth over the subsequent three years.

31. Under Basel II definitions, which were more lenient in the definition of capital, the corresponding change was from 11.6 to 14.2 percent.

(an increase of 14 percent in total assets moderated by an 8 percent decline in the ratio of risk-weighted to total assets). Three-fourths of the increase in risk-weighted capital ratios came from higher capital.

Cohen finds that higher capital requirements did indeed lead to higher spreads, amounting to 11 basis points per percentage point increase in the capital ratio, but notes that this increase is smaller than the 15- to 17-basis-point increase estimated by the MAG (2010) and much smaller than the 30- to 80-basis-point increase estimated by the IIF (2011). He also finds that the ratio of net income to book equity fell sharply, from almost 21 to 8 percent, driven by a decline for advanced economy banks. Price-to-book ratios also fell below unity after the crisis for many banks. In Europe lending growth lagged far behind asset growth, as banks shifted toward cash and government securities. The broad thrust of Cohen's findings is that the transition was going more smoothly than many had feared and that there had not been sharp cutbacks in assets that would have been contractionary (although there was "a pronounced shortfall in lending *growth* [emphasis added] among European banks" [p. 39]).

In late 2015 the Financial Stability Board released its first annual report to the G-20 on the implementation and effects of financial regulatory reform (FSB 2015b). It finds that "all large internationally active banks already meet the fully phased-in risk-based minimum capital requirements" (p. 7) of Basel III, three years ahead of the January 1, 2019 deadline. In addition, 80 percent of these banks met the fully phased-in targets for liquidity.[32] However, the report finds variations in banks' risk-weighting of assets based on internal models and indicates that the Basel Committee was working on improving the consistency of risk weighting. The report also notes that the Financial Stability Board had agreed to an international standard for TLAC for G-SIBs and that assessments indicated that "the benefits [of TLAC] exceed costs by a good margin" (p. 9).[33]

---

32. To meet the liquidity coverage ratio, banks are required to hold unencumbered high-quality liquid assets equal to liquidity needs over 30 days in a liquidity stress scenario (BCBS 2013). To meet the net stable funding ratio, banks must ensure that the portion of their capital plus liabilities that is expected to be reliable over the course of one year (the numerator) equals or exceeds the required amount of stable funding given short-term debt and residual maturities (BCBS 2014b).

33. The report estimates that shortfalls from the TLAC target amounted to €42 billion to €776 billion for advanced-economy G-SIBs and €265 billion to €354 billion for G-SIBs headquartered in emerging-market and developing economies. It estimates that meeting the TLAC requirement would boost average lending rates by 2.2 to 3.2 basis points, causing a median long-run loss of 2.0 to 2.8 basis points of annual GDP (with a conservative range of loss set as high as 10 to 15 basis points). Its central estimate is 48 basis points of annual GDP in macroeconomic benefits. Crisis avoidance was presumably the basis for the benefit estimate, but the report does not discuss the methodology behind the estimates.

Cecchetti (2014) reviews the experience of initial implementation of Basel III capital requirements. He notes the wide gap between the early predictions of the IIF (2011) and the MAG (2010) regarding economic consequences and observes that most analysts outside the banking and regulatory communities considered that the drag on output would be relatively small and closer to the MAG end of the spectrum. Noting that most large internationally active banks already met the 2019 requirements, he argues that "the jury is in. . . . The optimists were not optimistic enough. Capital requirements have gone up dramatically, and bank capital levels have gone up with them. In the meantime, lending spreads have barely moved, bank interest margins are down, and loan volumes are up" (p. 1). Cecchetti cites the Basel Committee's periodic quantitative impact studies showing an increase in common equity tier 1 from 5.7 percent of risk-weighted assets at end-2009 to 10.2 percent at end-2013 for 102 large global banks, noting that the increase is large (4.5 percentage points) and the 2019 target had already been reached.

Like Cohen (2013), Cecchetti emphasizes that most of the increase in the capital ratio came from the buildup of capital from retained earnings, not a collapse in assets. Presenting data indicating falling bank profitability from the average in 2000–07 to 2013, he infers that the costs of increased capital were borne by shareholders and emphasizes that net interest margins did not balloon.

Other data show that with the exception of Europe, lending spreads fell and lending standards eased—but these trends stem mainly from a contrast between the high-risk crisis period (2008–09) and the postcrisis (2010–13) period. Cecchetti acknowledges that weak demand could explain falling spreads and easing standards but cites rising ratios of total credit to GDP as inconsistent with a weak-demand explanation. Most of the big increases in the credit to GDP ratio were in emerging-market economies, however; the ratios were lower in 2013 than in 2006 for the United States, Germany, the United Kingdom, Belgium, Norway, and Ireland (p. 5).

Cecchetti's broad conclusion is that the social costs of raising capital seem to have been small so far and that policymakers should consider further increases—while being wary of a shift in intermediation to shadow banks. An alternative interpretation would be that the extraordinary conditions of this period, including zero interest rates and quantitative easing, mean that the observed trends may provide a less reliable guide to long-term impacts than do calibrated estimates based on more normal conditions.

DSGE Model Estimates

Angelini et al. (2011) provide what may be seen as a mainstream synthesis of DSGE model results for the long-term impact of higher capital requirements on economic output. Their study conducts simulations of 13 models, primarily for the United States and the euro area. All of the models allow for an influence of the capital requirement on steady-state output; they exclude models with strict M&M irrelevance of capital structure.

A second criterion for inclusion was that the model's steady state should be straightforward to compute, a criterion that tended to rule out most of the large-scale semistructural models used in BCBS (2010a). In the models considered, higher capital requirements "affect economic activity via an increase in the cost of bank intermediation . . . [as] banks increase lending spreads to compensate for the higher cost of funding. . . . This leads to lower investment, which then affects employment and output" (pp. 2–3). This framework is the same as that applied in chapter 4. The framework does not hinge on the notion that banks take excessive risks as a consequence of the implicit subsidy of deposit insurance, a premise that underlies some other DSGE analyses of bank capital.

Based on the median results of the model simulations, Angelini et al. (2011) arrive at a central estimate of a 0.09 percent reduction in steady-state output (and consumption) as a consequence of a 1 percentage point increase in capital requirements against risk-weighted assets. This estimate is close to the estimate of 0.10 percent reduction in BCBS (2010a). It is also close to the parameter estimated in chapter 4 (in the base-case specification of parameters): an increase in capital requirements of 1 percent of total assets causes a loss in long-term output of 0.15 percent. Given that the ratio of total assets to risk-weighted assets averages 1.78 for US and euro area banks (BCBS 2010b), 1 percent of risk-weighted assets amounts to only 0.56 percent of total assets. The Angelini et al. result of 0.09 percent output impact thus translates into a 0.16 percent loss of output.

Angelini et al. also investigate the long-term impact on output of higher liquidity requirements and of higher capital requirements on output volatility.[34] However, they do not attempt to model the benefits of increased capital requirements stemming from the reduced probability of financial crises.

In Clerc et al. (2015), eight authors from six central banks and one think tank analyze optimal capital requirements using a DSGE model. Their

---

34. They find that a 50 percent increase in the ratio of liquid to total assets has nearly the same impact reducing steady-state output as a 1 percent rise in the (risk-weighted) capital ratio, at 0.08 percent. They note, however, that the models tend to be less suited to providing estimates of liquidity effects.

model involves several "dynasties" that maximize welfare over an infinite horizon: households (a patient dynasty of net lenders and an impatient one of net borrowers), bankers, and entrepreneurs. Output is a function of labor and capital, and capital formation is lower when borrowing rates are higher. Because of limited liability and subsidized deposit insurance, banks have an incentive to undertake excessively risky projects. The dominant influence of an initial amount of required equity capital is thus to curb socially inefficient investments and defaults, increasing welfare. However, equity is more expensive than debt not only because it is not subsidized but also because "bankers' wealth is limited and in equilibrium appropriates some scarcity rents" (p. 34). (The paper does not mention the M&M offset.)

"Costly state verification" means that banks play a key role in credit allocation; when their leverage is excessively constrained, so is credit creation. As a consequence, "the negative effects on economic activity coming from the reduction in the supply of credit to the economy dominate when capital requirements are high enough" (p. 43). Welfare thus follows an inverted-U curve in relation to the capital requirements. The authors' base parameter values generate maximum welfare at an optimal capital requirement of 10.5 percent for business loans (risk weight 1.0) and 5.25 percent for mortgages (risk weight 0.5). Applying the ratio of total assets to risk-weighted assets identified by BCBS (2010a) for US and European banks, the corresponding optimal ratio of capital to total assets would be 5.9 percent (10.5/1.78).

It is unclear whether the model adequately captures the benefit of banking crisis avoidance. There is no explicit mapping from capital requirements to the probability of a banking crisis or any explicit calibration of the expected welfare loss from the occurrence of a banking crisis. The model does incorporate an influence of aggregate shocks that supplement idiosyncratic shocks in determining defaults, but the relationship of these shocks to past international experience in banking crises is opaque. No entry in the authors' table of parameter values corresponds to an estimate of welfare (or output) loss in the event of a banking crisis (p. 41). In addition, the study applies a loss given default ratio of only 30 percent (p. 40), far below the range of 50 to 75 percent suggested by Dagher et al. (2016).

Mendicino et al. (2015) apply the Clerc et al. (2015) model as calibrated to euro area banks for the period 2001–13. Bank lending is high, with mortgages set at 143 percent of GDP and loans to nonfinancial corporations representing an additional 182 percent of GDP (p. 19). Idiosyncratic risk gives a log-normal distribution of return shocks. Below a given threshold in the lower tail, the borrower defaults, with loss given default of 30 percent. The model calibration yields annual bank default rates of 1.68 percent (p. 21), which the authors note is for a period including bank crises. The optimization results depend on the weight assigned to borrower versus saver households.

A key finding is that "it is always optimal to impose an average capital requirement and a mortgage risk weight high enough to keep bank defaults low and to reduce the strength of bank-related amplification channels" (p. 3). Beyond a certain level, still higher capital requirements benefit savers (56 percent of households) by avoiding the tax costs of deposit insurance losses, but they reduce the welfare of borrowers (44 percent, p. 21) by reducing the supply of bank loans.[35]

At the authors' preferred benchmark weights of 0.3 to savers and 0.7 to borrowers, the two groups of households share the welfare gains from optimal capital requirements equally. The optimal capital ratio is 13.5 percent of risk-weighted assets—3 percentage points higher than the calibrated base-period actual capital ratio of 10.5 percent. The optimal ratio is also 3 percent above the Basel III ratio of 10.5 percent, including the capital conservation buffer (p. 26).[36] Of the welfare gains from a move to the optimal capital ratio, the gains from the influence of "aggregate uncertainty"—the model's apparent incorporation of systemwide banking crisis effects—accounts for almost the entirety for borrower households, but only about one-third of the gains for saver households (p. 30). The simulations show relatively little gain from altering the risk-weighting on mortgages from the base rate of 50 percent and relatively little gain from reducing volatility through larger variation in countercyclical capital levies. Overall, the optimal ratio for capital against risk-weighted assets is approximately the same as that identified in chapter 4, even though the methodology is completely different. Even so, considerable inherent opacity remains in the model and its results in comparison with the simpler but more transparent formulation suggested in chapter 4 and applied in such studies as BCBS (2010a) and Miles, Yang, and Marcheggiano (2012).

Begenau (2015) sets forth a DSGE model that finds that "higher capital requirements leading to a reduction in the supply of bank debt can in fact result in more lending" (p. 1). She argues that bank debt provides safe and liquid assets "coveted" by households, so that when banks reduce debt in response to capital requirements inducing lower leverage, the interest on debt falls substantially. The decline in the interest rate swamps the impact

---

35. Savers also benefit from the high capital requirements, because there are "higher bank profits" (p. 1), but the motivation for higher profits seems to be that depositors will accept lower deposit rates—although with deposit insurance it is unclear why this would be so.

36. The Basel III ratio the authors cite refers to total capital rather than common equity tier 1, for which the required minimum is 7 percent (4.5 percent plus the 2.5 percent capital conservation buffer).

of the higher funding cost from increased equity, resulting in a lower rather than a higher lending rate and more rather than less lending.

This approach seems to fail to distinguish between insured deposits (the safe liquid assets held by households) and bank debt to bondholders. The scope for interest reductions on bank deposits would seem limited. The model also includes other unusual assumptions (e.g., decreasing returns to scale in production in the production sector, which depends on bank finance). Sufficient questions and opacity characterize the study that it is unclear whether its quantitative estimate of optimal capital warrants much emphasis.[37]

Writing before the Great Recession, Van den Heuvel (2008) examined the welfare costs of bank capital requirements in a general equilibrium model in which households derive utility from liquid assets provided in the form of bank deposits. Capital requirements reduce banks' liabilities, which include deposits relative to equity, so they curb the provision of bank deposit services. Van den Heuvel treats the benefits of capital requirements as stemming solely from their effect in limiting moral hazard arising from deposit insurance. He pays no attention to the risk of a systemic banking crisis (or other macroeconomic shock) effectively imposing a shock from outside the individual bank as opposed to a disturbance originating from incentive distortions within the bank. Indeed, he states that "if one believes that deposit insurance does *not* create a moral hazard problem. . . then capital requirements have no benefits" (p. 315).

On the basis of the revealed willingness to pay for deposit liquidity (as indicated by the spread between the interest rate on deposits and that on subordinated debt as a proxy for the return on equity), Van den Heuvel estimates the gross welfare costs of the existing effective bank capital requirement of 10 percent of risk-weighted assets (including subordinated debt in capital) at 0.10 to 0.22 percent permanent reduction in annual consumption, a large number.[38] On the basis of a comparison with the relatively small costs of additional supervision as a means of substituting for bank capital requirements, he estimates the marginal costs of capital requirements as several times the marginal benefit and concludes that "capital requirements are currently too high" (p. 316). This type of general equilibrium model omits the main benefits in the calibrated optimal capital studies: the reduction in the probability of a banking crisis multiplied by the output loss in the event of a banking crisis. The study was written in

37. Note that whereas the extensive literature survey in BCBS (2016a) includes the study in its bibliography, it makes no mention of the study in the text.

38. He places the average spread between the deposit rate and the subordinated debt rate during 1986–2004 at 2.94 percent (p. 313).

late 2007, when it was still possible to refer to the "very low rate of bank failures in the United States, since the implementation of the Basel Accord" (p. 315).

De Nicolò, Gamba, and Lucchetta (2014) develop a DSGE model that finds an inverted U-shaped relationship between the amount of bank lending and the stringency of capital requirements and a corresponding inverted U-shaped relationship between welfare and capital requirements (p. 2099). They do not report the optimal level of capital requirements in the simulations. They do state that as their model is calibrated, if capital requirements are initially raised to a "mild" level, lending will rise to a peak of 15 percent above the no-regulation case (p. 2100). The reason for the initial increase is that "the capital requirement lowers the return of holding cash relative to the expected return on loan investment" (p. 2115). In other words, higher capital requirements would initially raise the ratio of loans to holdings of safe bonds in the portfolio of banks.

Why higher capital requirements would even initially boost rather than reduce the amount of lending is counterintuitive, contrary to the standard modeling of the impact of higher capital requirements, and relatively opaque in the paper. Considering that in practice there would tend to be a zero risk weighting on safebond assets, it is even more difficult to see why higher capital requirements would (initially) boost lending.

More fundamentally, the model excludes two elements that are central to the analysis. First, it does not include a production function, making it impossible to estimate the impact of a higher price of capital (resulting from higher lending costs) on output. Second, it does not include damages from a banking crisis—the centerpiece of the more usual calibrated model calculations of optimal capital requirements. As it turns out, at least for one interpretation of the main calibrations, the study arrives at an optimal capital ratio similar to that found in chapter 4 (about 7 percent).[39] However, questions about the underlying method suggest that great caution should be taken in weighing the study's findings.

---

39. From their equations (30) and (31), and using MVL to represent the marginal value of additional lending (left-hand side of both equations) and constants A and B to represent two right-hand side components common to the two equations (both having positive values), we have $MVL_c = A - B\left((1 + Z^L)/(1 + r_f)\right)$ for unregulated lending constrained only by collateral, versus $MVL_k = A - B(1 - k)$ for regulation at capital requirement ratio k. The marginal value of lending will be higher, and thus the quantity of lending lower (under concave returns to lending), in unregulated lending so long as $k < k^* = 1 - ((1 + Z^L)/(1 + r_f))$. Parameters implied by the authors place Z^L (the return shock at low return) at −0.05 and r_f (the bond rate) at 0.025. By implication, the optimal capital ratio would be 0.073 (1 − (0.95)/(1.025)). Note, however, that in a subsequent paper De Nicolò (2015) states that the turning point is lower, at $k = 0.03$.

3

Testing the Modigliani-Miller Theorem of Capital Structure Irrelevance for Banks

Like the banking crisis and Great Depression of the 1930s, the financial crisis and Great Recession of 2008–09 have provoked regulatory reform in the financial sector. Internationally, the new Basel III rules approximately double minimum capital requirements for most banks and triple them (or more) for systemically important financial institutions (SIFIs).[1] The new requirements also introduce a minimum "leverage ratio" capitalization of 3 percent of total (as opposed to risk-weighted) assets under the Basel rules and 4 percent under US rules (BCBS 2014a, Federal Reserve 2013).[2]

Some economists have called for far higher capital requirements. Admati and Hellwig (2013, 179) propose a leverage ratio requiring equity

---

An earlier version of this chapter appeared in Cline (2015c). The equations and quantitative estimates are unchanged.

1. In the change from Basel II to Basel III, common equity is to rise from 2 percent of risk-weighted assets (RWA) to 4.5 percent. Total tier 1 capital (which includes common equity) is to rise from 4 percent of RWA to 6 percent. There is an additional "capital conservation buffer" of 2.5 percent, bringing the total to 8.5 percent (BCBS 2010b, 69). In addition, SIFIs are to maintain extra capital, set at 2.5 percent of RWA in the Basel rules and up to 4.5 percent in the United States (Yalman Onaran, Jesse Hamilton, and Ian Katz, "Big US Banks Face Capital Requirements of Up to 4.5% on Top of Global Minimum," Bloomberg, December 9, 2014).

2. In the United States, for banks with assets over $700 billion the requirement will be 5 percent (*Forbes*, "Steep Leverage Ratio Requirements Will Force Banks to Rethink Their Capital Plans," April 9, 2014). Moreover, in the United States, the Volcker Rule of the Dodd-Frank legislation additionally seeks to constrain "trading" (as opposed to lending) activity that banks are allowed to pursue. Note that the Basel III asset base is "exposure" that includes off-balance-sheet items.

capital of 20 to 30 percent of total assets. As noted in chapter 2, this range would correspond to 36 to 53 percent of risk-weighted assets, about four to five times the risk-weighted capital target for SIFIs under Basel III. The empirical tests in this study are motivated in considerable part by the wide divergence in expert opinion about desirable capital requirements for banks.

A key theoretical element of the argument of Admati and Hellwig and some other economists favoring far higher capital ratios is the "capital structure irrelevance" proposition of Modigliani and Miller (1958). The M&M hypothesis maintains that there is no optimal relationship of equity finance to debt finance for a firm, because any increase in profitability through greater leverage will be offset by an increase in the unit cost of the remaining equity capital as a consequence of greater risk. Based on this premise, some argue that there should in principle be no reason for banks to oppose far higher equity capital requirements because the resulting reduction in their leverage would result in a fully compensating reduction in the cost of equity capital.[3]

In contrast, the few analytical attempts at identifying optimal capital requirements from society's viewpoint tend to acknowledge that higher capital requirements will make banks less profitable, and reduce lending and economic activity somewhat as a consequence. In these studies such reductions are set against the corresponding reductions in the probabilities of financial crises, and thus expected damages avoided, to arrive at the optimal increases in capital requirements.[4]

This chapter examines the empirical evidence on the M&M proposition as applied to the banking sector. It analyzes whether more highly capitalized banks do indeed enjoy lower costs of equity capital. The actual extent of such a relationship can then be used as an input into a broader analysis of optimal bank capital requirements from the standpoint of society, taking account of risks of financial crises from insufficient bank capitalization.

---

3. Admati and Hellwig (2013, chapter 5) emphasize the Modigliani-Miller theorem, although they recognize that subsidized funding through guaranteed bank deposits creates an incentive for banks to rely less on equity.

4. Thus, Miles, Yang, and Marcheggiano (2012, 18) apply an M&M offset of only about one-half in their cost of capital calculations, based on UK bank data. The Basel Committee on Banking Supervision (BCBS 2010a, 23) makes no allowance at all for an M&M offset, although it does so apparently in the spirit of concluding that its calculation of optimal capital requirements may correspondingly be conservative, and it cites Kashyap, Stein, and Hanson (2010) as supporting the M&M relationship of equity cost to leverage.

Is Banking Special?

At the outset it is useful to address in qualitative terms the question, "Why is banking different?" For the nonfinancial sector, shareholder equity capital typically accounts for about one-third of total assets, whereas debt and other liabilities amount to about two-thirds (see, e.g., Rajan and Zingales 1995, 1428). In contrast, in the postwar period US commercial banks have had equity-to-assets ratios (book value basis) of only 4 to 6 percent up to the 1970s, rising to 6 percent in the late 1980s and 9 percent by 2007 (Berlin 2011, 5). Leverage of debt to equity on the order of 10 to 1 (or higher) instead of 3 to 1 has meant that the literature in this area has tended to treat the financial sector as "different," typically excluding it from empirical tests.

It seems intuitively appealing that the sector of financial intermediation should rely more heavily on debt financing than nonfinancial sectors. The intensity of inputs in a sector should depend on the nature of the output of the sector. One would not expect oil refining to have the same ratio of crude oil to total output as, say, the computer industry. Financial intermediation is a sector that by definition involves debt (in the form of deposits by households and corporations) as its main input. The main product provided by the bank is a store of value that has a high degree of safety and liquidity: bank checking and saving accounts. The sector also is based on acting as the intermediary that transforms short-term claims (deposits) into long-term claims (e.g., mortgages). Deposits are financial liabilities. Replacing them entirely with equity would require that the public be told that henceforth bank deposits are not available and that households and corporations must instead hold liquid assets in the form of equity shares (e.g., in mutual funds).[5] Considering that deposits amount to about one-half of assets for the large banks and much more for smaller banks, the deposit-taking nature of the banking sector inherently means that the ratio of "debt" (including "debt" to depositors) to assets will tend to be higher than in most sectors.

There is a considerable tradition in the literature that debt/equity characteristics of banking are likely to be different from those of other firms. Thus, in their analysis of equity returns Eugene Fama and Kenneth French (1992, 429) "exclude financial firms because the high leverage that is normal for these firms probably does not have the same meaning as for nonfinancial firms, where high leverage more likely indicates distress." In a recent survey, Berlin (2011, 8) essentially adopts the proposition that financial intermediation is inherently levered when he states: "Since liquid liabilities are a primary output of the banking firm, we should expect banks to be highly levered." Similarly, Herring (2011, 9) observes that "Since some liabilities

---

5. As proposed by Kotlikoff (2010).

are really a product supplied by the bank rather than simply a means of funding the bank, we know that a 100 percent equity-to-assets ratio cannot be the correct answer." Although Miller (1995) himself informally discussed whether M&M applies to banking, his answer was an ambivalent "Yes and No" (the three-word abstract of his article).[6]

One key reason that has been given for observed high leverage in banking is that deposits are subsidized by publicly provided deposit insurance (e.g., Admati and Hellwig 2013). However, it turns out that nonbank financial firms that do not enjoy deposit insurance also have high leverage. Thus, in 2001–07, the median ratio of total assets to shareholder funds was 19.1 for banks, and 12.1 for nonbank financial firms, but only 3.0 for nonfinancial firms (Herring 2011, 17). Once again the implication is that something is different about leverage for the financial sector even after removing the influence of deposit insurance.

Perhaps the most explicit analysis finding that banking is different is that by DeAngelo and Stulz (2013, 1, 3), who conclude that "MM's leverage irrelevance theorem is simply inapplicable to banks . . . given a material market demand for liquidity, intermediaries will emerge to meet that demand with high leverage capital structures (made possible by asset structures optimized to produce liquidity)." In their model, with the bank choosing a portfolio of assets that is "not risky at the optimum" (p. 8), debt as a share of debt plus equity turns out to be the ratio $1/[1+\theta + \phi z]$. Here θ is the "liquidity spread" that those purchasing liquidity from banks accept for assured future access to capital, ϕ is the "loan spread" paid on bank loans by those with limited access to capital markets, and z is the fraction of capital invested in loans that yield $r(1 + \phi)$, with the remaining fraction $(1-z)$ invested in capital market securities at yield r. With reasonable values for θ and ϕ, this ratio will be high, relatively close to unity. Moreover, the contrast with lower bank leverage in earlier historical times can be explained by the bidding down of θ over time as financial markets developed. In a manner similar to the oil refining analogy suggested above, DeAngelo and Stulz (2013, 9) state that "Banks are different because financial flows are the inputs and outputs they utilize to generate value for their shareholders."

Calomiris and Herring (2013) also take issue with the notion that

---

6. In the article he also acknowledged that "taken literally, they [the M&M propositions] would not apply anywhere else either. Much of the research focus in finance in the last 30 years has been precisely on those departures from the strict M&M assumptions—things like taxes and agency costs—that will give a push or a tilt towards more or less leverage.... No very simple or coherent set of tilting principles has yet emerged, however, nor, for that matter, has any clear pattern of capital structures been observed across firms" (p. 487).

equity capital can be increased indefinitely without costs to the banks. They cite Kashyap, Rajan, and Stein (2008) regarding the adverse influence of too much equity on agency problems, as reduced leverage could insulate bank managers from market discipline if leverage is low and stock ownership is more fragmented than borrowing. Calomiris and Herring believe that although an increase in capital is necessary, "...we are convinced that there are negative—not just diminishing—social returns to achieving a higher amount of capital solely by raising equity capital requirements beyond a certain point" (p. 43). Their solution instead is to supplement the equity capital requirement with required contingent convertible (CoCo) capital in the form of debt that would convert to common equity upon a trigger (based on the 90-day average of bank stock prices). Their objective is to make the conversion so unattractive to the banks that managers would have an extreme incentive to issue more equity early in an emerging deterioration rather than wait too late. They propose a (book value) leverage ratio of 10 percent equity relative to assets, supplemented by required CoCo funding of 10 percent of book assets (Calomiris and Herring 2013, 29). Their equity capital requirement would thus be only one-third to one-half the level proposed by Admati and Hellwig (2013), although it would be about twice the Basel III level for SIFIs (9.5 percent of RWA, corresponding to about 5 percent of total assets).

Capital Assets Pricing Model Betas versus Direct Estimation

It is important to emphasize that, unlike the few existing empirical estimates of the M&M effect for banks, the tests in this study do not use the indirect route of identifying the stock price "beta" for banks within the framework of the Sharpe-Lintner-Black capital asset pricing model (CAPM). In that framework, the riskiness of a given stock relative to a diversified equity portfolio is measured by the parameter beta, which tells the percent by which the stock price rises when the overall market rises by 1 percent, or falls when the overall market falls by 1 percent. Given the CAPM theory, the equity yield of a stock should equal the risk-free return plus the stock's "beta" multiplied by the excess of the diversified market yield over the risk-free rate (the "equity premium"). For example, if the beta is 1.5, the risk-free return is 4 percent, and the general diversified stock market premium is an additional 4 percent (placing average equity return at 8 percent), then the return on the stock in question would be expected to be 10 percent.[7] The leading empirical studies of M&M for banks conduct statistical tests

---

7. That is: $4 + [1.5 \times (8 - 4)] = 10$.

that calculate beta as a function of the bank leverage ratio (capital relative to assets).[8] Considering that the analytical objective for policy purposes is to calculate the extent to which a reduction in the unit cost of equity can be expected to offset the shift from low-cost debt to high-cost equity in the process of increasing regulatory capital requirements, in principle the CAPM framework can provide a means of accomplishing this objective.

However, it is much more direct to apply the estimation form implied by the original M&M article (as set forth in equation 3.1 below) than to infer the M&M influence through the bank beta in the CAPM framework. Such a test provides direct evidence on how much the equity yield can be expected to decline when the ratio of debt to equity is reduced. Because the CAPM has been found to provide poor explanation of equity prices with regard to the beta coefficient, it is problematic to rely on use of the beta as the indirect means to identify the M&M influence.[9] Fama and French (2004) find that the response of the equity return to changes in the stock's beta is only about one-third the size of what is predicted by the CAPM, such that stocks with low betas have higher than expected return and stocks with high betas have lower than expected returns.[10] On this basis, those who apply a bank beta estimated in relationship to leverage to calculate the reduction in required equity yields in response to higher capital should presumably shrink their raw estimates by two-thirds.

At a broader level, it is curious to accept the CAPM beta framework to estimate how much additional bank capital would reduce equity capital cost without recognizing that the banking sector already has an average beta of about unity.[11] If bank stocks are already about as safe as the equity market as a whole, what are the grounds for arguing that the sector is unduly risky and needs deeper capitalization in comparison with other sectors?

---

8. King (2009); Kashyap, Stein, and Hanson (2010); Yang and Tsatsaronis (2012); and Miles, Yang, and Marcheggiano (2012).

9. Fama and French (1992, 428) state that "Our bottom line results are: (a) [beta] does not seem to help explain the cross-section of average stock returns, and (b) the combination of size and book-to-market equity seems to absorb the roles of leverage and E/P [earnings to price ratio] in average stock returns...."

10. The authors report that for 1928–2003, average monthly returns are what CAPM would predict for a beta of 1.25, but for a beta of 1.8 the predicted return is considerably higher (at 17 percent) than the actual observed (14 percent), whereas for a beta of 0.6 the predicted return (8 percent) is considerably lower than the actual observed (11 percent). The ratio of the actual difference between the two ends of the spectrum to the CAPM-predicted is thus $[14 - 11]/[17 - 8] = 0.33$ (Fama and French 2004, 33).

11. King (2009, 71) estimates that the banking sectors in Canada, France, Germany, Japan, the United Kingdom, and the United States had an average beta of 0.95 in 1990–2000 and 0.74 in 2005–09.

Arbitrage versus Optimization

A final introductory remark concerns the framework of M&M and its relationship to other frameworks of optimization. At its core, M&M is based on a syllogistic arbitrage proposition: (1) Any debt-equity configuration chosen by the firm can be "unwound" by investors, who can sell shares of a highly leveraged firm and purchase shares in unleveraged firms using the proceeds plus borrowed funds, bidding down the share price of the leveraged firm and bidding up the share price of the unleveraged firm. (2) Market arbitrage will eliminate any profitability advantage of a more highly leveraged firm. (3) Therefore the capital structure (ratio of equity to debt) is irrelevant. Modigliani and Miller do not formally introduce risk. It is telling that their equations do not include an investor utility function, and they do not posit a typical degree of risk aversion. Nor do their equations set forth a probabilistic profile of returns in relationship to the debt-equity ratio, nor any hypothesized distribution function for returns. With such a function it would be possible to explore the optimal debt-equity ratio as a function of the risk aversion characterizing financial markets. Instead the authors appeal to "risk" only qualitatively and by implication maintain that any risk aversion whatsoever will suffice to drive their arbitrage process and rule out any superiority of one debt-equity ratio over any other.

Specifying the Tests

As set forth in appendix 3A, the M&M proposition leads to a straightforward specification for an empirical test:

$$i_j = \rho + (\rho - r)\frac{D_j}{S_j} \tag{3.1}$$

where i is the cost of equity capital as measured by ratio of earnings per share to price per share (the earnings yield or inverse of the price-to-earnings ratio); ρ is the "capitalization rate" at which expected streams of future earnings are capitalized (discounted) for the "class" (by implication, sector) of the firms in question; r is the rate of interest at which both the firm and investors can borrow; D is the firm's debt, and S is shareholder equity in the firm. Subscript j refers to the firm observed. Because the capitalization rate exceeds the interest rate ($\rho > r$), reducing debt relative to equity will reduce the earnings yield demanded by the market, thanks to reduction in perceived risk. The formulation turns out to cause exactly the amount of reduction in the earnings yield that is needed to have the average cost of capital remain constant. Moreover, this average cost of capital must equal the capitalization rate ρ (see equation 3A.4 in appendix 3A).

The average cost of capital will be the weighted average of the cost of equity capital and the interest rate cost of debt. Defining V as the value of the firm, setting this value as being equal to debt plus equity ($V = D + S$), and defining the debt financing share y as the fraction of total value attributable to debt rather than equity (such that $y = D/V$), it follows that:

$$ACC_j = y_j r + (1 - y_j) i_j \qquad (3.2)$$

As demonstrated in appendix 3B, given equation (3.1), the derivative of ACC (average cost of capital) in equation (3.2) with respect to the ratio of debt to equity is zero. Capital structure (i.e., the decision to finance through debt as opposed to equity) therefore has no influence on the average cost of capital in the M&M framework.

For purposes of empirical implementation, equation (3.1) can be estimated as:

$$i = a + bz \qquad (3.3)$$

where z is defined as the debt to equity ratio ($z = D/S$), $a = \rho$, and $b = (\rho - r)$. To support the M&M hypothesis, the constant a should be found to have a value that plausibly represents the return to capital in the banking sector (ρ), and the coefficient b should be such that $a - b$ yields a plausible value for the interest rate r.

Data

The database developed for the tests in this study is drawn from the annual filings of form 10-K with the Securities and Exchange Commission for the 54 largest US banks, for the period 2001–13.[12] The asset sizes of the banks at the end of 2013 range from $6.5 billion for PacWest Bancorp (Los Angeles, California) to $2.4 trillion for JPMorgan Chase. The 54 banks had combined assets of $13.2 trillion at the end of 2013, representing 83 percent of total assets of US depository institutions (Federal Reserve 2014, 77) and about 75 percent of assets including the nondepository subsidiaries of bank holding companies (see chapter 7).

The 10-K data report total assets, total liabilities, and shareholder equity (the difference). Total liabilities are used as the estimate of debt (D in equation 3.1), and shareholder equity as the estimate of equity (S). The depen-

---

12. For most banks, the corporate website provides the 10-K filings on its investor portal (see, for example, www.citigroup.com/citi/investor/sec.htm). Note that for four large banks the data end in 2007 because during the financial crisis they were either taken over by other banks (Washington Mutual by JPMorgan Chase, Countrywide by Bank of America, and Wachovia by Wells Fargo) or failed (IndyMac).

dent variable i, cost of equity capital, is estimated as the inverse of the price-to-earnings ratio for the year in question, using the fourth-quarter average stock price and trailing 12-month earnings.[13] (For most banks, these data are from the 10-K filings and data for a few banks are from Bloomberg.)

It is a standard principle of corporate finance that the "earnings yield," or inverse of the price-to-earnings ratio, should be higher when the riskiness of the asset is greater.[14] There should be no ambiguity whatsoever that the "expected" earnings yield should be higher for higher risk, other things being equal. Ambiguity does arise, however, in measuring what investors expect future returns to be, because recently observed actual returns may or may not reflect those expectations. The price of a stock should be the discounted present value of its future stream of earnings. Expected future earnings depend on the base period earnings and the expected rate of growth of earnings in the future. The appropriate discount rate to apply equals the risk-free rate of return plus a premium to reflect the riskiness of the firm. In the M&M framework, this riskiness varies directly with the ratio of debt to equity. The discount rate will thus be higher for a more leveraged firm. Accordingly, for a specific class of firms (such as banks) in which the growth rate of future earnings is expected to be similar among the firms in question, the earnings yield is expected to be higher for firms with greater risk. Application of a higher risk premium in the discount rate will translate the future stream of earnings into a lower present value (stock price) relative to earnings.

Although stock valuation is based on expected future earnings, empirical estimates require the use of actual observed earnings as the proxy for expected future earnings. However, use of the observed earnings yield as the measure of the cost of equity capital raises the problem of interpreting data for a year of losses. The problem is that in such years actual net earnings will not be a meaningful proxy for the expected stream of future earnings, the relevant concept in M&M. Investors would not supply capital if they believed future earnings would be negative, so by definition a year of losses does not provide a meaningful proxy of future expected earnings. Negative net earnings occur in about 8 percent of the bank-year observations, with heavy concentration (83 percent of negative instances) in the Great Recession years of 2007–10. The solution adopted here is to constrain the earnings yield observation to be no lower than the real return on US

---

13. Modigliani and Miller (1958, 271) identify i as the inverse of the price-to-earnings ratio in stating that "...the market price of any share of stock is given by capitalizing its expected return at the continuously variable rate i_j."

14. See, for example, Damodaran (2007, chapter 2). Or, for standard analysis for the general investing public, see Malkiel (2015, 125).

Treasury inflation-protected (TIP) five-year bonds, plus a risk spread of 100 basis points, as the lowest meaningful rate at which investors might be prepared to provide equity capital.[15] Choice of the real rate reflects the fact that when inflation is expected the nominal stream of earnings will be expected to rise over time, automatically providing inflation protection, such that inclusion of the inflation rate for the year in question would be double-counting expected inflation.

As an alternative measure of the cost of equity capital, a second test uses the ratio of net income in the year in question to the book value of equity at the end of the previous year. The same imposed floor replaces observations for years with negative income.

Figure 3.1 shows the trends in the simple averages of these ratios for the 54 large US banks in 2002–13. The earnings yield (ey) refers to the inverse of the price-to-earnings ratio using trailing earnings and fourth-quarter average stock price, in percentage terms. Flanking confidence intervals at the 95 percent level for two standard errors for each year are also shown. Net income relative to equity (NI/E) refers to net income for the year shown as a percent of equity (assets minus liabilities) at the end of the previous year, again in percentage terms. Both series are the constrained observations, overriding observations that are negative or too small as just discussed. The unconstrained series are shown in appendix 3D, figure 3D.1. They indicate average losses in 2008 and 2009 for the earnings yield measure and near zero averages for the net income relative to equity measure.

Figure 3.1 also shows the ratio of debt to equity (lagged one year), this time as a pure number. It turns out that there has been significant develeraging for US banks since 2007 (i.e., 2008 in the figure with respect to the debt/equity ratio). The ratio of debt to equity fell from an (unweighted) average of about 10.5 in 2007 to about 8 in 2013. Based on the same 10-K filings data, tier 1 capital is persistently an average of about 83 percent of book equity. By implication, the ratio of tier 1 capital to total assets rose from about 7.2 percent of assets to about 9.2 percent of assets over this period.[16]

The (constrained) earnings yield, in contrast, has remained relatively steady within a range of 6 to 8 percent during this period, with the exception

---

15. The five-year Treasury inflation-protected rate averaged 1.27 percent in 2003–05, 1.91 percent in 2006–08, but fell to an average of –0.23 percent in 2009–14 (Federal Reserve 2015a).

16. For a given ratio of debt to equity (D/E), the corresponding ratio of assets to equity (A/E) is higher by unity. That is: $A/E = (D + E)/E = (D/E) + 1$. With tier 1 capital at 83 percent of equity, a reduction in the debt/equity ratio from 10.5 to 8 represents an increase in the (inverse) leverage ratio of tier 1 capital to assets from 7.2 percent (= $1/(11.5/0.83)$) to 9.2 percent (= $1/(9/0.83)$).

Figure 3.1 Net income relative to equity, earnings yield, and debt to equity ratio, averages for the 54 largest US banks: Constrained data, 2002–13[a]

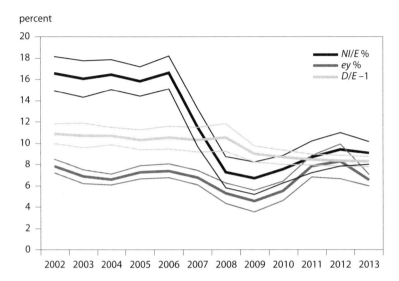

percent

NI/E = net income relative to equity; ey = earnings yield; D/E –1 = debt to equity (lagged one year)

a. For observations with earnings constrained to exceed minimum thresholds; see text.

Note: Also shown in the figure are 95 percent confidence intervals of two standard errors for each year.

Source: Calculated from the annual filings of Form 10-K with the Securities and Exchange Commission.

of a dip to as low as about 4 percent in 2009 in the Great Recession. However, the (constrained) ratio of net income to book equity capital has substantially declined, from about 16 percent to a range of 8 to 10 percent. The contrast between the income-book equity ratio and the earnings yield is a manifestation of the decline in the ratio of market capitalization to book value of equity, which fell from an average of 2.26 in 2001–06 to 1.23 in 2007–09 and 1.15 in 2010–13 (market capitalization data are from Bloomberg).

It is informative to consider the distribution of net income for these large banks over the 12-year period 2002–13. Figure 3.2 is a histogram showing the distribution of net income as a percent of total assets at the end of the previous year. The first panel shows the full distribution. The second panel shows the distribution for just the cases of losses. In the second panel, the right-hand bucket "0" refers to the percent of bank-year observations with net income between –1 percent and zero. A total of 8.3 percent of bank-year cases had negative income in this period (which included the worst

Figure 3.2   Distribution of annual bank net incomes relative to assets, 54 largest US banks, 2002–13

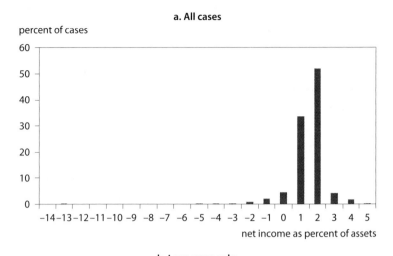

a. All cases

percent of cases

net income as percent of assets

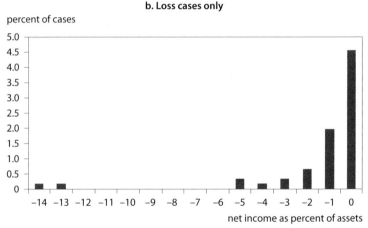

b. Loss cases only

percent of cases

net income as percent of assets

Sources: Calculated from annual filings of Form 10-K with the Securities and Exchange Commission and Bloomberg.

recession since the 1930s). Only 1.1 percent had losses exceeding 3 percent of assets (the new Basel III capital leverage standard) and only 0.7 percent had losses exceeding 5 percent of assets (the US largest-bank capital leverage standard). Critics of the low Basel ratio often seem to consider it self-evident that the 3 percent level is far too low given the losses that might be expected, but it turns out that the frequency of larger losses is relatively low. Of course, a major caveat is that book income may be overstated (and losses understated) by failing to capture erosion in market value of assets in periods of stress.[17] Nonetheless, the distribution of income results in figure 3.2 suggests that setting the capital leverage ratio far higher than the US level would amount to addressing a small fraction of cases based on the most recent decade's experience.

Test Results

The tests here estimate equation (3.3) using a pool of 12 years' observations on 51 of the 54 largest US banks.[18] Because of the unusual conditions during the Great Recession, the tests include a dummy variable for the years 2008–10. For the earnings yield variant of the unit cost of equity capital, the results are:[19]

$$ey_t = 6.63 + 0.0513\ z_{t-1} - 1.89\ D_{0810};\ adj.\ R^2 = 0.088 \qquad (3.4)$$
$$(19.5)\ (1.62)\qquad (-7.2)$$

where *ey* is the earnings yield (percent), or inverse of the price-to-earnings ratio; *z* is the ratio of debt to equity (with equity defined as the excess of book assets over book liability); and *D* is a dummy variable with value 1 for 2008–10 and 0 otherwise. *T*-statistics are in parentheses.

The coefficient on the leverage ratio is not significant. Importantly, the size of the coefficient is relatively small, about 5 basis points for each unit change in the leverage ratio. Instead, the M&M value for the coefficient should be $\rho - r$. It seems unlikely that the interest rate r would be so close to the bank "class" rate of return on capital that the difference would be this small.

When the net income/equity variant is applied instead as the measure of the unit cost of equity capital, there is a considerably stronger relationship:

$$NI_t/E_{t-1} = 7.206 + 0.636\ z_{t-1} - 5.823\ D_{0810};\ adj.\ R^2 = 0.268 \qquad (3.5)$$
$$\phantom{NI_t/E_{t-1} = }(10.0)\quad (9.4)\qquad (-10.5)$$

---

17. Thus, IndyMac consistently had positive earnings in 2002–06, and its losses in 2007 were only 2.1 percent of end-2006 assets. Those losses amounted to only 30 percent of book equity at the end of 2006, so technically the bank does not seem to have been insolvent when it was closed down.

18. The tests exclude three of the top 54 banks: Ally Financial (which was not publicly listed during most of this period), UnionBanCal (which was acquired by Mitsubishi UFJ in 2008), and, as an outlier, Synovus Financial (which had extreme swings in earnings yield from –164 percent in 2008 to +41 percent in 2011).

19. Tests on the earnings yield variant apply 564 bank-year observations; tests on net income relative to equity apply 579 bank-year observations.

where NI_t / E_{t-1} is the ratio of book net income to equity at the end of the previous year (percent). This time the coefficient on the leverage ratio is highly significant. Moreover, its size is substantial, at about 60 basis points for each increment by unity in the ratio of debt to equity. Nonetheless, even this magnitude is small as a likely gauge of the excess of the banking sector return on capital minus the interest rate.

Application of fixed-effects tests for an unbalanced panel yields results that are very close to those of equations (3.4) and (3.5).[20] Because of their simplicity and transparency, the results in equations (3.4) and (3.5) are applied in the impact estimates below.

A potentially important statistical question is whether the estimates are biased because of endogeneity. It could be argued that treating the capital ratio as an exogenous right-hand-side variable misses the point that investors might put pressure on a highly leveraged bank to raise its capital. If they do, the observed capital ratio might already reflect some moderation prompted by market forces.[21] Appendix 3E investigates this question. It concludes that if such endogeneity does exist, the measured M&M coefficient (b in equation 3.3) should not be affected (and hence is unbiased) even though the observed range of variation in debt leverage would be smaller than the ex ante range.[22]

Implications for the Average Cost of Capital

Table 3.1 considers the implications of a sharp increase in bank capital requirements on the average cost of capital for banks. The table uses the estimates in equations (3.4) and (3.5) to assess the effects of raising bank capital from a benchmark of 10 percent of total assets to 25 percent (the midpoint of the range suggested by Admati and Hellwig 2013). This increase is equiv-

---

20. Using fixed effects, which is equivalent to having individual dummy variables for each bank and each year, yields the following coefficients on the debt/equity ratio z_{t-1}: 0.063 (1.31) for the earnings yield (instead of 0.0513, equation 3.4) and 0.708 (8.12) for net income relative to equity (instead of 0.636, equation 3.5), with t-statistics in parentheses.

21. One participant in the study group that discussed the penultimate draft of this study emphasized this point, arguing that in this case the measured coefficient would tend to *understate* the influence of debt leverage on the unit cost of equity capital, thereby underestimating the true M&M offset.

22. The same participant posited the possibility that the relationship would also be affected by the capital behavior of peer banks. This view implies that investors would be less inclined to penalize a bank with a high debt to equity ratio if peer banks were also following this strategy. The implications of this proposition for the empirical tests are unclear, however. As noted, fixed-effects tests made little difference, yet a pronounced swing in behavior of a large group of banks from one period to another would be captured by fixed-time effects.

Table 3.1 Impact of raising the capital-to-assets ratio from 10 to 25 percent[a]

Concept	Symbol	*ey* model (equation 3.4)	*NI/E* model (equation 3.5)
Debt/equity (ratio)	z_0	9	9
	z_1	3	3
Cost of equity (percent)	i_0	7.09	12.93
	i_1	6.78	9.11
Interest rate (percent)	r_A	3	3
	r_B	2	2
Average cost of capital (percent): A	ACC_{A0}	3.41	3.99
	ACC_{A1}	3.95	4.53
Change (percentage points)		0.54	0.54
Average cost of capital (percent): B	ACC_{B0}	2.51	3.09
	ACC_{B1}	3.2	3.78
Change (percentage points)		0.69	0.69
Change if M&M effect 0 (percentage points)	Change A	0.61	1.49
	Change B	0.76	1.64
M&M offset (percent of potential)	A	12.5	64
	B	10.1	58.2

ey = earnings yield; M&M = Modigliani and Miller; *NI/E* = net income/equity
a. Refers to total assets, not risk-weighted.
Source: Author's calculations.

alent to reducing the debt/equity ratio from 9 to 3.[23] The cost of equity capital is obtained using equation (3.4) or (3.5) (with no dummy variable) as applied first to $z = 9$ and next to $z = 3$.[24] The table considers two cases: one (A) with the interest rate at 3 percent and the other (B) at 2 percent.

The table then shows average cost of capital before the reform (0) and after (1), for each of the two alternative interest rate assumptions. The table also shows the corresponding changes in average cost of capital. Surprisingly, the two models show identical changes in the average cost of capital: an increase of 54 basis points if the real interest rate is 3 percent, and 69 basis points if the real interest rate is 2 percent. Essentially the larger coefficient *b* in the *NI/E* model and higher base level of equity cost provide a

---

23. That is, with the shares of *D* and *E*, respectively, at 0.9 and 0.1, $D/E = 0.9/0.1 = 9$. With these shares instead at 0.75 and 0.25, $D/E = 0.75/0.25 = 3$.

24. The value for *b* estimated in equation (3.4) is applied even though it is not significantly different from zero.

substantially larger absolute reduction in the cost of equity, but because the equity cost (both before and after) is substantially higher in the NI/E model than in the equity yield model, there is a fully offsetting effect from a more powerful impact of shifting from low-cost debt to high-cost equity.

The table next shows the change in average capital cost that would occur if there were no M&M effect at all (namely, the unit cost of equity capital after the reform is identical to that before the reform). Finally, the table reports the corresponding percent of total potential increase in average cost of capital that is offset by the induced reduction in equity capital cost as a consequence of the M&M effect. As expected from the small size of coefficient b in the ey model and large size of this coefficient in the NI/E model, the percentage offset is much smaller in the earnings yield model (only about 10 percent) than in the net-income model (about 60 percent).

Taking the averages over the two models and two alternative interest rates, the expected change in the average cost of capital from the higher capital requirement would amount to 61.5 basis points. In the absence of any M&M offset the average increase would be 112.5 basis points. So on average, the M&M offset amounts to 45 percent of the potential increase in the weighted-average cost of capital.[25] Banks could be expected to pass along the net increase to household and corporate borrowers. Permanently higher real interest rates would reduce the amount of capital formation and thus reduce future GDP from levels otherwise reached.

The central estimate, an increase of approximately 62 basis points in average cost of capital for an increase in capital of 15 percent of total assets, is considerably more modest than would be implied by the findings of Cohen and Scatigna (2014) for actual behavior of lending rates so far during the phase-in of Basel III. They estimate that for a sample of 94 banks in both advanced and emerging-market economies, common equity capital rose from 11.4 percent of risk-weighted assets in 2009 to 13.9 percent in 2012 (p. 12). Net interest income rose from 1.37 percent of total assets to 1.67 percent. The authors state that the 30 basis point increase translates to 12 basis points per percentage point increase in the (risk-weighted) capital-to-assets ratio. Considering that risk-weighted assets would likely be no more than 50 percent of total assets going forward (the 2012 ratio was only 0.42; p. 11), each percentage point of total assets increase in capital would impose at least 24 basis points increase in lending cost based on the Cohen-Scatigna results. In the exercise of this study, the 15 percentage point increase in capital relative to total assets would thus boost bank lending costs by 360 basis points. So the estimates here can be seen as substantially on

---

25. Note that this turns out to be the same offset as identified by Miles, Yang, and Marcheggiano (2012). See appendix 3C.

the conservative side in comparison with actual experience under increased capital requirements in 2009–12.

Similarly, the increase of 62 basis points estimated here is more modest than the corresponding increase implied by the estimates of Miles, Yang, and Marcheggiano (2012), which would amount to 81 basis points for the same increase in capital. As discussed in appendix 3C, they estimate that raising capital by 3.33 percent of total assets (reducing the asset/capital leverage ratio from 30 to 15) would increase the weighted-average cost of capital by 18 basis points after taking account of the M&M offset (induced reduction in equity cost). Applying an increment of 15 percentage points of assets would thus imply an increase of 81 basis points (= 18 × [15/3.33]).

Another study discussed in appendix 3C, by Yang and Tsatsaronis (2012), obtains results that imply a 15 percentage point increase in the ratio of capital to total assets would boost the weighted-average cost of capital by 120 basis points. The findings of these two studies thus also imply that the estimates in the present study for the impact on lending rates from a 15 percentage point increase in capital relative to assets may be understated rather than overstated, although not by as wide a margin as implied by comparison to the findings of Cohen and Scatigna (2014) for increases that have already occurred from the much smaller capital increases as a result of the initial phase-in of Basel III.

Lower Borrowing Cost for Banks?

The original M&M analysis held all unit costs of debt fixed. But some authors emphasize that higher equity capital would reduce unit borrowing costs for banks as well. The reason would be the same as that for equity: Creditors (as well as equity investors) would perceive less risk than before.

Gambacorta and Shin (2016) examine the borrowing cost question using data for 105 international banks in 14 advanced economies over the period 1995–2012. They conclude that a 1 percentage point increase in the ratio of equity to total assets reduces the average cost of bank debt funding by 4 basis points. The authors use an example in which equity capital is raised from 5.6 percent of total assets to 6.6 percent, equity unit cost is held constant at 10 percent, and debt unit cost is 3.1 percent. Whereas a "naïve" direct calculation shows an increase of 7 basis points in average cost of total funding, the net increase is only 3 basis points after applying their estimated regression coefficient to calculate the reduction in unit cost of debt.[26] A problem with their presentation, however, is that they neglect to

---

26. Namely, the unit cost of borrowing falls from 3.10 to 3.06 percent (the 4-basis-point reduction).

point out that the same exercise yields a far smaller impact if the empirical estimate for the most directly comparable alternative specification in their tests is applied instead.[27] Although more research examining the impact of capital on borrowing cost would seem warranted, the main basis for analyzing the economic cost of higher capital requirements remains the M&M influence on equity cost.

Conclusion

The M&M offset is a key building block in any analysis of the optimal capital requirement for banks. The central finding of this chapter is that this offset parameter is 0.45. Namely, although equity capital has a higher unit cost than debt, slightly less than half of the increase in average unit cost of capital to banks that would otherwise result from raising bank equity capital requirements as a consequence of this differential is offset by the reduction in the unit cost of equity capital demanded by investors, thanks to the reduction in risk provided by the reduction in leverage. The calculations of chapter 4 apply this value for the M&M offset parameter in arriving at estimates of optimal capital requirements.

---

27. In the specification using the ratio of total assets to common equity, the coefficient is only 0.0012 percentage point impact on unit debt cost. Following their example of boosting equity from 5.6 to 6.6 percent of total assets, the assets/capital variable would move from 17.86 to 15.15. Applying the coefficient of 0.0012, unit cost of debt funding would change by $(15.15 - 17.86) \times 0.0012 = -0.0033$ percent, or less than one-tenth as large as the 4 basis points in the variants the authors choose to discuss.

Appendix 3A

The Modigliani-Miller Model

Modigliani and Miller (1958, 267–71) posit that for any given "class" of firms (implicitly, for example, a particular industrial sector), in the absence of any debt financing the price of a share of a given firm j will be the expected annual stream of income earned ("expected return") discounted by the expected rate of return for that class. Thus:

$$p_j = \frac{1}{\rho}\bar{x}_j, \tag{3A.1}$$

or equivalently:

$$\frac{\bar{x}_j}{p_j} = \rho \tag{3A.2}$$

where p_j is the share price of firm j, $\bar{x}_j$ is the annual future steady stream of returns (earnings, abstracting from taxes) per share, and ρ is the characteristic rate of return to that class of firms.[28]

They then introduce debt financing and examine its influence on share pricing. Their first proposition is that "the market value of any firm is independent of its capital structure and is given by capitalizing its expected return at the rate ρ_k appropriate to its class" (p. 268). Thus:

$$V_j \equiv \left(S_j + D_j\right) = \bar{X}_j/\rho \tag{3A.3}$$

where V_j is the market value of the firm, S_j is the market value of its common shares, $\bar{X}$ is expected return on assets owned by the company (before deduction of interest), and D_j is the market value of the debt of the company.[29]

The authors define the "average cost of capital" as the ratio of expected return to the market value of all the firm's securities. Their proposition is then that this average cost is constant at the rate ρ applicable to the class in question, and consequently is "completely independent of the capital structure and is equal to the capitalization rate of a pure equity stream of its class" (p. 268). Thus:

$$ACC_j \equiv \frac{\bar{X}_j}{S_j + D_j} \equiv \frac{\bar{X}_j}{V_j} = \rho \tag{3A.4}$$

---

28. For convenience and because this study refers to a single sector, banking, I omit the subscript "k" that M&M include for the "class." Note further that M&M are not explicit about the role of inflation, but by implication their setup refers either to real values or to nominal values under the assumption of a constant rate of inflation.

29. D would thus include preferred shares. M&M do not address a situation in which default risk has sharply depressed the market value of a firm's debt below nominal value, considering that their construct treats D at face value (hence it can be applied directly to arrive at interest costs).

where *ACC* is average cost of capital (my addition). This proposition challenged the then dominant view that average cost of capital was a declining function of leverage until leverage reached so high that the average cost rose once again because of rising risk, with the implication that there was some optimal leverage ratio.[30] The conventional view apparently reflected the sense that debt capital was cheaper than equity capital so higher leverage would reduce the average cost of capital, whereas the central proposition of M&M was that higher leverage would introduce higher risk and increase the cost of equity capital enough to offset the rising share of debt capital.

To demonstrate this proposition, the authors invoke arbitrage between the share prices of two firms, one leveraged and the other not. Both firms have the same expected return (gross of interest), stated thus as simply X. The authors first suppose that the value of the levered firm, V_2, is larger than that of the unlevered one, V_1. They then consider an investor holding s_2 dollars' worth of shares in firm 2, constituting the fraction α of total shares in the firm worth S_2. The return to this investor, Y_2, will be the owned fraction of the firm times its income net of interest costs, or:

$$Y_2 = \alpha(X - rD_2) \tag{3A.5}$$

where D_2 is the amount of debt of firm 2, r is the interest rate, and $\alpha \equiv s_2/S_2$.

The authors next have the investor sell his αS_2 worth of shares in company 2 and purchase the larger amount $s_1 = \alpha(S_2 + D_2)$ of shares in company 1. In doing so, the investor borrows the amount αD_2 to supplement the proceeds of the sale of company 2 shares. Keeping in mind that in firm 1 there is no debt so the value of the firm is solely total equity share value S_1, the investor's income from the new holding in company 1 net of interest paid on the amount borrowed is then:

$$Y_1 = \frac{\alpha(S_2+D_2)}{S_1}X - r\alpha D_2 = \alpha\frac{V_2}{V_1}X - r\alpha D_2 \tag{3A.6}$$

So long as $V_2 > V_1$ other holders of company 2 shares will find it attractive to imitate the first investor, because Y_1 (equation 3A.6) will exceed Y_2 (equation 3A.5). This process will bid up the price of company 1 shares and bid down the price of company 2 shares until $V_2 = V_1$. The authors conclude "levered companies cannot command a premium over unlevered companies because investors have the opportunity of putting the equivalent leverage into their portfolio directly by borrowing on personal account" (p. 270).

Of course, this conclusion requires that the outside investors can borrow at the same interest rate as that paid by company 2 on its debt, "r". It is not clear in general that this would be the case; certainly retail investors

---

30. M&M attributed this view for example to Graham and Dodd (1951).

seem likely to pay higher interest on stock margin debt than the typical borrowing cost of a sound firm. For banking, it is even more unlikely that outside investors can borrow at the same rate, because one-half or more of the funding of the bank is likely to come from deposits that bear extremely low interest rates (if any). One can thus begin to see limitations on application of the model, especially for banks.[31]

Modigliani and Miller then show that conversely, if the unlevered firm were more valuable than the levered firm, the investor in the unlevered firm could sell stock, use the proceeds to buy shares in the levered firm and invest what is left over in bonds, until the value of the levered firm were bid up to that of the unlevered firm. This process would amount to "an operation which 'undoes' the leverage" (p. 270). However, the general presumption had been that if there were any difference, levered firms would be more valuable, so the algebra going in the opposite direction need not detain this appendix.

The authors then turn to the result that is key for the empirical test here: The earnings yield of the stock in question should equal the capitalization rate appropriate to the class of the firm plus a constant times the ratio of debt to equity. The constant in question is the excess of the capitalization rate over the interest rate. This result is derived as follows. The earnings yield on a share of the stock will be:[32]

$$i_j = \frac{\bar{X}_j - rD_j}{S_j} = \frac{\rho(S_j + D_j) - rD_j}{S_j} \qquad (3A.7)$$

That is, total net earnings are the gross return less interest paid. But gross earnings are simply the constant capitalization rate for the class, ρ, times value of the firm $(S+D)$. Simplifying:[33]

$$i_j = \rho + (\rho - r)\frac{D_j}{S_j} \qquad (3A.8)$$

The earnings yield should thus be a linear function of the ratio of debt to equity, with a constant intercept equal to the capitalization rate for the class, and a coefficient on the debt/equity ratio equal to the excess of the capitalization rate over the borrowing rate. To illustrate, Modigliani and Miller set $\bar{X} = 1000$, $D = 4000$, $S = 6000$, $\rho = 10$ percent, and $r = 5$ percent.

---

31. In particular (but not discussed by M&M), if the investor can borrow only at the higher rate r', then the interest rate applicable to equation (3A.6) becomes r', and (setting equation 3A.5 equal to 3A.6) arbitrage will stop when $V_2/V_1 = 1 + (r' - r)(D_2/X)$.

32. Equation (9) in Modigliani and Miller (1958).

33. That is: dividing each part of the numerator of the final right-hand-side of equation (3.A7) by S, and rearranging. Equation (8) in Modigliani and Miller (1958).

Expected yield or rate of return per share is then 13.3 percent.[34] In their example, if the capital structure reverses from 60 percent equity to 40 percent equity, the earnings yield should rise from 13.3 to 17.5 percent.[35] This linear relationship of earnings yield to leverage (defined as the debt-equity ratio) holds the average cost of capital constant regardless of leverage. Thus, in the first case capital costs an average of $0.4 \times 0.05 + 0.6 \times 0.133 = 0.1$, or 10 percent. In the second case, capital costs an average of $0.6 \times 0.05 + 0.4 \times 0.175 = 0.1$, again 10 percent.

In the case of US banks, with equity capital at about 10 percent of total assets and thus the debt-equity ratio at about 9, these same postulated rates would place the earnings yield implausibly high at 55 percent (and the price-to-earnings ratio implausibly low at 1.8). Instead, at the end of 2014 the median trailing price-to-earnings ratio for the seven largest US banks was approximately 16, placing the earnings yield at about 6 percent.[36] For the same banks, the median credit default swap (CDS) rate spread above 5-year US Treasury bonds in 2013 was 78 basis points, placing the corresponding borrowing rate at 2.73 percent.[37] By implication equation (3A.8) would require that the bank sector capitalization rate (ρ) was only 3.06 percent.[38] This capitalization rate is implausibly low, however. By implication, the sensitivity of the earnings yield to leverage may be overstated by the M&M model.

---

34. That is: $0.1 + (0.1 - 0.05)(4000/6000) = 0.133$.

35. Or: $0.1 + (0.1 - 0.05)(6000/4000) = 0.175$.

36. See www.finance.yahoo.com. The seven largest banks are JPMorgan Chase, Bank of America, Citigroup, Wells Fargo, Goldman Sachs, Morgan Stanley, and Bank of New York Mellon.

37. CDS rates are from Bloomberg. The 5-year Treasury rate averaged 1.95 percent in 2013 (Federal Reserve 2015c).

38. That is: $0.06 = 0.0306 + (0.0306 - 0.0273) \times 9$.

Appendix 3B

Demonstrating Constant Average Cost of Capital in Modigliani and Miller

The original equations in Modigliani and Miller (1958) show a clear negative relationship between the unit cost of equity and the amount of debt leverage. The authors use a numerical example to demonstrate that as a consequence the average cost of capital is constant and does not depend on leverage. It is useful to show that this result is general for their setup. Especially for banks, with high leverage, the ratio of debt to equity might be thought to have nonlinear consequences for the average cost of capital as leverage rises even higher, if only because in the limit this term (the final variable in equation 3A.8, appendix 3A) would approach infinity.[39] This appendix shows that the derivative of the average cost of capital with respect to the debt/equity ratio is zero, demonstrating that the result of constant average cost of capital is general.

Define w as the average cost of capital, and y as the ratio of debt to total enterprise value. (In the terms of appendix 3A, $y = D/V = D/(D + S)$.) With the interest rate at r and the cost of equity capital at the rate i (and with i in turn equal to the net earnings yield per share), average cost of capital will be:

$$w = yr + (1 - y)i \tag{3B.1}$$

Because debt will be $D = yV$ and equity value $S = (1 - y)V$, it follows that the key debt to equity ratio (D/S, equation 3A.8) can be written as:

$$z \equiv \frac{D}{S} = \frac{y}{1-y} \tag{3B.2}$$

From equation (3A.8) of appendix 3A, the unit cost of equity capital will be:

$$i = \rho + (\rho - r)z \tag{3B.3}$$

It will be helpful to use the relationship:[40]

$$y = \frac{z}{1+z} \tag{3B.4}$$

---

39. Their numerical example involves intermediate levels of leverage, with the debt to equity ratio rising from only 2/3 to 1.5, well below the range observed in the banking sector.

40. That is: from equation (3B.2), $z(1 - y) = y$, so $z = y + yz = y(1 + z)$. Rearranging yields equation (3B.4).

From equation (3B.1), the derivative of the average cost of capital with respect to the leverage ratio will be:[41]

$$\frac{dw}{dz} = r\frac{dy}{dz} + (1-y)\frac{di}{dz} + i\frac{d(1-y)}{dz} \tag{3B.5}$$

From equation (3B.4), the derivative of y with respect to z will be:[42]

$$\frac{dy}{dz} = \frac{d\frac{z}{z+1}}{dz} = \frac{(1+z)(1)-z(1)}{(1+z)^2} = \frac{1}{(1+z)^2} \tag{3B.6}$$

Similarly, it can be shown that:[43]

$$\frac{d(1-y)}{dz} = -\frac{1}{(1+z)^2} \tag{3B.7}$$

From equation (3B.3),

$$\frac{di}{dz} = \rho - r \tag{3B.8}$$

Substituting into equation (3B.5),

$$\frac{dw}{dz} = \frac{r}{(1+z)^2} + \left(1 - \frac{z}{1+z}\right)(\rho - r) + [\rho + (\rho - r)z][\frac{-1}{(1+z)^2}]$$

$$= \frac{r}{(1+z)^2} + \frac{\rho - r}{1+z} + \frac{-\rho - \rho z + rz}{(1+z)^2} \tag{3B.9}$$

Combining the first and third terms and cancelling $(1+z)$ yields:

$$\frac{dw}{dz} = \frac{r-\rho}{1+z} + \frac{\rho-r}{1+z} = 0; QED \tag{3B.10}$$

---

41. The last two terms in equation (3B.5) apply the standard formula for the derivative of a product of two variables, uv, namely: $d(uv) = u\,dv + v\,du$, where $u = (1 - y)$ and $v = i$.

42. Applying the standard derivative formula $d(u/v) = (v\,du - u\,dv)/v^2$.

43. This result is also intuitive as it should be simply the negative of dy/dz.

Appendix 3C

Alternative Analyses of the Modigliani-Miller Offset for Banks

As discussed in chapter 2, there is a surprisingly wide divergence of expert opinion on the costs of increasing bank capital requirements (let alone on the social benefits). Several academic studies tend to invoke the M&M theorem as grounds for judging these costs to be minimal. The official sector studies have tended to quantify costs without explicit allowance for the M&M offset (lower cost of equity capital thanks to less risk as leverage declines) but with qualitative recognition of the potential offset. One important industry study, in contrast, took note of the theorem but rejected it and arrived at relatively high costs of increased capital requirements. This appendix examines both that study (IIF 2011) and three leading papers on the other side of this spectrum to shed further light on the debate.

The literature survey in appendix 2A provides a summary of an important study by the Institute of International Finance (IIF 2011). Whereas that study had predicted a sizable increase in bank lending rates and spreads above risk-free rates for the period 2011–15 as a consequence of the phasing in of Basel III capital requirements, such increases did not occur, as shown in figure 3C.1.

In panel A for the United States, the spread between the prime rate and the 5-year US Treasury rate was an average of 362 basis points in 2007, fell to an average of 173 basis points in 2011, and instead of rising fell slightly further to 163 basis points for 2014 and early 2015. The corresponding spreads for consumer installment loans averaged 334, 429, and 262 basis points, so on this measure, from 2011 to 2014–15 the lending cost to private borrowers relative to the risk-free benchmark fell rather than rising.[44] In panel B for France and Germany, interest rates for new bank lending to nonfinancial corporations are shown, along with the 5-year rate for the German treasury bond. The average spread for the two countries above the 5-year German bund did edge up, from 130 basis points in 2011 (already up from 89 basis points in 2007) to 173 basis points in 2014–January 2015. The increase of 43 basis points from 2011 to 2014–15 is consistent with some impact of higher capital requirements on lending rates, but far less than had been projected in the IIF study.[45]

---

44. The IIF estimate instead was that the lending cost (and hence spread) should have risen by 468 basis points from 2011 to 2015 for the United States. For the euro area, the corresponding estimate was 291 basis points (IIF 2011, 54).

45. As noted in the main text, Cohen and Scatigna (2014) found that for 94 large banks internationally, actual experience in 2009 to 2012 showed an increase of 30 basis points in

Figure 3C.1 Bank lending rates in the United States and euro area, 2001–15

a. United States

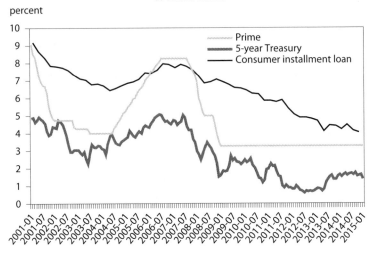

b. France and Germany

Sources: European Central Bank (ECB 2015); Federal Reserve (2015a, 2015b); Thomson Reuters Datastream.

Miles, Yang, and Marcheggiano (2012) conduct tests for 7 UK banks for the period 1997–2010 to estimate the influence of leverage on the cost of equity capital. They apply the CAPM framework and thus focus on estimating market betas rather than directly investigating the relationship of equity yield to leverage. In their main finding, the equity beta equals a constant 1.07 plus the estimated coefficient 0.03 times the ratio of assets to capital (pp. 10, 13). With an average asset to capital ratio of 30, by implication the average beta was approximately 2.[46] They translate the implications for equity cost of higher capital requirements as follows. They place average return on equity at approximately 15 percent, average bank borrowing cost at 5 percent, and average leverage at 30, implying weighted-average cost of capital (WACC) of 5.33 percent.[47] They then consider the impact of doubling required capital, or lowering the leverage ratio from 30 to 15. In the absence of any M&M offset the effect would be to boost WACC to 5.66 percent, an increase of 33 basis points.[48]

The authors then calculate the impact of higher capital requirements taking account of their estimated M&M offset. In the CAPM, the equity cost of a firm equals the risk-free rate plus the firm's beta multiplied by the market average risk premium. They place the risk-free rate at 5 percent, and the general market risk premium at 5 percent. With their regression estimate, the cost of equity capital at the lower leverage ratio (15 instead of 30) would fall to 12.6 percent.[49] As a consequence, the new WACC would be 5.51 percent.[50] The rise in the WACC would be 18 basis points instead of 33, indicating that the M&M effect would offset 45 percent of the potential rise in average cost of capital.

As it turns out, the central estimate in this study is also that the M&M offset would be 45 percent of the potential rise in the average cost of capital for bank lending. That estimate involves a more ambitious increase in capital (reducing the asset to capital ratio from 10 to 4, rather than from 30 to 15).

---

lending rates in association with an increase of 2.5 percentage points in capital relative to risk-weighted assets.

46. The authors do not clarify why this ratio is about twice the average beta shown in their figure 3. Moreover, King (2009, 71) places the UK bank betas at a median of 0.87 in this period, more consistent with the level shown in that figure.

47. That is: $(1/30) \times 14.85 + (29/30) \times 5$.

48. That is: $(1/15) \times 14.85 + (14/15) \times 5$.

49. That is: 5 percent risk free + 5 percent market premium $\times (1.07 + 0.03 \times 15)$.

50. That is: $(1/15) \times 12.6 + (14/15) \times 5$.

Finally, the authors acknowledge that the alternative of directly testing the relationship of required return on bank equity to bank leverage "has the advantage of not assuming the CAPM holds" (p. 14). Unlike the present study, they find that in a regression of realized earnings relative to price (the equity yield) on leverage, "the impact on the required return on equity of changing leverage is about as big as if MM held exactly" (p. 15). Unfortunately, they do not report these results.[51]

Yang and Tsatsaronis (2012) use a CAPM framework incorporating leverage as a shift variable affecting estimated betas. They find a statistically significant influence of leverage on the cost of equity capital. However, this influence turns out to be relatively small. The estimates indicate that "if the ratio of a bank's total assets to its equity increases by 10 and the market return is 4 percent in excess of the risk-free rate, the bank pays 0.4 percent more for every unit of equity" (p. 51). Correspondingly, the authors calculate that if average leverage fell from 20 to 10, the cost of equity capital would fall from 13.4 to 13.0 percent. Taking into account a 5 percent cost of debt, the weighted-average cost of capital would rise from 5.4 to 5.8 percent.[52]

The M&M offset in the study by Yang and Tsatsaronis is also relatively small. With no induced change in the cost of equity capital, doubling equity from 5 to 10 percent of total assets would raise the average cost of capital from 5.42 to 5.84 percent, an increase of 42 basis points. After taking account of induced reduction in the cost of equity capital, the average cost of capital would still rise to 5.80 percent, a net increase of 38 basis points.[53] The M&M offset from induced reduction in the equity rate would thus be only 4 basis points, or about one-tenth of the increase at ex ante returns. The main text above instead places the offset at about 45 percent.

An increase of 40 basis points in the average cost of capital for an increase in capital of only 5 percent of total assets, moreover, would imply an increase in average cost of capital of 120 basis points for a capital increase amounting to 15 percent of total assets, the exercise considered in the main text here. This increase would be considerably larger than the corresponding increase of 62 basis points estimated in the main text.

---

51. Note also that testing earnings yield as a function of the asset/capital ratio would be a misspecification of M&M, which instead has the earnings yield as a linear function of the debt/equity ratio. At high leverage ratios the difference is not great but at intermediate and low ratios more characteristic of nonbank corporations the difference becomes large.

52. That is: $(0.95 \times 5) + (0.05 \times 13.4) = 5.42$ percent; and $(0.90 \times 5) + (0.10 \times 13.0) = 5.8$ percent.

53. That is: $(0.90 \times 5) + (0.10 \times 13.4) = 5.84$ percent.

In another study employing the CAPM framework for US banks, **Hanson, Kashyap, and Stein (2010)** estimated that the long-run steady-state impact of higher capital requirements on lending rates should be modest, only 25 to 45 basis points for a (large) 10 percentage point increase in capital relative to total (not risk-weighted) assets. They noted, however, that short-run frictions associated with raising capital could be substantial, implying the need for gradual phase-in. They also suggested increased regulation of the shadow-banking sector to avoid increased fragility in the system as a consequence of possible migration of financing out of banking in response to higher capital requirements.

The authors regress bank betas on the capital-to-assets ratio for US banks in 1976–2008. They find a significant coefficient of –0.045. With the median bank beta at 0.90 and capital-to-assets ratios at a median of 7 percent, they argue that this finding is "broadly in line with what is predicted by the [M&M] conservation-of-risk principle" (p. 17). Namely, doubling capital to 14 percent of assets would reduce the beta by 0.32 (= 0.045 × 7) to a level of 0.58, not far from the level of 0.45 that would be half the original median beta. However, they do not formally demonstrate that the original M&M formulation should translate to a reduction in bank market beta proportionate to a reduction in the assets-to-capital ratio.[54]

The authors apply a prior assumption of strong M&M effects to calibrate the impact of higher capital requirements on lending rates. In their preferred variant, the effect is complete except for the distortion from corporate tax deduction for interest but not dividends. They estimate this effect as causing a 25-basis-point increase in the lending rate as a consequence of 10 percent of assets in additional capital. With a corporate tax rate of 35 percent, the effect of shifting this amount of finance from debt to equity, even with induced reduction in the unit cost of equity, would be 0.35 × 700 × 0.1 = 25 basis points. The upper bound of their range adds another 10 basis points for loss of convenience of short-term debt as well as a further 10 basis points catch-all for all other violations of M&M ("arbitrary fudge factor," p. 18), to arrive at a maximum 45-basis-point increase in the bank lending rate (for a 10 percentage point increase in the capital-to-assets ratio). Surprisingly, the authors do not specify the ex ante equity capital cost. They do cite a debt cost of 7 percent (which seems high, certainly for a real concept that should be used for comparison to equity). By implication, if they considered the equity cost to be 14 percent ex ante, then in the absence of any M&M effect at all the total increase in weighted-average cost

---

54. It would be surprising if this transform could be shown to be exact, considering that M&M employ the debt-to-equity ratio rather than the assets-to-equity ratio.

of capital would be 70 basis points.[55] The authors thus implicitly judge that the M&M offset amounts to at least 36 percent of the otherwise potential increase in lending cost ([70 – 45]/70) and, in their preferred estimate, as much as 64 percent ([70 – 25]/70).

The authors further seek to show that lending rates have not been influenced much by capital-to-assets ratios in the past (from the 1920s to the present), but their message is somewhat clouded by the fact that of their three alternative measures the only one with a statistically significant coefficient on the capital-to-assets ratio must be rejected out of hand because it indicates an excessively large increase in lending cost for a given rise in capital.

Despite their strong prior on full M&M effects, the upper end of the range identified by the authors is surprisingly similar to the estimate of the present study. The lending-cost impact for 15 percentage points of assets in additional capital would be 67.5 basis points (applying their upper-bound 4.5 basis points per percentage point increase in the capital-to-assets ratio), slightly above the 62 basis points estimated in the main text of the present study.

---

55. The initial weighted average would be $(0.07 \times 14) + (0.93 \times 7) = 7.49$ percent. The ex post weighted average with no offset would be $(0.17 \times 14) + (0.83 \times 7) = 8.19$ percent.

Appendix 3D

Trends in Unconstrained Earnings Indicators of the Cost of Equity Capital

The tests in the main text constrain observations on equity yield and net income relative to equity to be positive. For cases where earnings are negative, these two proxies for cost of equity capital are constrained to be greater than zero and are set equal to the real 5-year Treasury bond rate plus a moderate spread, as discussed in the main text. Figure 3D.1 shows the paths of the averages for the 54 banks using the unconstrained data, whereas figure 3.1 in the main text shows the constrained data. Confidence intervals (5 percent level) for each year are shown as well.

Figure 3D.1   Net income relative to equity and earnings yield, averages for the 54 largest US banks: Unconstrained data, 2002–13

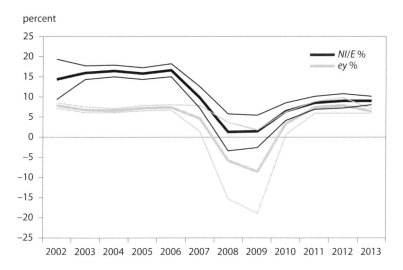

NI/E = net income relative to equity; *ey* = earnings yield

Note: Also shown in the figure are 95 percent confidence intervals for two standard errors for each year.

Source: Calculated from annual filings of Form 10-K with the Securities and Exchange Commission and Bloomberg.

Appendix 3E

Possible Endogeneity Bias

Suppose that a risk-averse bank plans on an ex ante basis to employ debt to equity leverage z represented by the horizontal distance at point "a" in figure 3E.1, and expects to have to pay the unit cost for equity i represented by the vertical distance at that point. Suppose a risk-prone bank plans to employ corresponding debt/equity leverage shown by the horizontal distance to point "c", anticipating equity unit cost of the vertical distance at that point. Now consider the influence of "market pressure" on equilibrium positions. The endogeneity proposition is that investors will press the risk-prone firm to be more cautious (reducing z) and even then will require higher unit equity cost than the firm had sought (raising i), shifting the firm's position to point "d". Similarly, investors considering the plans of the risk-averse firm will admonish it to be more aggressive (boosting z) and even so are willing to provide equity at lower unit cost than the firm had anticipated (reducing i), moving the firm to the somewhat more risk-prone position at point "b".

Figure 3E.1 Relationship of unit cost of equity to debt-to-equity ratio

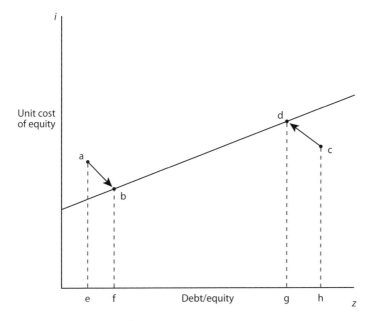

Source: Author's illustration.

What will be the consequences of this endogeneity for the measured relationship of unit cost of equity to the observed debt/equity leverage? The initial positions *a* and *c* have no meaning because the market would not make equity available at the ex ante terms expected by the firms. The meaningful relationship will be shown by the line *bd*. The M&M proposition is that there is a linear relationship between unit cost of equity and debt/equity leverage, so the empirical measurement process should not be distorted.

It is completely another matter whether the resulting measured line *cd* has a sufficiently steep slope that the M&M offset is complete. The findings in equations (3.4) and (3.5) indicate not. But there should be no bias in the observed slope from the influence of the narrowing of the range of variation of the debt/equity leverage resulting from endogeneity to market pressures, so long as the relationship is linear as posited in M&M.

The induced reaction of banks in moving from *a* to *b* and from *c* to *d* does narrow the range of observed variation in debt leverage. The observed range will be distance *fg* instead of distance *eh* for ex ante leverage. Nevertheless, in the US bank data there remains a wide range of variation in observed leverage. Thus, for the full period in the estimates of equations (3.4) and (3.5), the bank at the 12th percentile showed an average debt/equity ratio of 6.0 whereas the bank at the 88th percentile had an average debt/equity ratio of 13.1.

4

Benefits and Costs of Higher Capital Requirements for Banks

This chapter provides new estimates of the likely economic losses from banking crises. It also provides new estimates of the economic cost of increasing bank capital requirements, based in part on the estimate in chapter 3 of the empirical magnitude of the Modigliani-Miller (M&M) effect in which higher capital reduces the unit cost of equity capital. The study applies previous official estimates (BCBS 2010a) of the impact of higher capital on the probability of banking crises to derive a benefits curve for additional capital, which is highly nonlinear. It examines the benefit and cost curves to identify the socially optimal level of bank capital, which it estimates at about 7 percent of total assets (corresponding to about 12 percent of risk-weighted assets). A more cautious alternative (75th percentile across 2,187 possible outcomes under alternative parameter assumptions) places the optimum at about 8 percent of total assets, corresponding to about 14 percent of risk-weighted assets. These levels are, respectively, about one-fourth to one-half higher than the Basel III capital requirements for the large global systemically important banks (G-SIBs).

Higher bank capital requirements reduce the probability of banking crises. Combining this reduction with estimates of the economic cost of banking crises provides a basis for calculating the "benefit" of higher capital requirements. This benefit is the expected damage avoided by reducing the risk of occurrence of a banking crisis. This chapter first quantifies the expected costs and frequency of banking crises, paying special attention to

An earlier version of this chapter appeared in Cline (2016a). The equations and quantitative estimates are unchanged.

avoiding overstatement of recession losses if the economy has an unsustainable positive output gap prior to the crisis, as well as to finite life of losses considered to persist after the first few years of a crisis. The benefits section then calibrates a "benefits curve" relating damages avoided to the level of bank capital, based on the most important official survey of the influence of bank capital on the likelihood of banking crises (BCBS 2010a).

The analysis then turns to the cost curve relating economic costs to the level of the capital requirement. This relationship turns out to be an upward-sloping straight line. The cost line is steeper if the M&M offset is lower, the excess unit cost of equity versus debt is higher, there is spillover to nonbank finance, the capital share in output is higher, and the elasticity of substitution between capital and labor is higher. The optimal level of capital will then be the amount at which the slope of the benefits curve equals the slope of the (straight-line) cost curve. Requiring still higher amounts of capital will not provide sufficient further reduction in expected damages from banking crises to warrant the additional loss of output caused by less capital formation. The calibrations explore a range of alternative parameter estimates to obtain a sense of the sensitivity of this optimal capital ratio, in addition to arriving at a central estimate.

Benefits of Higher Capital Requirements

Actual GDP losses in past episodes of banking crises provide the point of departure for estimating the benefits of higher capital requirements. This section first sets forth a method for calculating losses from banking crises. It then translates these losses into a curve relating benefits of higher capital requirements to the level of these requirements.

Trend Output and Cumulative Losses in the Initial Years. The first step in calculating losses is to identify a benchmark baseline for GDP that could have been expected in the absence of the banking crisis, for comparison against actual GDP realized. Defining year T as the year the crisis begins, crisis losses over an initial five-year period can be estimated as:

$$L_{cum5} = \sum_{t=T}^{t=T+4} \hat{Q}_t - Q_t \tag{4.1}$$

where $\hat{Q}_t$ is expected GDP and Q_t is actual GDP in year T and the four subsequent years. Expected output is calculated by applying a trend growth rate for output relative to working-age population to the annual growth in working-age population, with the base set as potential GDP in the year before the crisis. The use of working-age population is important because of the sharp demographic changes in the period after the Great Recession.

Adjusting the base output level to the potential level addresses the problem of otherwise overstating the level of output that might have been expected by failing to recognize an unsustainable boom prior to the crisis.

For its part, expected output is calculated as:

$$\hat{Q}_t = \frac{Q_{T-1}}{(1+\Omega_{T-1})}\Pi_t(1+g)\times(1+n_t) \tag{4.2}$$

where Ω_{T-1} is the output gap in the year before the crisis, g is the long-term rate of growth of output per working-age population, and n_t is the rate of growth of working-age population in year t. The multiplication operator Π_t refers to the cumulative product from period 1 to period t.

Long-Term Losses. In most of the banking crises, output does not fully return to its trendline by the end of the fifth year.[1] A crucial question is then how to treat ongoing losses in later years. The approach here is to apply a finite lifespan of the "missing" capital stock and worker skills caused by the crisis, rather than interpreting the loss as persisting over an infinite horizon. In contrast, simply capitalizing the gap between output and trend still present in year 5 (or another year chosen as marking the end of the crisis) by dividing by the discount rate would implicitly assume that the extra capital equipment that would have been created during the crisis under normal circumstances would have had an infinite life. The approach here is to identify a lifetime M of the relevant productive capacity, and to apply straight-line depreciation. The present value of losses subsequent to year 5 (LT for long-term) is calculated as:

$$L_{LT} = L_5 \sum_{t=6}^{t=M+5} \left\{1 - \frac{1}{M}(t-5)\right\}/(1+\rho)^{t-5} \tag{4.3}$$

where $L_5 = \hat{Q}_5 - Q_5$ and ρ is the discount rate. I set this rate at 2.5 percent, based on US experience in 1962–2008.[2] For productive capacity lifetime I use 15 years.

The damage of the banking crisis is then expressed as a proportion of precrisis potential output, in two components: the initial cumulative five-year loss, d_{cum5}, and the longer-term loss over the subsequent 15-year horizon, d_{LT}. The first is the value in equation (4.1) divided by potential

---

1. This outcome is consistent with the finding by Blanchard, Cerutti, and Summers (2015) that in two-thirds of recessions in advanced economies in the past 50 years, output after the recession is below the prerecession trend.

2. The 10-year Treasury bond rate after deflation for the consumer price inflation rate in the same year showed an average of 2.45 percent in 1962–2008. The inflation-adjusted 10-year Treasury bond had an average rate of 2.25 percent in 2003–08 (earlier periods are not available). Calculated from Federal Reserve (2016c), IMF (2015a), and BLS (2016).

Figure 4.1   Losses from a banking crisis

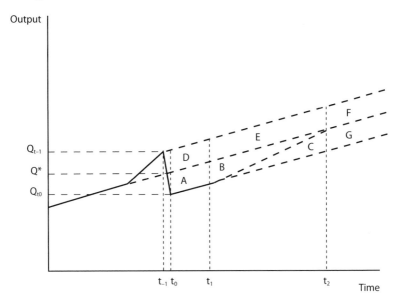

Source: Author's illustration.

output in the base year prior to the crisis; the second is the value in equation (4.3) divided by the same base potential output.[3] Total damage is the sum of the two measures: $d_{tot} = d_{cum5} + d_{LT}$.

Figure 4.1 illustrates the losses from a banking crisis. The solid line in the figure is the path of actual output. It initially peaks in the year before the crisis, t_{-1}, falls in the year of the crisis, t_0, and rises thereafter to the fifth year of observed data, t_1. Potential output at the outset of the crisis is Q^*, but actual output is higher at Q_{t-1}, reflecting a positive output gap. Output then falls well below potential in the crisis, to Q_{t0}. The approach here calculates potential output rising at trend rates (the middle of the three upward-sloping dashed lines). The period t_2 is set here at 15 years after the fifth year. The approach here calculates output loss as the sum of areas A and B. If areas C and G were also included in the loss estimate, the implicit assumption would be that the capital equipment that was not created because of the crisis would have had an infinite life.

In an upper-bound estimate of output loss, there would be no reduc-

---

3. Note that the first five years involve no discounting, in part because with typically falling per capita income the usual intertemporal consumption basis for discounting (rising per capita consumption combined with diminishing marginal utility) is not present but also because the period is short enough for discounting to have limited influence.

tion from the initial positive output gap, and losses would be assumed to last forever. In that case the loss would add not only areas C+G but also areas D+E+F (presumably with some time discounting to address the infinite horizon). Such an estimate, however, would be seriously exaggerated.

Estimates of Losses from Banking Crises. By now a relatively standard set of episodes is recognized as banking crises (see BCBS 2010a, 39; Reinhart and Rogoff 2008; Laeven and Valencia 2012). For several decades after the Great Depression, banking crises were essentially absent in industrial countries. Even so, US and other industrial-country banks barely avoided a crisis from large exposure to Latin America in the region's sovereign debt crisis of the early 1980s, in part thanks to concerted lending and official sector support of adjustment programs (Cline 1984). Failure of one large US bank (Continental Illinois) in 1984 did not metastasize into a banking sector crisis, as the Federal Deposit Insurance Corporation guaranteed all depositors and creditors and the failure stemmed from bank-specific rather than systemic shocks. By the late 1980s crises began to occur, notably in the savings and loan banks in the United States. The early 1990s witnessed banking crises in some Nordic economies (Finland, Norway, and Sweden), and by 1997 Japan experienced a crisis that had built up in the aftermath of the collapse of the bubble economy in the late 1980s. By far the most severe postwar banking crisis, however, has been that associated with the Great Recession. In 2007–08, 16 industrial countries experienced banking crises, accounting for about two-thirds of all the banking crisis episodes among industrial countries in the past three decades.[4]

Table 4.1 reports estimates for equations (4.1) through (4.3) for 22 banking crises in 1977–2008 in advanced industrial countries.[5] It also reports corresponding estimates for six advanced economies that escaped a banking crisis in the 2007–08 period. Column 1 indicates the year the crisis began. Column 2 reports the average growth rate of real GDP per working-age population from 1980 through 2014, for crisis episodes in 2007 or 2008. For earlier crises, the column shows the corresponding growth rate during the two decades prior to the crisis through year 5 after the crisis.[6]

---

4. The countries are Austria, Belgium, Denmark, Finland, France, Germany, Greece, Iceland, Ireland, the Netherlands, Portugal, Spain, Sweden, Switzerland, the United Kingdom, and the United States (Laeven and Valencia 2012, 24–26).

5. The crises are as identified in Laeven and Valencia (2012).

6. These rates are from log-linear regressions of real GDP per working-age population on time. Real GDP is from IMF (2015b, 2015c). Data on the size of the population of ages 16–64 are from OECD (2015b, 2015c). For Germany, growth is postunification, with data beginning in 1991.

Table 4.1 Estimates of output losses from banking crises in advanced industrial countries, 1977–2015

	(1)	(2)	(3)	(4)	(5)	(6)	(7)	(8)	(9)
Country	Crisis year	g	Ω_{T-1}	n	d_{cum5}	$gap5$	d_{LT}	d_{tot}	$LV{:}d_{cum4}$
				Crisis countries					
Austria	2008	1.76	3.20	0.32	11.5	4.4	23.9	35.5	14.0
Belgium	2008	1.72	2.99	0.64	18.4	6.8	36.9	55.3	19.0
Denmark	2008	1.60	3.94	0.05	24.3	8.5	46.0	70.3	36.0
Finland	1991	1.97	2.34	0.28	57.6	11.7	63.7	121.2	69.6
France	2008	1.53	1.99	0.03	16.1	4.6	25.0	41.1	23.0
Germany	2008	1.52	2.25	−0.57	0.2	0	0	0.2	11.0
Greece	2008	1.46	10.62	−0.77	21.5	18.7	101.8	123.3	43.0
Iceland	2008	1.51	4.30	−0.16	13.1	6.6	35.7	48.7	43.0
Ireland	2008	3.50	9.69	−0.46	31.1	11.7	63.5	94.6	106.0
Italy	2008	1.27	2.70	0.24	34.8	12.2	66.4	101.2	32.0
Japan	1997	2.50	0.98	−0.31	25.6	8.5	46.1	71.7	45.0
Netherlands	2008	2.04	1.00	−0.01	28.6	9.8	53.1	81.7	23.0
Norway	1991	2.76	−1.99	0.51	7.1	0	0	7.1	5.1
Portugal	2008	2.10	1.46	−0.48	32.9	13.7	74.5	107.4	37.0
Spain	1977	3.25	2.58	1.24	35.9	16.5	90.0	125.8	58.5
Spain	2008	1.86	2.88	−0.30	25.1	10.4	56.8	81.8	39.0
Sweden	1991	1.75	1.63	0.39	27.8	5.4	29.6	57.4	32.9
Sweden	2008	1.79	4.90	0.21	9.3	3.1	16.9	26.2	25.0
Switzerland	2008	1.03	1.00	1.08	10.8	3.9	21.1	31.9	0

Country	Year								
United Kingdom	2007	2.05	2.51	0.76	25.9	10.9	59.5	85.4	25.0
United States	1988	1.76	−0.32	0.97	0	0.8	4.5	4.5	0
United States	2007	1.74	2.66	0.69	19.1	7.2	39.4	58.5	31.0
Median		1.76	2.54	0.23	22.9	7.8	42.7	64.4	31.5
Noncrisis control countries (2008)									
Australia		1.91	1.08	1.46	12.0	3.3	17.8	29.7	n.a.
Canada		1.42	1.75	0.81	14.7	3.0	16.2	30.9	n.a.
Finland		2.04	6.09	−0.16	19.5	7.6	41.6	61.1	n.a.
Japan		1.85	0.43	−0.81	29.5	5.7	31.2	60.7	n.a.
New Zealand		1.47	0.08	0.55	23.1	4.5	24.3	47.4	n.a.
Norway		1.88	2.30	1.18	34.8	10.8	58.9	93.7	n.a.
Median		1.87	1.41	0.68	21.3	5.1	27.7	54.0	n.a.

g = long-term growth of output relative to working-age population (1980–2014; or for crises before 2007, 20 years before to 5 years after crisis) (percent per year); Ω_{T-1} = output gap in year before crisis (percent); n = average growth of working-age population (16–64) in 5 years beginning in crisis year; d_{cum5} = cumulative damage over 5 years as percent of potential GDP in year prior to crisis (Q^*); $gap5$ = shortfall of output in year 5 of crisis from benchmark baseline, as percent of Q^*; d_{LT} = long-term damage after year 5, as percent of Q^*; d_{tot} = total damage as percent of Q^*; LV: d_{cum4} = Laeven-Valencia: cumulative damage over 4 years as percent of trend output in year 4; n.a. = not applicable

Sources: Author's calculations; IMF (2008a, 2008b, 2015c); OECD (2015b, 2015c); Laeven and Valencia (2012).

Column 3 reports the International Monetary Fund's estimate of the output gap (in percent) in the year prior to the crisis (IMF 2015c).[7] There is a positive output gap in all but two of the 22 episodes, suggesting the importance of adjusting the trend GDP estimates downward by the amount of the positive output gap (equation 4.2). In both Greece and Ireland, actual output was about 10 percent above potential in 2007, making the adjustment particularly important in these cases.

Column 4 reports average annual growth in the size of the working-age population in the five years beginning the year of the crisis. This potential labor force shrank relatively rapidly in Germany, Greece, and Ireland after 2008; it also shrank in Portugal and Spain. The steepest decline, at about 0.8 percent per year, was in noncrisis Japan.

Column 5 indicates the cumulative five-year loss of output against the benchmark potential GDP path, as a percent of potential GDP in the year before the crisis. The median five-year loss amounted to about 23 percent of base-year potential GDP. The final column of the table reports a similar estimate for four-year loss of output as calculated by Laeven and Valencia (2012). Those estimates are broadly similar, albeit somewhat larger—with a median of about 32 percent. The higher estimates reflect the absence of an adjustment for above-potential GDP in the base year in the Laeven-Valencia estimates, as well as their use of trend GDP growth (rather than actual working-age population growth). These differences make the estimates much more modest here for Ireland (31 percent, instead of 106 percent of GDP in the Laeven-Valencia estimates) and Greece (22 percent instead of 43 percent). There is also a sizable difference for the United States (19 percent of base GDP instead of 31 percent).

Column 6 indicates the shortfall of output in year 5 from the benchmark baseline for potential GDP, expressed as a percent of the base-year potential GDP (in the year prior to the crisis). Column 7 indicates the long-term loss subsequent to year 5 (equation 4.3), as a percent of the base-year potential GDP.[8] With a median of 43 percent of GDP, this cost is relatively large. Column 8 is the sum of the five-year cumulative loss and long-term cost, again as a percent of base-year potential GDP. The median total loss is 64 percent of GDP.

The bottom panel of table 4.1 carries out the same calculations for what may be seen as a "control" group of advanced economies that did not ex-

---

7. No estimate is available for Spain in 1976. The output gap used here is estimated by applying a Hodrick-Prescott filter to output for 1957–82.

8. With $\rho = 0.025$ and $M = 15$, the value of the summation on the right-hand-side of equation (4.3) is 5.44. The long-term cost d_{LT} in column 7 in table 4.1 equals this constant times column 6, $gap5$, which in turn equals L_5/Q_0 in equations (4.1) and (4.2).

perience banking crisis in the Great Recession. Three of these economies (Finland, Japan, and Norway) experienced banking crises in the 1990s but escaped the banking crises of 2007–08.[9] It turns out that the "losses" that would have been attributed for this period are also relatively high for these economies. The median five-year cumulative loss is about 21 percent of base-year potential GDP, surprisingly close to the 23 percent median for the crisis cases. The median total cost (including long-term) is about 54 percent of GDP, compared with 64 percent for the banking crisis cases. At the extreme, then, it could be posited that the contribution of the banking crisis to losses should be calculated as the excess of the estimates for the crisis group over the control group. If this approach were adopted, the marginal cost of the banking crisis, including the long-term cost, would be small—only 10 percent of base-year potential GDP even for the total cost including long-term.

It might be argued that the losses in economies such as Canada and Japan were driven by external diseconomies of the banking crises in the United States and the euro area, and thus that the problem is underestimation of the banking crisis costs (rather than overestimation) for lack of including externalities. However, all of these control economies had some degree of excess demand as measured by the output gap in 2007, and it would have required dexterous macroeconomic management to avoid some degree of subsequent shortfall from potential output even in the absence of international spillover from economies with banking crises. Moreover, much of the loss of output in the euro area reflected a sovereign debt crisis, and with the exception of Ireland and to a considerably lesser extent Spain, this crisis did not stem primarily from banking crises (Cline 2014a, chapter 3). Essentially the worst global recession in 80 years imposed severe losses, and attributing the entirety of these losses to banking crises may overstate the cost of a typical banking crisis and thus the welfare gains from reducing the probability of such a crisis.

Another complication is that the IMF's calculations of the output gap might be seen as endogenous to hindsight reflecting actual history rather than what might have been. For example, in October 2007 the IMF's estimate of the US output gap for 2007 was –0.5 percent of potential GDP, whereas in October 2015 its estimate of the 2007 output gap was +2.66 percent of potential GDP (IMF 2007b, 2015b). Similarly, whereas the median value of the initial output gap in table 4.1 is +2.5 percent, the corresponding median value for contemporary estimates by the IMF in 2008 (or, for the United

9. For purposes of comparability with the main advanced industrial economies, this set of control countries excludes several economies that the IMF (2015c) also designates as "advanced": Eastern European, newly industrialized East Asian, and small economies.

States and United Kingdom, 2007) was –0.4 percent (IMF 2007a, 2008c). Yet it would seem inappropriate to completely ignore the benefit of hindsight. In the US economy, for example, the jeopardy that arose from the housing market bubble is now evident but was much less recognized in 2007.

The analytical challenge is that an extremely wide range can arguably be asserted for the magnitude of banking crisis damages. As noted, the estimate could be as low as 10 percent of the base year's GDP, using the control group approach. At the opposite extreme, if it is assumed that there was no positive output gap before the crisis, and that the entire gap from the no-crisis baseline by year 5 should be seen as permanent, then the median damage from a banking crisis could be estimated as high as 450 percent of GDP![10]

In the empirical estimates developed below, the central estimate of damage is placed at the 64 percent benchmark reported in table 4.1. The main calculations include alternatives at 30 percent and 100 percent of base-year GDP as what might be considered plausible-low and plausible-high estimates. However, in the discussion of the final results, the outcomes are also reported for two extremes: damage of 10 percent and 450 percent of base-year GDP. As will be shown, the resulting optimal ratio of capital to assets turns out to be considerably narrower than might have been thought for this 45-fold variation in the damage parameter. That outcome essentially reflects the sharp curvature of the function relating the probability of a banking crisis to the capital ratio, as developed below.

Finally, it warrants mentioning that the damage estimates here are formulated in a binary nature: either zero, for no crisis, or a fixed estimate (64 percent of base-year GDP in the central estimate), if a banking crisis occurs. It would be useful to provide a graduated estimate of output loss that relates the depth of the loss, given a banking crisis, to the amount of bank capitalization. However, the few studies that attempt to link crisis severity to level of bank capitalization are insufficient to draw significant conclusions (BCBS 2010a, 17).

Comparison with Basel Committee Estimates. In its 2010 survey of damages from banking crises, the Basel Committee on Banking Supervision (BCBS) assessed the long-term economic impact (LEI) at 19 percent of GDP with no permanent effects; 158 percent of GDP with permanent effects and an infinite horizon; and 63 percent for the "median cumulative effect across all studies," which it also characterized as the case in which "crises have a

---

10. With no initial output gap, the median output loss is larger by 2.5 percent of initial GDP, boosting the median five-year loss to 35.4 percent. The median gap in year 5 becomes 10.3 percent of initial year GDP. Assuming this gap persists forever, and discounting at 2.5 percent, the "permanent" portion of the loss becomes $10.3/0.025 = 412$ percent of base-year GDP. Adding the loss in the first five years boosts the total to 447 percent.

long-lasting or small permanent effect on output" (BCBS 2010b, 10, 13). On the basis of the existing studies, the BCBS argued that a 1 percentage point reduction in the annual probability of a banking crisis would thus generate gross benefits of 0.19 percent, 0.63 percent, or 1.58 percent of GDP, depending on the degree of permanency of the losses.[11]

It turns out that the estimates in table 4.1 are extremely close to the middle case of the BCBS. Namely, the median total loss of 64 percent of base GDP is almost the same as the survey median of 63 percent found by the BCBS for the middle (as opposed to high permanent) estimate, even though in contrast the present study is heavily dominated by actual experience from the 2007–08 crisis rather than for earlier periods (and includes a wider range of countries, including emerging-market economies). Similarly, the cumulative initial effect during the crisis years, 19 percent in the BCBS estimates, is fairly close to the median five-year cumulative effect estimated here (22.9 percent). The key difference in the damage estimates, then, is in the long-term "permanent" effects, as table 4.1 shows no estimates anywhere near 158 percent. The central reason again is the judgment that nothing lasts forever and that some form of productive resource lifespan must be taken into account in arriving at a meaningful "permanent" effect.

There is another key contrast, however. It concerns the baseline frequency assumed for the incidence of banking crises. This incidence is crucial, because the product of the annual probability of a crisis and the damage cost of a crisis determines the expected damage from a banking crisis, and thus the amount of benefit that can be achieved by reducing the likelihood of a crisis.

The BCBS (2010a, 39) places the annual probability of a banking crisis at 3.6 to 5.2 percent for "all BCBS countries" and 4.1 to 5.2 percent for G-10 countries. The slightly lower range for both concepts is from the compilation of crises by Laeven and Valencia (2008) and the higher range from Reinhart and Rogoff (2008). The frequency estimates are for the period 1985–2009.[12]

---

11. Curiously, the study states that "These results from the existing literature are obviously based on crises prior to the current one." It then cites Haldane (2010) as arguing that the current crisis would impose much higher losses, ranging from 90 to 350 percent of (one-year's) world GDP (BCBS 2010a, 11). Yet in appendix A1 of the study about one-half of the crises examined are indeed from the "current" crisis, and show dates of 2007 or 2008 (BCBS 2010a, 39).

12. With 25 years and 10 countries, there are 250 country-years. In this period, there was at least one crisis in all G-10 countries except Canada. The frequency measure represents dividing the total of 9 (Laeven-Valencia 2012) to 13 (Reinhart-Rogoff 2008) crises by 250 country-years. All G-10 countries except Canada and Sweden experienced crisis in 2007 or 2008 (BCBS 2010a, 39). Seven of the crises in Laeven-Valencia and Reinhart-Rogoff

It is by no means clear, however, why the starting point should be 1985. In table 4.1, there is a banking crisis recorded for Spain in 1977. If we begin the period at 1977 and bring it up to 2015, then there is a span of 38 years to consider. If we consider all the industrial countries listed in table 4.1 (including the "control" group with no crisis in 2008), there are 22 countries. The number of country-years in this full span is thus 836. The number of banking crises in table 4.1 is 22. On this basis, the annual frequency of a (new) banking crisis is 2.6 percent.

At the upper end of the BCBS range for both frequency of and damage from banking crisis, the expected annual loss from a banking crisis under conditions of 1985–2009 was 5.2 percent × 158 percent = 8.2 percent of one year's GDP. By this reckoning, if it were possible to purchase an insurance policy that would completely eliminate the risk of a banking crisis, it would be worth spending 8.2 percent of GDP every year to pay the premium on this policy. This amount would be several times what most countries pay for national defense.

If instead the estimates of table 4.1 are adopted and the time span is set at 1977–2015, then the expected annual loss from banking crises amounts to 1.7 percent of GDP (2.6 percent × 64 percent). Although still high, this estimate (which includes long-term effects) would seem more plausible than the 8.2 percent of GDP expected loss in the high end of the BCBS estimates. Even this lower figure could be exaggerated, however, to the extent that it mainly captures the extreme outcomes of the Great Recession, something broadly comparable to a 100-year flood that included losses from uncertainty associated with sovereign debt distress not necessarily triggered by banking crises.

The Capital Requirements Benefits Curve. Let the probability of a banking crisis when the capital requirement is at its base level k_0 be P_{cr0}. Let the total output loss from a banking crisis (including the long-term loss) be L_{cr}. Defining the crisis loss as the fraction λ of one year's base GDP (Y_0), where $\lambda_0 = L_{cr}/Y_0$, the annualized expected loss from a banking crisis expressed as a fraction of base year GDP will be:

$$D_0 = P_{cr0}\lambda_0 \tag{4.4}$$

Now suppose that increasing bank capital requirements from their base level k_0 to a higher level k reduces the annual probability of occurrence of a banking crisis to P_{crk}. Suppose that the relationship between the probability of a crisis and the ratio of capital to (total) assets, k, is of the form:

---

were from 2007 or 2008, constituting 54 percent of the G-10 banking crises in the period according to the first study and 78 percent according to the second.

$$P_{crk} = Ak^\gamma;$$
$$\ln P_{crk} = \ln A + \gamma \ln k \tag{4.5}$$

where $\gamma < 0$.

The gross benefits of increasing the capital ratio from its base value of k_0 to level k, expressed as the reduction in expected annualized crisis losses, will then be:

$$B = -(P_{crk} - P_{cr0})\lambda_0$$
$$= -(Ak^\gamma - Ak_0^\gamma)\lambda_0 \tag{4.6}$$
$$= -A\lambda_0(k^\gamma - k_0^\gamma)$$

Because $\gamma < 0$ (that is, the probability of crisis declines as k rises), the final expression within parentheses is negative (considering that $k > k_0$), yielding a positive benefit in equation (4.6). The derivative of the benefit equation is:

$$\frac{dB}{dk} = -A\lambda_0\gamma k^{\gamma-1} \tag{4.7}$$

Again with $\gamma < 0$, this derivative is positive, so the benefit is a rising function of the capital ratio. The final exponent of k is a strictly negative number, such that increasing k reduces the overall value of the right-hand side. The benefit function is thus concave with respect to the capital ratio; there are diminishing returns to increases in the capital ratio.

Calibrating the Benefits Curve. Arguably the most crucial and also the most uncertain building block in implementing the benefits model set forth in equations (4.4) through (4.7) is the curve describing the response of the probability of a banking crisis to the level of the bank capital requirement (equation 4.5). The most authoritative estimates on this question still seem to be those compiled in a survey by the BCBS in 2010 (BCBS 2010a). It is worth quoting from the study on its method:

> Mapping tighter capital and liquidity requirements into reductions in the probability of crises is particularly difficult. This study relies mainly on two types of methodology. The first involves reduced-form econometric studies. These estimate the historical link between the capital and liquidity ratios of banking systems and subsequent banking crises, controlling for the influence of other factors. The second involves treating the banking system as a portfolio of securities. Based on estimates of the volatility in the value of bank assets, of the probabilities and of correlations of default and on assumptions about the link between capital and default, it is then possible to derive the probability of a banking crisis for different levels of capital ratios. (BCBS 2010a, 3).

Table 4.2   BCBS synthesis of impact of capital on the probability of systemic banking crises (percent)

TCE/RWA	TCE/TA	P_{cr}: All models, NCLA	P_{cr}: NSFR
6	3.37	7.2	4.8
7	3.93	4.6	3.3
8	4.49	3.0	2.3
9	5.06	1.9	1.6
10	5.62	1.4	1.2
11	6.18	1.0	0.9
12	6.74	0.7	0.7
13	7.30	0.5	0.5
14	7.87	0.4	0.4
15	8.43	0.3	0.3

BCBS = Basel Committee on Banking Supervision; TCE = tangible common equity; RWA = risk-weighted assets; TA = total assets; P_{cr} = probability of crisis; NCLA = no change in liquid assets. The NCLA variant reflects model results when liquid assets are not changed; NSFR = meeting net stable funding ratio. The NSFR variant is for results modeling an increase in the ratio of liquid assets to total assets by 12.5 percent; TCE/TA = based on TA/RWA = 1.78 for US and euro area banks

Source: BCBS (2010a, 15, 57).

Key studies of the first type include Barrell et al. (2010) and Kato, Kobayashi, and Saita (2010). An example of the second category is Elsinger, Lehar, and Summer (2006).

Table 4.2 shows the resulting synthesis of the BCBS mapping of capital ratios to banking crisis probability.

The third and fourth columns of table 4.2 provide a basis for estimating the probability function in equation (4.5). If the logarithm of the crisis probability (column 3 or 4) is regressed on the logarithm of the ratio of capital to total assets (column 2), the resulting constant and coefficient estimates provide an estimate of A and γ.[13]

---

13. With $\ln (P_{cr}) = a + b \ln k$, in equation (4.5) the constant $A = \exp(a)$, and the coefficient $\gamma = b$. The estimations yield: for column 3, and using pure numbers rather than percentages, $\ln (P_{cr}) = -14.41 \, (-85) -3.50 \, (-60) \ln (TCE/TA)$; adj. $R^2 = 0.997$, with t-statistics in parentheses. For column 4: $\ln (P_{cr}) = -13.16 \, (-63) -3.016 \, (-42) \ln (TCE/TA)$; adj. $R^2 = 0.995$. The extremely high R^2 and t-statistics likely reflect the fact that the BCBS numbers are already syntheses in stylized form rather than underlying empirical observations. Note that these log-log regressions achieve a higher explanation than either quadratic or cubic specifications.

The point of departure for increasing capital ratios is a base of 7 percent tangible common equity relative to risk-weighted assets (3.9 percent of total assets), near the lower bound of the range considered in BCBS (2010a), as shown in table 4.2. At this level of capital, the probability of banking crisis is 4.6 percent in the all-models estimate and 3.3 percent in models considering liquidity and assuming that the net stable funding ratio (NSFR) liquidity targets are met. However, both these estimates are higher than the 2.6 percent benchmark identified above, based on 1977–2015 experience. As a result, in the main estimate here, the constant A is adjusted downward by the ratio 2.6/4.6.[14]

Figure 4.2 shows the benefits curve relating the main estimate of losses avoided annually as a percent of total GDP in response to alternative ratios of capital to total assets. The zero point in these benefits is set at a starting point of 3.9 percent capital relative to total assets. The damages use the all-models estimates in table 4.2 (after the shrinkage from base crisis frequency of 4.6 to 2.6 percent). As can be seen, after the ratio of capital to total assets exceeds about 7 percent, the curve levels off, reaching a plateau of 1.67 percent of output. Thus, whereas the benefits of reducing the incidence of banking crises would amount to about 1 percent of GDP annually at a capital ratio of 5 percent, about 1.3 percent of GDP at a capital ratio of 6 percent, and about 1.5 percent at a capital ratio of 7 percent, boosting the capital ratio far higher to 25 percent would boost the benefits only marginally higher to 1.67 percent of GDP. This concave nonlinearity stems directly from the survey findings in BCBS (2010a).

It is evident in figure 4.2 that the curvature of the benefits curve is quite pronounced in the range of capital to total assets of about 5 to 7 percent, but thereafter the curve is nearly flat. This phenomenon is a key driver of the optimal capital ratio estimates obtained below. The curvature of benefits is in turn driven by the curvature in the probability of banking crisis in response to alternative capital ratios (table 4.2). In explicating this crisis probability curvature, the Basel Committee report states the following:

> Another consistent result across models is that the incremental benefit of higher capital and liquidity requirements declines as the system becomes better capitalized. That is, when banks have low levels of capital, even small increases have a very significant impact, but the marginal benefit of further increases in capital ratios declines as banks move further away from the insolvency threshold.... These results are fairly intuitive. The

---

14. As discussed below, an optimistic alternative uses the adjustment factor 2.6/3.3 applied to the constant A in the curve for the NSFR models. A pessimistic alternative uses no downward adjustment in the constant and applies the curve for the all-models with no change in liquid assets.

Figure 4.2   Benefits of additional bank capital

benefit (fraction of GDP)

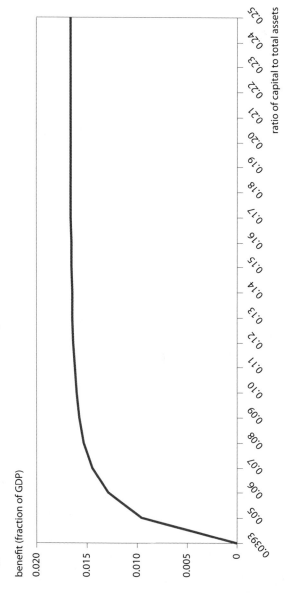

ratio of capital to total assets

Source: Author's calculations.

rationale is quite similar to that applying in the context of risk models applied to individual banks. For a given volatility in the value of assets, the further away a bank is from the insolvency threshold, the lower is the benefit of additional protection. (BCBS, 2010a, 16.)

It is important to recognize that the 1.67 percent potential upper-bound benefit refers to the level of GDP, not the annual growth rate. Thus, if extremely high capital requirements were set (say 20 to 25 percent of total assets), and there were no costs, the long-term path of GDP would be expected to lie about 1.7 percent higher than if there had been no change from the pre-Basel III requirements. The corresponding increase in the growth rate—again if there were no costs at all from higher requirements because of complete M&M offset—would amount to 0.055 percent annually over a 30-year period.[15]

Costs of Higher Capital Requirements

If the Modigliani-Miller offset is incomplete, however, higher capital requirements for banks will increase their costs. As they pass along these extra costs to borrowers, lending rates will rise. Firms borrowing capital will find it is no longer profitable to borrow as much and make plant and equipment investments as large as before. With less capital formation, total output will reach levels lower than otherwise. As will be shown, the output cost of higher capital requirements turns out to be a linear function of the level of the requirement, expressed as the ratio of equity capital to total (not risk-weighted) assets.

Average Cost of Capital. The initial and driving force in the output cost is the increase in the interest rate banks must charge on loans as a consequence of shifting from cheaper debt finance to more expensive equity finance (under incomplete M&M effects). Thus, defining z as the average cost of capital to banks, one has:

$$z = z_0 + (k - k_0)(\rho_B - r_d)(1 - \mu) \tag{4.8}$$

where k is the ratio of equity capital to total assets, ρ_B is the unit cost of equity capital for banks, r_d is the real interest rate on debt financing of the banks, and μ is an M&M offset factor.[16] Subscript 0 refers to the base period prior to the regime shift raising capital requirements.

---

15. That is: $1.00055^{30} = 1.0166$.

16. It is the real interest rate that is comparable to the cost of equity as measured, for example, by the inverse of the price-to-earnings ratio. The reason is that nominal earnings will tend to rise with inflation so the equity cost is already stated in real terms.

The analysis here refers to the ratio of equity capital to total assets, not risk-weighted assets. This ratio is sometimes called the "leverage ratio," although it is actually a close transform of the inverse of the leverage ratio of debt to equity.[17] Note further that regulatory requirements refer to capital required relative to "risk-weighted" assets. The values of risk-weighted assets (RWA) are considerably lower than those of unweighted assets because of the low risk weights for some assets (especially for highly rated sovereign obligations but also for home mortgages).

In equation (4.8), if the capital ratio is increased from a modest base (say 5 percent) to a high level (say 25 percent), there will be a corresponding increase in the weighted-average cost of capital, reflecting the excess of the equity cost rate (ρ_B) over the borrowing rate facing the banks (r_d). The final term in the equation shrinks this increase in average cost of capital by the factor μ. If offset is complete ($\mu = 1$), the average cost of capital to banks remains unchanged at z_0 regardless of how high the capital requirement k is raised.

The real interest rate paid by banks on debt is the risk-free rate i plus the spread facing banks, S_B.

$$r_d = i + S_B \tag{4.9}$$

In the calibration applied to the calculations of this chapter, the base case values for the parameters in equation 4.8 are as follows: $z_0 = 2.79$ percent, $\rho_B = 10$ percent, $r_d = 2.5$ percent, and $\mu = 0.45$ (tables 4.3 and 4.4). If there were no M&M offset ($\mu = 0$), the differential of 750 basis points between unit equity cost and the interest rate on debt would mean that increasing the capital requirement by 1 percent of assets would raise the average unit cost of capital to banks by 7.5 basis points. Considering the offset, the increment is $0.55 \times 7.5 = 4.1$ basis points. If the capital ratio is stated in terms of risk-weighted assets, an increase of 1 percentage point would translate to an increase in average cost of $0.55 \times 4.1 = 2.3$ basis points.[18] This estimate is at the low end of the range calculated by Kashyap, Stein, and Hanson (2010) for the same concept (2.5 to 4.5 basis points), and considerably below the median of 9.4 basis points identified across the 10 studies surveyed in BCBS (2016a, 11). From this standpoint, then, the cost estimates of this study

---

17. If $L = D/E$, where L is the debt-equity leverage ratio, D is debt, and E is equity; and $k = E/A$, where A is assets, then considering that debt plus equity equals assets, $L = (A - E)/E = A/E - 1$, so $L = 1/k - 1$.

18. As discussed below, on average, total assets in euro area and US banks are 1.78 times as large as risk-weighted assets (BCBS 2010a, 57).

Table 4.3 Alternative parameter values for simulations

Parameter	Concept	Low OCR	Base	High OCR
λ_0	Total loss (including long-term) from banking crisis as fraction of one year's base GDP	0.3	0.64	1
ρ_B	Cost of equity capital to banks	0.13	0.1	0.07
μ	Modigliani-Miller offset factor	0.35	0.45	0.6
θ	Spillover coefficient, banks to nonbanks	0.7	0.5	0.2
α	Elasticity of output with respect to capital	0.43	0.4	0.33
σ	Elasticity of substitution, capital and labor	0.8	0.5	0.4
	Crisis probability curve (jointly):			
A	Constant	1.50E–06	3.14E–07	5.52E–07
γ	Exponent	–3.016	–3.5	–3.5

OCR = optimal capital ratio
Source: Author's calculations.

Table 4.4 Other parameter and base values

Parameter	Concept	Value
ρ_f	Unit cost of equity capital for nonfinancial firms	0.066
i	Real risk-free interest rate	0.015
S_B	Risk spread in banks' borrowing rate	0.01
S_f	Risk spread in nonfinancial firms' borrowing rate	0.015
φ_B	Share of firms' financing provided by banks	0.333
φ_{NB}	Share of firms' financing provided by nonbanks	0.333
φ_f	Share of firms' financing provided by firms' equity	0.333
k_0	Base level of bank capital relative to total assets	0.0393
z_0	Base average cost of capital to banks	0.0279
w_0	Base average cost of capital to nonfinancial firms	0.046

Source: Author's calculations.

may be on the low rather than high side, and correspondingly the optimal capital requirement may tend to be overstated rather than understated.

For nonfinancial firms, the average cost of capital is a weighted average of the interest rate charged by banks, the interest rate charged by nonbank financial entities and on corporate bonds, and the firm's equity cost:

$$w = \phi_B(z + S_f) + \phi_{NB}r_{NB} + \phi_f\rho_f \qquad (4.10)$$

The interest rate charged by banks is their average cost of capital (z) plus the risk spread applicable to the firms (S_f).

Some spillover effect is likely to occur to lending rates by nonbanks when banks must charge more. If banks increase their lending rates by the same amount that their average cost of capital increases as a consequence of higher capital requirements, and nonbanks raise their rates by the fraction θ of the increase in bank lending rates, then:

$$r_{NB} = r_{NB,0} + \theta \times (z - z_0) \tag{4.11}$$

where $r_{NB,0}$ is the nonbank lending rate in the base period prior to regulatory reform.

With the elements for calculating average cost of capital to firms in hand, the proportionate increase in the cost of capital to the economy (v) resulting from a bank capital ratio of k rather than the base period level k_0 will be:

$$v = \left(\frac{w_k}{w_0} - 1\right) \tag{4.12}$$

Impact on the Economy. As suggested by Miles, Yang, and Marcheggiano (2012) and followed in Cline (2015c), the proportionate output cost to the economy from placing the bank capital requirement at k rather than at the prereform level of k_0 will then be:

$$C = \frac{v \times \alpha \times \sigma}{(1-\alpha)} \tag{4.13}$$

where α is the elasticity of output with respect to capital (capital's factor share) and σ is the elasticity of substitution between capital and labor.

The derivative of this output cost with respect to the required capital ratio is then:

$$\frac{dC}{dk} = \frac{dC}{dv} \times \frac{dv}{dw} \times \frac{dw}{dz} \times \frac{dz}{dk} \tag{4.14}$$

$$= \frac{\alpha\sigma}{1-\alpha} \frac{1}{w_0} (\phi_B + \theta\phi_{NB})\{(\rho_B - r_d)(1-\mu)\} \equiv \psi$$

All the terms in the final right-hand side of equation (4.14) are constants, so the derivative of the proportionate output loss with respect to the capital requirement is a constant (set equal to ψ in the final right-hand-side expression). The expressions containing differences are all greater than zero, so this constant is positive. A graph representing the proportionate output cost on the vertical axis and the capital requirement on the horizontal axis will thus be a straight line sloping upward.

In the base case for the calculations developed below, the parameters and base values of the variables in equation (4.14) are as follows: $\alpha = 0.4$; $\sigma = 0.5$; $w_0 = 0.046$; $\phi_B = 0.333$; $\theta = 0.5$; $\phi_{NB} = 0.333$; $\rho_B = 0.10$, $r_d = 0.025$;

and $\mu = 0.45$. The resulting value of ψ, the constant derivative of output with respect to the capital ratio, is 0.15. Thus, for example, if the capital requirement is increased by 10 percent of total assets, the level of output will decline by 1.5 percent from the path it otherwise would have followed. Over 30 years, cumulative output loss would amount to 45 percent of the initial base-year output level, ignoring time discounting as well as the baseline growth rate.[19] This illustration makes it evident that the economic cost of a large increase in capital requirements would be substantial. Identifying the optimal level of capital thus requires a close examination of the marginal cost in comparison to the marginal benefit.

The estimate for ψ developed here is extremely close to that identified for the corresponding concept in the LEI study (BCBS 2010a, 26). That study found that across 13 models, the median impact of an increase by 1 percentage point in capital relative to risk-weighted assets was a reduction of 0.09 percent in the level of production. With risk-weighted assets only 56 percent of total assets, the corresponding impact of an increase in capital by 1 percent of total assets would amount to an output reduction of 0.16 percent, almost the same as the parameter $\psi = 0.15$ estimated in the present study. Because the LEI analysis conservatively sets the M&M offset at zero, it follows from equation (4.14) that the BCBS parameter for ψ should be more than twice as large as the magnitude in the analysis here.[20] By implication, the LEI study seems to understate the long-term output cost resulting from a specific realized increase in the unit cost of capital to firms. Two sources of that underestimation seem likely. First, the studies surveyed in the LEI study may tend to use a higher base unit cost of capital than the level applied here (4.6 percent in real terms; see table 4.3). If so, a specific increment in the unit cost of capital in the LEI study would be a smaller proportionate increase than in the calculations here. Second, the LEI survey includes simulation results from large macroeconomic models. These models may understate output effects by inappropriately including monetary policy offsets reducing the policy interest rate, even though an environment of less capital stock formation would imply greater scarcity and if anything more severe inflationary pressures. Moreover, these models seem more likely to be relevant for evaluating consequences of shifts in demand than long-term shifts in capacity and underlying supply.

---

19. If the baseline growth rate is approximately equal to the social discount rate, the two influences cancel each other out.

20. That is: from (4.14), if $\mu_{LEI} = 0$, then $\psi_{LEI} = \psi/(1 - \mu)$. In chapter 3 of the present study μ is found to be 0.45, the value applied in the estimates below. With the analysis here estimating ψ at 0.15, the corresponding parameter under the LEI assumptions should be $\psi_{LEI} = 2.22\ \psi$, other things being equal.

Optimal Capital Requirements

With the marginal social cost of additional capital given by equation (4.14) and the marginal social benefit given by equation (4.7), the optimal capital ratio k^* will occur where these two marginal effects are equal, at:

$$-A\lambda_0\gamma k^{*\,\gamma-1} = \psi \tag{4.15}$$

Solving for the optimal capital ratio k^* yields:

$$k^* = \left[\frac{\psi}{-A\lambda_0\gamma}\right]^{\frac{1}{\gamma-1}} \tag{4.16}$$

In graphical terms, this optimal capital ratio will occur where the slope of the convex benefit function equals the slope of the linear cost function.

Tables 4.3 and 4.4 report parameter values applied in implementation of the model using equations (4.4) to (4.16). For seven key influences shown in table 4.3, three alternative parameter values are considered: a base case using the central estimates; a "low" case in which the parameters will generate a lower optimal capital ratio (with other parameters unchanged); and a "high" case in which the parameters will generate a higher optimal capital ratio (OCR).

The first parameter, λ_0, is the expected present value of damage from a banking crisis, as a fraction of one year's base GDP. The estimates in table 4.1 provide the central value of 0.64 for this parameter. The low OCR variant is set at 0.30 (effectively treating most of the damages as those occurring within the first five years); the high OCR variant, at 1.0, represents much longer persistence of damages.

For the second parameter, ρ_B, the unit cost of equity capital, the base case uses 10 percent. This is the rate indicated in IIF (2011). For the two alternative rates, 13 percent and 7 percent, the source is chapter 3, table 3.1. These were the rates identified for 54 large US banks in 2001–13 for the earnings yield (inverse of price-to-earnings ratio) and the ratio of net income to equity, respectively. The 13 percent equity cost variant will impose greater costs from forcing a shift away from debt to equity, so it represents a low-OCR case; conversely, a 7 percent equity cost represents a high-OCR case.

The base case places the M&M offset, μ, at 0.45, again based on the estimates in chapter 3. The low-OCR alternative posits a smaller offset of 0.35; the high-OCR alternative sets the offset at 0.6. For the spillover effect, θ, the base estimate assumes that nonbank lending rates rise by one-half of the increase in bank lending rates. The low-OCR variant sets this spillover effect at 0.7, raising the economic cost of higher capital requirements for banks; the high-OCR variant assumes a spillover coefficient of only 0.2, making higher capital requirements less costly. The base elasticity of output with respect to capital, α, is set at 0.4, reflecting the high share of capital in GDP in recent years. As can be seen in equation (4.13), the economic cost of higher capital requirements is positively associated with α. Higher cost translates to a lower optimal capital ratio. The low-OCR variant of α is set at 0.43. Conversely, the high-OCR variant is set at the more traditional notional value of $\alpha = 0.33$.[21] The elasticity of substitution, σ, is set at 0.5 in the base case (following Miles, Yang, and Marcheggiano 2012). Again equation (4.13) reveals the direction of influence of this parameter on economic cost of higher capital requirements as being positive. The low-OCR variant is thus set at 0.8 (higher cost will lead to a lower optimal capital ratio), and the high-OCR variant, at 0.4.[22]

The final two rows of table 4.3 show alternative sets of parameters for the crisis probability curve. The base case applies the "all models" column of table 4.2, but imposes the base crisis probability estimate of 2.6 percent developed in the initial section above. The high-OCR alternative instead accepts the BCBS (2010a) base crisis probability of 4.6 percent and applies the curvature of the all-models estimates (table 4.2). That is, with higher crisis damages and hence benefits of curbing the probability of crisis, there will be a higher return to additional bank capital. The low-OCR variant imposes the lower 2.6 percent base probability of crisis, and applies the somewhat more favorable curvature of the net stable funding ratio estimates in the BCBS (2010a) study. For the other parameters and base values in the model, single estimates are applied, as shown in table 4.4.

Equity cost to firms is based on a typical price-to-earnings ratio of 15.[23] A real risk-free interest rate of 1.5 percent is meant to represent medium- to long-term rates under conditions more normal than those following the Great Recession. The risk spread for banks is based on observed credit default swap rates.[24] The share of equity in corporate financing is set at one-third on the basis of data for G-7 countries (Rajan and Zingales 1995, 1428). The share of debt financing by corporations is also set at one-third as estimated by Miles, Yang, and Marcheggiano (2012, 16), who note that this share would be lower for the United States and "slightly higher" in some

---

21. In 2013–14, compensation of employees accounted for 61.3 percent of national income in the United States; in 1990, this share was 66.4 percent (BEA 2016).

22. The intuition regarding this influence is that if the elasticity of substitution is higher, raising the cost of capital will have a greater impact in reducing the amount of capital applied in production, which in turn will drive lower output.

23. This ratio is consistent with the estimate by Damodaran (2015) that the average earnings yield in the United States in 1960–2014 was 6.8 percent.

24. For the six largest US banks, credit default swap rates in 2015 averaged 76 basis points (Bloomberg). The rate of 100 basis points makes allowance for higher rates at other banks.

European countries. The remaining share of capital financing, in the form of nonbank debt (including corporate bonds) is then also one-third.

The base value of the capital-to-assets ratio is set at 3.93 percent, based on the base value of 7 percent for tangible common equity relative to risk-weighted assets and a ratio of 1.78 for total assets to risk-weighted assets for US and euro area banks (BCBS 2010a, 57). The two final entries in table 4.4 are the estimated base values of average cost of capital to banks and average cost of capital to nonfinancial firms, obtained by applying equations (4.8) and (4.10) to the parameters and base values in tables 4.3 and 4.4.

Results

Application of the base case values for the parameters in tables 4.3 and 4.4 yields an optimal capital-to-assets ratio of $k^* = 0.0656$. Figure 4.3 shows the paths of benefits (equation 4.6) and costs (equation 4.13), using the base case. As noted, in this case the total potential benefit of higher capital ratios plateaus at about 1.7 percent of annual GDP. If the capital-to-assets ratio were raised all the way to 25 percent, the cost would reach 3 percent of annual GDP. The two curves intersect at a capital-to-assets ratio of about 15 percent. But the optimal capital ratio, the point at which the slopes of the two curves are parallel, occurs at a capital-to-assets ratio less than half as high, at 6.56 percent. This optimal ratio would correspond to a ratio of capital to risk-weighted assets of 11.7 percent.

Figure 4.4 provides a histogram of the estimates of the optimal capital-to-assets ratio across all 2,187 possible combinations of parameters in table 4.3 (again calculated using equation 4.16). The lowest optimal ratio is 0.0411. The highest estimate finds $k^* = 0.1164$. At about 12 percent, even the highest case is slightly less than half of the midpoint of the 20 to 30 percent range recommended by Admati and Hellwig (2013, 179).

The median estimate of the optimal capital ratio is $k^* = 0.0694$ percent, slightly higher than the base case estimate ($k^* = 0.0656$). When arrayed from lowest to highest, the 25th percentile shows a value of $k^* = 0.0611$, and the 75th percentile places k^* at 0.0787. On this basis, it seems reasonable to place the central estimate of the optimal capital ratio at about 7 percent of total assets, and a more risk-averse main estimate at about 8 percent.

Returning to the issue of potentially wide variation in the estimated damage from a banking crisis, it is useful to consider the optimal capital ratios implied by the extreme ends of the spectrum discussed above. If a banking crisis causes output loss of only 10 percent of base-year GDP ($\lambda_0 = 0.1$), and if all other parameters in tables 4.3 and 4.4 are set at their base values, then the optimum capital ratio reaches only 4.3 percent of total assets ($k^* = 0.043$). If instead banking crisis damage is set at 450 percent of

Figure 4.3   Benefits and costs of additional bank capital

benefit or cost (fraction of GDP)

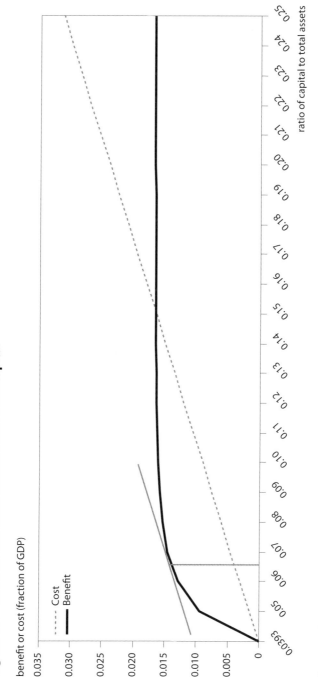

Source: Author's calculations.

Figure 4.4   Frequency of estimates for optimal capital-to-assets ratio

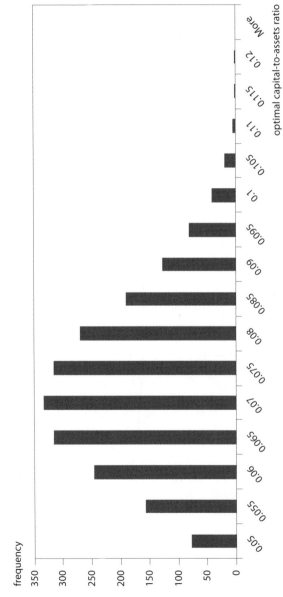

Source: Author's calculations.

GDP ($\lambda_0 = 4.5$), the optimal capital ratio rises to 10.1 percent of total assets ($k^* = 0.101$), higher than the 75th percentile in the main estimates but lower than the very highest estimate (11.6 percent) identified from the most extreme combination among the alternative parameters already considered.

An important question is whether the optimal range identified here should be substantially different for European as opposed to US banks, in view of the greater reliance on bank finance in Europe. This question can be examined by changing the shares of debt finance to the economy between banks (ϕ_B) and nonbanks (ϕ_{NB}). The consequence of a higher bank share will be to raise the economic cost of higher capital requirements for banks.

Merler and Véron (2015, 54) estimate that whereas 88 percent of corporate borrowing in the euro area comes from banks, this share is only 30 percent in the United States. Applying these shares to the combined two-thirds of finance coming from debt, the parameter ϕ_B would be placed at 0.59 for the euro area but only 0.2 for the United States (leaving the parameter ϕ_{NB} at 0.08 or 0.47, respectively). From equation (4.14), the effect of applying these tailored financing shares is to change the cost parameter ψ from 0.15 percent of GDP for each percentage point increase in the capital-to-total assets ratio, to 0.19 percent for the euro area and 0.13 for the United States.

Equation (4.16) can then be applied to obtain the corresponding changes in optimal capital ratios. With k^* as the optimal capital requirement in the base case, the tailored debt-sourcing shares place the optimal capital ratios at $k_E^* = 0.965\ k^*$ for the euro area and $k_U^* = 1.022\ k^*$ for the United States.[25] So even a seemingly high divergence between bank and nonbank sourcing of debt has only a modest impact on the optimal capital ratio. Namely, the US optimal ratio would be proportionally higher than the euro area optimal ratio by only about 6 percent, even though the unit economic cost of capital would be 46 percent higher ($\psi = 0.19$ versus 0.13).

This exercise once again underscores the importance of the high degree of curvature in the benefits curve, which is based on the BCBS (2010a) estimates of the sharp drop-off in crisis probability as the capital ratio increases (table 4.2). This same influence is the driving force behind the relatively modest change in the optimal capital ratio (from 4.3 to 10.1 percent of total assets) as crisis damage is multiplied 45-fold between the extreme variants just noted. Because of this key influence, further research is warranted on

---

25. From equation (4.16), $k_E^*/k^* = (\psi_E/\psi)^{\wedge}(1/\gamma - 1)$. With the base case value $\gamma = -3.5$ (table 4.3), the optimal capital ratio varies approximately with the inverse of the fourth root of the unit cost parameter ψ.

whether the BCBS estimates provide the right degree of curvature in the relationship of crisis probability to the capital ratio.[26]

Comparison with Other Estimates

Alternative estimates in four other studies warrant special discussion. The first two are important in their own right but also provide key inputs for the estimates here. The third is a benchmark academic study, and the fourth a recent empirical study conducted at the IMF.

First, in its summary assessment, the 2010 Basel Committee study that provides the basis for the crisis probability estimates here identified an optimal ratio of capital to risk-weighted assets (TCE/RWA) of 10 percent if there are no permanent effects of banking crises, and 12.5 percent if there are "moderate" permanent effects (BCBS 2010a, 2). The moderate permanent effects case is close to the 11.7 percent identified here (6.56 percent of total assets). There is, nonetheless, an important difference. As shown in figure 4.3, net benefits—the vertical distance between the benefits curve and the cost line—show a steady and sizable decline after capital exceeds the optimal ratio. In contrast, in the BCBS study the net benefits remain almost flat at about 1.7 percent of GDP even as the ratio of capital to risk-weighted assets reaches 16 percent. This level corresponds to a ratio of about 9 percent for capital relative to total assets. At this level, net benefits (the distance between the upward-sloping line for cost and the convex curve for benefits) would be significantly smaller than at the optimal ratio.[27] The reason for the seeming flatness of the net benefits curve in the BCBS study is not clear. This pattern appears to reflect a nonlinear cost curve that allows for costs to plateau almost as fully as benefits. The study's cost estimates are opaque, however, as they are based mainly on several dynamic stochastic general equilibrium (DSGE) models without details reported.

Second, Miles, Yang, and Marcheggiano (2012) use a framework similar to that applied here. Although specific components and calibrations differ, their overall results are similar to those obtained here. On the side of economic costs of additional capital, their cost curve is only about half as steep as that developed here, largely because they set their base value for the average cost of capital to firms at about twice the level assumed here.[28]

---

26. As discussed in appendix 4A, the curvature of the benefits curve is much milder in the analysis of the Minneapolis Plan (2016). However, that analysis seriously understates the initial benefits and overstates the benefits at high capital ratios, as discussed in the appendix.

27. In the base case here, at the optimal capital ratio of $k^* = 0.0656$, $B - C = 1.0$ percent of GDP; at $k = 0.09$, $B - C = 0.82$ percent of GDP.

28. Miles, Yang, and Marcheggiano posit a shift from bank leverage of 30 to 15, meaning

Their benefits curve is quite different in concept, and is premised on the proposition that a given decline in GDP causes an equal and proportionate decline in risk-weighted assets. The distribution of asset reductions is then compared with capital to estimate the implied incidence of banking crises. They obtain a distribution of GDP declines based on 200 years' data for 31 countries. The authors set the present value of a banking crisis at a loss of 55 percent of one year's GDP—a benchmark similar to the 64 percent base estimate here. If they exclude the most extreme cases (where GDP falls by 35 percent), it turns out that their optimal capital ratio lies in the range of 7 to 9 percent of total assets.[29] That range is surprisingly close to the range identified here: 6.56 percent of total assets (base case) to 7.9 percent (conservative 75th percentile).

The third and fourth studies warranting special mention are those by Admati and Hellwig (2013) and Dagher et al. (2016). Both are reviewed in chapter 2. The Admati-Hellwig recommendation of bank equity capital of 20 to 30 percent of total assets is far above the range found optimal here. It is not based on an optimization model. The recent IMF study by Dagher et al. (2016), in contrast, arrives at a desired range for capital that is comparable to that estimated in this chapter.

Finally, the "Minneapolis Plan," issued in preliminary form by the Minneapolis Federal Reserve in late 2016, uses the Dagher et al. (2016) data on the relationship of crises to nonperforming loans and bank capital, together with simulations of the Federal Reserve's large macroeconomic model to arrive at an optimal capital ratio of 23.5 percent of risk-weighted assets. For the reasons set forth in appendix 4A, this estimate appears to be seriously overstated.

---

k rises from 0.033 to 0.066. They calculate the resulting rise in average cost of capital to banks at 18 basis points, and a resulting increase in average cost of capital to firms of 6 basis points. They place base capital cost to firms at 10 percent, so 6 basis points is an increase of 0.63 percent in the cost of capital. Their calculation of the resulting output loss is the same as in equation (4.13) here. They use $\alpha = 0.33$ and $\sigma = 0.5$, so $C = 0.148$ percent. The corresponding change here from base to optimal is as follows. The capital ratio k rises from 0.0393 to 0.0656; average bank capital cost z rises by 11 basis points; average cost of capital to firms rises by 5 basis points, after taking account of spillover to nonbanks ($\theta = 0.5$). But because average capital cost to firms begins at 4.6 percent (real) rather than 10 percent, the proportionate increase of capital cost to firms is 1.1 percent. Applying equation (4.13) (and using $\alpha = 0.4$ instead of 0.33) yields a decrease in output by 0.37 percent, more than twice the Miles, Yang, and Marcheggiano estimate.

29. The authors state this range as 16 to 20 percent of risk-weighted assets. They use a ratio of 0.45 for RWA/TA, or 2.22 for TA/RWA, implying an optimal range of 7 to 9 percent of total assets.

Implications for Regulatory Capital

The Basel III regulatory reform requires that by 2019 banks hold a minimum of 4.5 percent of risk-weighted assets in common equity, plus another 2.5 percent as a capital buffer (BCBS 2010b, 69). The total requirement of 7 percent of RWA in common equity corresponds to 3.9 percent of total assets.[30] G-SIBs are to hold additional capital of up to 2.5 percent of RWA, bringing the ratio to 9.5 percent of RWA (BCBS 2014c).[31]

A capital ratio of 9.5 percent against risk-weighted assets corresponds to a ratio of 5.3 percent against total assets. Against the optimal ratio estimated here—6.6 percent central estimate and 7.9 percent for the conservative 75th percentile estimate—the Basel III capital requirements are too low. They would need to rise by about one-fourth to reach the central estimate, and by about one-half to reach the more risk-averse 75th percentile estimate. Even so, the increases needed to reach the optimal capital ratios are far less than the five-fold multiple called for by Admati and Hellwig (2013).

In the United States, the additional amount for G-SIBs is to range up to 4.5 percent, bringing the ratio to as high as 11.5 percent of RWA.[32] This level would correspond to 6.5 percent of total assets. That level would be almost exactly the same as the base case optimal capital ratio identified in the present study. However, in practice the highest G-SIB increment by early 2016 was 3.5 percent (for JPMorgan), and the amount for the US G-SIBs was centered at about 3 percent.[33] So the principal G-SIB rate stood at about 10 percent of RWA, or 5.6 percent of total assets. On this basis, even for US G-SIBs the capital requirement would need to increase by about one-sixth to reach the central-estimate optimal capital ratio and by about two-fifths to reach the more conservative benchmark (6.56 and 7.9 percent, respectively).

The G-SIBs account for a large portion of assets in the international banking system. The broad implication is thus that capital requirements on track under Basel III are below optimal levels, but not nearly as far below as some past studies have suggested.

---

30. As noted above, this study uses the BCBS (2010a, 57) estimate that for US and euro area banks the ratio of total assets to risk-weighted assets is an average of 1.78.

31. The top "bucket" in the 2014 survey of 75 large banks was set at 2.5 percent, though a higher bracket at 3.5 percent was identified for larger banks in the future (BCBS 2014c, 4).

32. Federal Reserve Press Release, July 20, 2015, www.federalreserve.gov/newsevents/press/bcreg/20150720a.htm.

33. Hugh Son, "JPMorgan Shares Rise on Surprise Drop in Capital Surcharge," Bloomberg, January 14, 2016; Ian Katz and Jesse Hamilton, "JPMorgan $12.5 billion Short in Fed Systemic-Risk Charges," Bloomberg, July 20, 2015.

Table 4.5   Basel III and FSB capital requirements for G-SIBs

Capital requirement	Percent of risk-weighted assets	Percent of total assets
Tangible common equity (TCE)		
Minimum	4.5	2.5
Capital conservation buffer	2.5	1.4
G-SIB surcharge	2.5	1.4
Total	9.5	5.3
Other Tier 1 capital[a]	1.5	0.84
Tier 2 capital[b]	2	1.12
Total Basel III capital (G-SIBs)	13	7.3
Other TLAC[b]	5	2.8
Total TLAC (FSB)	18	10.1

FSB = Financial Stability Board; G-SIBs = global systemically important banks; TLAC = total loss-absorbing capacity

a. Includes goodwill, deferred tax assets, some contingent convertible debt.
b. Other contingent convertible debt, subordinated debt.

Sources: BCBS (2010b, 2014c); FSB (2015d).

Table 4.5 summarizes Basel III requirements for G-SIBs, and in addition reports the TLAC requirements recommended by the Financial Stability Board in response to the St. Petersburg Summit of the Group of Twenty (G-20) in 2013 (FSB 2015d). The Basel III requirements are to be met by 2019; the TLAC target is to be met by 2022. The table shows the requirements in the usual form, against risk-weighted assets, and also the corresponding central estimate of the implied ratios against total assets.[34] Because the TLAC target is to be assessed on an individual bank basis, the 18 percent shown in the table is a minimum for G-SIBs.[35]

The analysis in this study is based on the tangible common equity concept of capital. This metric is used to calibrate the relationship between the probability of banking crisis and the level of capital (table 4.2). The proper comparison thus contrasts a Basel III target of 9.5 percent of RWA against an optimal range of about 12 to 14 percent identified in the present study.

---

34. Based on TA/RWA = 1.78. Note that Dagher et al. (2016) use a corresponding estimate of 1.75.

35. As noted in chapter 2, for 8 US G-SIBs the average TLAC requirement is 19.9 percent, and the highest requirement (that for JPMorgan Chase) reaches 23.5 percent. Federal Reserve press release, October 30, 2015.

As shown in table 4.5, however, the further requirement for TLAC pursued by the G-20 and Financial Stability Board would bring TLAC up to 18 percent of RWA. A key question is thus whether this additional layer would constitute an effective achievement of the optimal 12 to 14 percent range.

Chapter 5 examines contingent convertible (CoCo) debt and subordinated debt that would constitute the increment that would approximately double TCE to reach the TLAC level. The discussion there suggests that TLAC does not adequately address the basic purpose of capital, which is to ensure that the bank remains solvent. Instead, it is designed to ensure that a large bank can indeed go bankrupt without requiring a call on taxpayer funds. Subordinated debt could be subtracted from the bank's debt liabilities only upon bankruptcy. Bankruptcy of large banks is precisely what capital requirements should be designed to avoid, considering that episodes of failure of large banks would be difficult to envision without an associated banking crisis. As for CoCo debt, in a panic the collapse of market values of this debt would hardly contribute to an atmosphere favorable to avoiding broader crisis (Persaud 2014).[36] Moreover, US banks have not used CoCo debt because its interest does not qualify as a tax-deductible expense.

Further Considerations

Three major additional issues warrant reflection in interpreting the results of the estimates here. The first is whether consideration of social versus private returns substantially alters the diagnosis. The second concerns the relationship between capital actually held by banks and the amount required by financial regulations. The third concerns the possibility that decisions in monetary policy could change the regulatory policy calculus.

Social versus Private Returns. Admati et al. (2011, 22–23) argue that even if higher bank capital requirements cause an increase in bank lending rates, the result is likely to be welfare-enhancing from the viewpoint of society as opposed to private shareholders and borrowers. Their reason is that existing government guarantees of deposit, as well as implicit guarantees of too big to-fail, give a distorted incentive to banks to take excessive risks that can damage the economy in a financial crisis. These distorted incentives are additive to the general distortion from tax favoritism to debt relative to equity.

Identifying socially optimal increases in bank capital, however, would require taking into account a realistic evaluation of costs to the economy from raising bank lending rates and as a consequence reducing capital for-

---

36. In early 2016 there was a sharp sell-off in CoCo debt of European banks in an environment of heightened uncertainty and falling bank equity prices. See Thomas Hale, Joel Lewin, and Katie Martin, "Eurozone bank coco bonds extend slide," *Financial Times*, February 8, 2016.

mation. It may well be that the corresponding reduction in expected social losses from financial crises would warrant substantial costs from lower capital formation. But in principle there is likely to be some optimal limit to the socially beneficial increase in capital if the operational effect is some loss in output because the M&M offset is in fact far from complete. It is further worth noting that social benefits are associated with the service of providing bank deposits, because they constitute money performing its three basic functions: liquidity, store of value, and medium of exchange. It is not clear that the social subsidy to banks from government deposit guarantee is greatly larger than the social externality provided by banks in the form of providing money in the form of deposits.

In short, although recognition of the need to take societal externalities into account could indeed lead to identification of optimal capital requirements that are significantly higher than in the past, the calibration of appropriate policy is considerably more complicated than implied by a general proposition that higher capital requirements are costless and existing capital arrangements subsidize banks and encourage them to take risks at the expense of the public.

Behavioral Cushions. In practice, in the United States (at least) the large banks have already reached capital ratios that not only exceed the Basel III requirements but also are close to the optimal levels identified in this study. In the fourth quarter of 2014, 31 large bank holding companies (representing more than 80 percent of total bank assets) held Tier 1 common equity amounting to 11.9 percent of risk-weighted assets (Federal Reserve 2015c, 3). The Basel III requirement, including the G-SIB surcharge as applied in the United States (an average of 3 percent), is 10 percent of RWA.[37] So these banks held one-fifth more capital than the regulatory requirement (and well before the 2019 deadline). For these large banks, the ratio of total assets to RWA was an average of 1.53 (ibid.). So their common equity was 7.8 percent of total assets—effectively at the conservative (75th percentile) side of the optimal level estimated here.

The question thus arises as to whether the Basel regulatory requirement should be raised to the optimal level or instead placed significantly below the optimal level because of the banking practice of maintaining a cushion. As a principle of public policy, it would seem unwise to count on voluntary overachievement of regulatory requirements. The proper approach would be to set the capital requirement at the socially optimal level, and to antici-

---

37. That is: 4.5 percent plus 2.5 percent capital conservation buffer plus 3 percent G-SIB surcharge (table 4.5).

pate that at the newly higher level banks would no longer maintain such large cushions of additional capital beyond the required amounts.

In the estimates above, the central result for optimal capital is 6.6 percent of total assets. If banks maintained a cushion of an additional one-fifth, their capital would stand at 7.9 percent of total assets. As it turns out, this is the same as the conservative alternative (75th percentile) estimated here for the optimal ratio. The reasonable policy approach, then, would seem to be to set the regulatory requirement at the central estimate of the optimal level, in the expectation that in practice the banks would add a cushion that places their actual capital levels at the conservative (75th percentile) optimal target.

Monetary Policy Offset? Another key consideration is whether the costs of additional capital could easily be offset by more expansionary monetary policy, essentially achieving greater bank capitalization at no cost to the economy. The problem with this line of thinking is that monetary policy should stick to its central mandate—maintaining price stability along with high employment—and not be burdened with extraneous obligations. Superficially the numbers do look congenial to the monetary offset argument. Specifically, increasing the capital requirement by as much as 10 percent of total assets would raise the cost of capital to the economy by "only" about 20 basis points.[38] This amount is substantial relative to the average cost of capital to the economy (4.6 percent in the base case, with the increment representing a proportionate increase of 4.3 percent in the unit cost of capital). However, it would be equivalent to only a modest loosening of monetary policy (e.g., reducing the policy interest rate from 3 to 2.8 percent, or by 20 basis points).[39] But an environment of reduced capital formation and consequently lower output would tend to be one of supply scarcity rather than demand deficiency. Supply scarcity would tend to boost inflationary pressures, so that if anything a monetary policy response could be more likely a tightening than a loosening. Essentially, long-term financial regulatory structure should not be premised on the pursuit of monetary policy more expansionary than otherwise advisable.

---

38. Using the base values of the parameters above, shifting the financing of 10 percent of total assets from debt (paying 2.5 percent) to equity (paying 10 percent) would boost average cost of capital to banks by 75 basis points ($0.1 \times [0.1 - 0.025]$) with no M&M offset, and by 41 basis points applying the base-case offset of 45 percent. Including the 50 percent spillover to nonbank financial intermediaries, and applying the weights of alternative finance to the economy, the overall effect would be an increase of 20.5 basis points ($[0.333 \times 41] + [0.333 \times 20.5]$).

39. If the long-term rate moves less than the short-term policy rate, as would seem likely, the shift in this example might need to be, say, from 3 to 2.6 percent.

Conclusion

This chapter finds that long-term damage of a banking crisis amounts to 64 percent of base-year potential GDP and that in the past three decades the annual probability of such a crisis was about 2½ percent. The probability of a banking crisis can be reduced by requiring banks to hold more capital. The response of crisis probability is highly nonlinear, such that the most impact in reducing chances of a crisis comes from the initial increases in capital above pre-Basel III levels. After taking account of the additional cost to the economy from imposing higher capital requirements (thereby raising lending rates and curbing new investment and future output levels), it is found that the optimal ratio for tangible common equity is about 6.6 percent of total assets and a conservative estimate at the 75th percentile is about 7.9 percent. These benchmarks would correspond to 11.7 and 14.1 percent of risk-weighted assets, respectively. On this basis, the Basel III benchmarks are below optimal capital requirements, at only 7 percent of RWA (9.5 percent for G-SIBs). Further international banking reform could usefully consider phasing in capital requirements on the order of one-fourth to one-half higher than the Basel III requirements.

Appendix 4A

An Evaluation of the Minneapolis Plan to End Too Big to Fail

In late 2016 the Federal Reserve Bank of Minneapolis issued a Plan to End Too Big to Fail (Minneapolis Plan 2016).[40] The Minneapolis Plan (MP) study finds that the optimal level of capital for banks is 23.5 percent of risk-weighted assets. This level is nearly twice as high as the optimal level identified in the present study, a range of 12 to 14 percent. As a separate policy issue, the report goes on to argue that global systemically important banks (G-SIBs) should face a capital requirement of 38 percent, providing a strong incentive for these banks to split into smaller entities. The 38 percent level is chosen on grounds that it is at this level that the cumulative costs to the economy of higher bank capital requirements would begin to exceed the cumulative benefits from reduced risk of banking crises. The marginal costs would exceed the marginal benefits already at the lower optimal level, 23.5 percent. This appendix replicates the MP method and findings and seeks to clarify why its results are so different from mine. The discussion closes with additional observations about the too big to fail (TBTF) surcharge.

Replicating the Minneapolis Plan Results

The Minneapolis Plan (2016, 31) uses the Dagher, Dell'Ariccia, Laeven, Ratnovski, and Tong (2016, 13), or DDLRT, compilation of data on non-performing loans in 28 banking crises in 24 OECD countries over the period 1970–2011 as the basis for mapping the probability of crisis to the amount of bank capital. The MP authors reason that there is a base crisis risk that equals 28 episodes divided by 42×24 country years, resulting in a probability of 2.78 percent in any given year that a country will have a crisis. They accept the DDLRT proposition that in each case the crisis would not have happened if banks had held capital equal to losses. They impute losses at either 50 percent of reported nonperforming loans (NPLs) or 75 percent of NPLs. DDLRT compare these imputed losses to total bank assets, which are typically about twice the loan book. After taking account of the fact that risk-weighted assets (RWA) are typically only about 57 percent of total assets, DDLRT are then able to identify the ratio of capital to RWA that would have been needed to cover the losses and avoid the crisis.

DDLRT present a figure with the probability of avoiding a crisis mapped against the ratio of capital to risk-weighted assets, k. The MP authors use

---

40. The study is preliminary and was to be in a phase of commentary until January 17, 2017.

this mapping to calculate the probability of a crisis. I have estimated the following equation using the DDLRT figure and setting the value of k halfway between the 50 and 75 percent loss given default (LGD) lines shown separately in their figure (with t-statistics in parentheses):

$$P_{crav} = 0.118 + 0.0527\ k - 0.00084\ k^2;\ adj.\ R^2 = 0.94 \qquad (4A.1)$$
$$\phantom{P_{crav} = 0.118 +} (2.8) \quad\ (8.4) \qquad (-5.1)$$

where P_{crav} is the cumulative probability of avoiding a crisis (pure number) and k is the ratio of capital to risk-weighted assets (percent). Figure 4A.1 shows the cumulative probability of avoiding a banking crisis as a function of the ratio of capital to risk-weighted assets, and displays the corresponding estimated curve.

The MP authors use the same DDLRT dataset and also use the midpoint of the 50 to 75 percent LGD alternatives. They then translate these probabilities into benefits from higher capital in the following way. First, they set the damage from a crisis at 158 percent of one year's GDP. This high level is meant to emphasize permanent losses; in contrast, I estimate the loss at 64 percent of one year's GDP after recognizing that the base year output is typically above potential and (more importantly) that "permanent" losses are not eternal because the capital assets that would have been built in the absence of a crisis would not have had infinite life (table 4.3). So in short, the MP authors apply crisis damage that is 2.47 times the size of the corresponding damage in the present study.

Second, the MP authors identify the actual probability of a crisis as being equal to the base average of 2.78 percent, *minus* the influence of the reductions in the probability at successively higher levels of capital. Namely:

$$P_{cr} = P_{cr0} \times (1 - P_{crav}) \qquad (4A.2)$$

However, this formulation would seem to involve a logical ellipsis. The procedure implicitly assumes that the observed average incidence of crises (2.78 percent) would have been no higher if there had been *zero* capital, but surely that is not the case. A major problem with the MP study is thus that it understates the probability of crisis at the lower end of the capital ratio spectrum.

Third, the benefit to the economy from any given level of capital is then calculated as the base expected loss from crises multiplied by the probability of avoiding a crisis. With the crisis loss set at 158 percent of GDP and a base crisis probability of 2.78 percent annually, the expected crisis cost annually is 4.4 percent of GDP. The benefit of bank capital in the MP study is thus:

$$B = 0.044Y \times P_{crav} \qquad (4A.3)$$

Figure 4A.1 Probability of avoiding a banking crisis as a function of capital/risk-weighted assets

probability of avoiding banking crisis

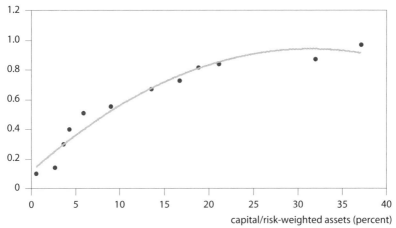

Source: Author's calculations from data in Dagher et al. (2016, 15).

From equation (4A.1), the derivative of the benefit with respect to the capital ratio is:

$$\frac{dB}{dk} = 0.044Y \times [0.0527 - 0.00168k] \tag{4A.4}$$

On the cost side, the MP authors simulate the Federal Reserve's macro model to arrive at the estimate that 1 percentage point increase in the capital/RWA ratio causes a reduction of 0.058 percent in GDP (Minneapolis Plan, p. 22).[41] The cost curve is a straight line, so this coefficient is the marginal cost of additional capital:

$$\frac{dC}{dk} = 0.00058Y \tag{4A.5}$$

We can then identify the optimal capital ratio as that which equates marginal benefit with marginal cost. This optimal level will occur where:[42]

$$0.044Y \times [0.0527 - 0.00168k^*] = 0.00058Y; \; k^* = 23.5 \tag{4A.6}$$

---

41. In principle this parameter would imply an ongoing annual cost of 1.36 percent of GDP. This amount is modestly larger than the total increment they show in their relevant table: 0.52 percent already included in current regulations plus 0.6 percent of GDP as the increment to their optimal ("Step 1") level.

42. That is: $[(5.27 \times 10^{-2}) - 1.68 \times 10^{-3}k^*] = \frac{[5.8 \times 10^{-4}]}{[4.4 \times 10^{-2}]} = 1.318 \times 10^{-2}; \; -1.68 \times 10^{-3}k^* = -3.952 \times 10^{-2};$ $k^* = [-3.952 \times 10^{-2}]/[-1.68 \times 10^{-3}].$

These calculations thus successfully replicate the MP result for the optimal capital ratio when that study's parameters are applied for benefits of crisis avoidance achieved and cost to the economy of additional bank capital.

Problems with the Estimates of Benefits

There are two problems, in my view, with the MP estimates of crisis avoidance benefits as a function of bank capital. First, as noted, they implicitly assume that if bank capital were zero, there would be no more crises than had actually been observed in the reference period. Second, they assume a level of damage (158 percent of one year's GDP) that is implausibly high after taking account of the finite life of any capital assets that failed to be built during the crisis-induced recession.

Figure 4A.2 compares the MP crisis probability curve to that presented in BCBS (2010a). The BCBS analysis is based on models developed by the UK's Financial Services Authority, Bank for International Settlements, and the central banks of Canada, Japan, and the United Kingdom. The estimates are based on econometric studies of historical experience relating crises to the amount of bank capital, as well as models of the banking system as a portfolio of securities. The models show a relatively rapid drop-off in the probability of a crisis as the capital/RWA ratio rises, a phenomenon familiar from risk models applied to individual banks (BCBS 2010a, 16). Although the BCBS study remains the most authoritative evaluation of the relationship of crisis probability to bank capitalization, the MP authors prefer the DDLRT approach because it is "easier for an outsider to re-create and judge" and because "the direction of the worldwide regulatory community" more recently has been toward higher capital than implied by the BCBS estimates (Minneapolis Plan 2016, 20).[43]

As shown in figure 4A.2, the MP crisis probability starts out far lower than that of the BCBS, and follows an extremely flat path such that after bank capital exceeds about 10 percent of RWA the MP crisis probability exceeds that in BCBS (2010a). The extreme flatness of the MP crisis probability curve means it is highly likely that the point at which its slope equals that of the economic cost curve will be at a much higher capital ratio than in the BCBS curve. As can be seen in figure 4A.2, the two alternative crisis probability curves are still not quite parallel (i.e., still do not have identical slopes) even at the top end of capital considered by the BCBS (15 percent of RWA).

---

43. However, the reference the MP authors cite in support of the second reason (FSB 2015a) does not contain an analysis of the relationship of the probability of crisis to the amount of bank capital.

Figure 4A.2   Probability of a banking crisis as a function of bank capital/risk-weighted assets, Basel Committee on Banking Supervision versus Minneapolis Plan

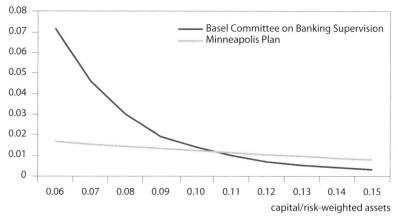

probability of avoiding banking crisis

Sources: BCBS (2010a, 15); Dagher et al. (2016, 15); Minneapolis Plan (2016); and author's calculations.

One reason for the flat MP curve is that the top four observations among the 28 OECD cases involve crises with exceptionally high losses, namely Iceland (2008) with peak NPLs at 60 percent of loans, and Japan and Korea (both 1997) and Greece (2008) at peak NPLs of about 35 percent of loans. In contrast, the median peak NPLs for the OECD crisis cases were only 10 percent of loan value (Dagher et al. 2016, 13). It would seem questionable whether it is socially cost effective to base US capital requirements in part on such extreme experiences.[44]

Understatement of the Cost Curve

Unlike Admati and Hellwig (2013), the MP authors do not obtain a low cost of capital requirements by assuming a complete "Modigliani-Miller offset" whereby shifting from low-cost debt to high-cost equity does not

---

44. The case of Iceland seems particularly irrelevant. In Iceland, claims of depository institutions reached 687 percent of GDP in 2007, far higher than the US level of 113 percent of GDP (IMF 2015a). In Greece the crisis was one of sovereign debt that had an impact on banks, not vice versa (Cline 2014a). In Korea the crisis reflected an exchange rate collapse associated with high short-term external debt. As for Japan, the 35 percent NPL figure in the underlying database (Laeven and Valencia 2012) looks seriously overstated. Fukao (2003, 12) estimates that a broader measure of troubled loans, "classified loans," peaked at 14.5 percent of total loans in 2002.

raise the average cost of capital because equity markets reduce the unit cost of equity in response to the resulting reduction in risk. They apply an offset parameter of one-half, about the same as the 0.45 magnitude estimated in chapter 3.

Instead, the low cost in MP appears to stem from the use of the large macroeconomic model of the US Federal Reserve to calculate the impact of higher bank capital cost on GDP. The authors apply the Taylor rule to allow monetary policy to respond to a shock in the loan rate. But the Taylor rule is designed to address relatively short-term cyclical issues for which the concern would be excess capacity. Instead, the long-term economic cost of higher capital cost involves less underlying capital stock and productive capacity, such that if anything the relevance of the Taylor curve would be that it would recommend raising the policy interest rate rather than reducing it given incipient inflationary pressure from supply constraints. It is misleading to assume that there is a monetary policy offset that can substantially reduce the cost of lesser supply as a consequence of higher capital requirements. Nor is it clear that the Fed model is appropriate for long-term analysis more generally.[45]

The resulting cost parameter in MP is that an increase in the capital requirement by one percentage point of RWA causes a reduction of the long-term output path by 0.058 percentage point. The corresponding parameter in this study is 0.084.[46] My estimate is based on the much more transparent approach proposed by Miles, Yang, and Marcheggiano (2012), which uses a simple aggregate production function. The higher unit cost of capital reduces capital formation and output declines in response to the factor share of capital and the elasticity of substitution between capital and labor.

A simple test of the plausibility of the MP cost parameter is to consider the output impact of a specified capital cost increase. In their "step 2" G-SIB exercise, the MP authors set the capital requirement at 38 percent of RWA. They calculate that this level would boost loan rates by 1.43 percentage points above those under current regulatory requirements. The same increase would apply to nonbank financial intermediaries in the MP (to avoid regulatory arbitrage). If we assume that banks and nonbanks together supply two-thirds of finance to nonfinancial corporations and the

---

45. The authors indicate that "The simulations start in 2050Q1, at which point the model is in its steady state. We assume the standard FRB/UF VAR-based expectations...." (p. 33). Doubts are warranted about starting the analysis so far in the future, and applying VAR equations that are based on a short period of several quarters.

46. The estimate here is that 1 percentage point increase in capital required relative to total assets reduces output by 0.15 percent ($\psi = 0.15$; see chapter 4). Because RWA are only 56 percent of total assets on average, this parameter becomes 0.084 when expressed in terms of RWA.

rest comes from retained earnings and new equity issuance, the economy-wide cost of capital would rise by 0.96 percentage point. I place the average real unit cost of capital to nonfinancial firms at 4.6 percent (table 4.4). So an increase of 96 basis points would amount to a 21 percent proportionate increase in the cost of capital to the economy.

In the simple aggregate production function approach, a proportionate increase of z in the unit cost of capital causes a reduction of $z \times [\alpha\sigma]/[1-\alpha]$, where α is the share of capital in output and σ is the elasticity of substitution between capital and labor. In the example here, with $z = 21$ percent, a capital share of 40 percent ($\alpha = 0.4$) and an elasticity of substitution of $\sigma = 0.5$, the impact would be a reduction of output by 7 percent. Yet the MP estimate for the step 2 impact is a reduction of output by only 1.41 percent (Minneapolis Plan 2016, 22). The mechanics of the Fed macro model, including induced monetary policy responses, seem to cause a substantial understatement of the output cost resulting from higher capital cost.[47]

Comparison of the Minneapolis Plan Results and Those of This Study

The MP study finds that the optimal capital ratio is 23.5 percent of RWA. The estimates in chapter 4 of the present study find that the optimal ratio is 12 percent of RWA at the median outcome of about 2,200 simulations of alternative combinations of low, central, and high values of key parameters. At a more risk-averse 75th percentile, the optimal capital ratio is 14 percent of RWA. The driving force behind the difference between my results and the MP estimate is the lower cost parameter used in MP. If my cost parameter (0.084 percent of GDP decline for 1 percentage point additional capital requirement, k) is applied while keeping the MP crisis probability and crisis damage parameters, the optimal capital ratio turns out to be $k^* = 12$ percent of RWA, the same as the median outcome in chapter 4. The reason for this identical outcome seems to be that on the benefits side, the serious understatement of the initial crisis probability in MP is offset by the overstatement of the long-term damage from a crisis. The marginal benefit of damage avoided turns out to be the same as in my estimates at the point where marginal benefit equals marginal cost using my cost function.

---

47. Note further that my output impact is not as much larger than the MP estimate as this exercise might seem to imply, because I assume that only one-half of the loan rate increase is induced in the nonbank financial sector.

The Questionable Link to a Too Big to Fail Surcharge

Finally, an important policy recommendation in MP is that for G-SIBs, the capital ratio should be set at 38 percent rather than the optimal level of 23.5 percent. The MP intent is to make it punitively costly to maintain a bank as large as a G-SIB, on grounds that such a bank will cause unacceptable taxpayer costs when it fails. This diagnosis is premised on the strong MP view that for the United States, seamless resolution of bankrupt G-SIBs using the Orderly Liquidation Authority of the Dodd-Frank bill is wishful thinking. This process would involve imposing losses on creditors at a moment of potential crisis, as well as requiring a complicated system whereby the holding company is in bankruptcy but the subsidiaries are not.

There are two fundamental problems with the G-SIB leap to a 38 percent capital requirement. The first is that the G-SIBs were already a large presence in the database used to construct crisis probabilities. So imposing a second level of damage that should be avoided because of G-SIBs amounts to double-counting on the benefits side. The second is that the MP authors commit a logical ellipsis when they choose 38 percent as the right punitive level for G-SIBs. Their basis for this threshold is that in their model this is the point where the cost line rises high enough to intersect the curve of benefits from crisis avoidance, such that net benefits (the vertical distance between the two curves) disappear. Yet surely it would be poor public policy formation to consciously seek to reduce the net benefits of bank regulation back to zero. More fundamentally, doing so would essentially shift potential output away from other activities into the activity of minimizing bank crisis risk. Indeed, this shift is evident in the fact that under the optimal capital ratio the chance of one crisis in one-hundred years is 39 percent, whereas under the 38 percent capital level this chance falls to 9 percent (Minneapolis Plan 2016, 20). The additional reduction in GDP under the more aggressive threshold amounts to 0.81 percent of GDP (p. 22). The MP authors are making a value judgment that the public would prefer to sacrifice 0.81 percent of potential output year after year over the next century in order to cut the chance of a single banking crisis over this period from 39 to 9 percent. It seems unlikely that the public is so risk averse that it would be willing to sacrifice this much output and consumption to reduce the chances of the 100-year storm from 39 to 9 percent. Nor do the MP authors present any utility analysis that clarifies what degree of risk aversion would suffice to warrant their aggressive "Step 2" threshold of 38 percent for G-SIB capital requirements.

Conclusion

The MP study substantially overstates the optimal capital requirement for banks. It does so primarily because its use of the Federal Reserve macro model understates the cost to the economy of higher unit cost of capital. A better method for assessing this cost is to apply a straightforward aggregate production function, as done in chapter 4. The MP study also seriously understates the curvature of the crisis probability function. However, its unduly low probability of crisis in the initial range of capital is offset by an unduly large estimate for the damage to be expected from a crisis. As a result, the MP approach would actually confirm my estimate of the optimal capital ratio if its damage avoidance benefit estimates were combined with my capital cost estimate. Moreover, the MP study is mistaken to imply that its 38 percent of RWA "step 2" capital requirement for G-SIBs would be socially cost-beneficial, as the influence of G-SIBs is essentially already included in the "step 1" optimal capital ratio as a consequence of the large banks' dominant role in the historical data for the banking system.

5

Total Loss-Absorbing Capacity for Large Banks

Total loss-absorbing capacity (TLAC) considers the scope for a bank to absorb losses. It thus adds two types of debt to the amount of common equity: subordinated debt and contingent convertible debt (CoCos). In the case of CoCos, conversion of debt to equity (or simply the sacrifice of principal) would occur before bankruptcy upon reaching a specified trigger. In the case of subordinated debt, there is also loss-absorbing capacity because in bankruptcy this debt can in principle be extinguished in the queue of claims following the wiping out of shareholders but before touching senior debt.

For global systemically important banks (G-SIBs), the Basel III reforms include the requirement that TLAC reach 18 percent of risk-weighted assets by the beginning of 2022 (FSB 2015c). Considering that the benchmark Basel III requirement for common equity for G-SIBs is 9.5 percent of risk-weighted assets, in effect the TLAC requirement approximately doubles the absorptive capacity of equity alone.[1]

There has long been a literature on how subordinated debt can act as a salutary discipline on bank risk taking; recently, studies on the incentive benefits of CoCos have proliferated. Despite the emphasis in the literature on incentive effects, in practice much of the motivation for the adoption of TLAC requirements seems to have come from the political imperative to limit taxpayer costs of future bank bailouts, as opposed to pursuit of effec-

---

1. The 9.5 percent benchmark comprises 4.5 percent plus 2.5 percent capital conservation plus another 2.5 percent for G-SIBs.

tive system incentives. Regardless of the motivation, the central policy question is whether the TLAC requirement, taken together with Basel III requirements for equity capital, is sufficient to ensure that banks are adequately capitalized in some broad meaningful sense. This question is equivalent to asking whether subordinated and CoCo debt are reasonable substitutes for capital and, if so, at what rates of equivalence.

At an important level, simple subordinated debt cannot be a substitute at all for equity capital. This level pertains to the key objective of avoiding bankruptcy. By definition subordinated debt only helps the balance sheet once a bankruptcy takes place and certain asset classes are ruled to have lost their claim. Subordinated debt may thus serve an important function in terms of monitoring and disciplining risk by sending market signals of rising spreads, but its relief cannot be mobilized without entering into what is dangerous for the system if even a few G-SIBs are involved at the same time: a financial sector crisis.[2] At the outset, then, it seems useful to rule out subordinated debt as an effective substitute for equity capital with respect to systemic risk. Subordinated debt may be more useful as a vehicle to limit taxpayer losses, but if that is the objective, it is important that TLAC not be conflated with equity as insurance against financial crisis.

CoCos might be seen as closer substitutes for equity if in practice they could be mobilized without contributing to a deterioration in market confidence and escalation of incipient crisis conditions. Importantly, in the case of the United States, tax authorities have not permitted CoCos to enjoy deductibility of interest expense, essentially ruling out their use by banks. CoCos have been more widely used in Europe, but they were the subject of new doubts in early 2016, when fears that Deutsche Bank issues might reach conversion triggers caused a sharp decline in equity prices for European banks.

Survey of the Literature on Total Loss-Absorbing Capacity

This chapter is based primarily on a survey of the literature on the role of subordinated debt and CoCos in providing greater systemic stability. It then examines the experience of large banks in the United States during the Great Recession as an event study of whether the larger banks took risks that revealed too big to fail (TBTF) behavior. It then draws policy implications for the role of TLAC in the overall regime of capital requirements.

---

2. Indeed, several of the studies reviewed in this study use the joint failure of two large banks as a benchmark for a financial crisis.

Disciplinary Role of Subordinated Debt and CoCos

The idea that subordinated debt can impose market discipline on banks is longstanding. Sironi (2003) notes that there have been numerous proposals for mandatory subordinated debt since the late 1980s. He provides new tests for European banks that confirm a statistical relationship between the spreads on subordinated debt and measures of bank default risk. He finds that this sensitivity increased in the 1990s, a phenomenon he attributes to the gradual erosion of TBTF perceptions as the more rigid public sector budget constraints of the European Monetary Union came into effect.

Using data for US banks in 1980–2004, Ashcraft (2008) examines the influence of an increase in the ratio of subordinated debt to regulatory capital (the sum of subordinated debt and equity capital). He begins with recognition that the standard (Merton model) influence of greater debt leverage is higher risk and hence that the disciplining role must be great enough to more than offset the higher leverage risk for the net influence of subordinated debt to be favorable. His empirical tests deal with endogeneity by using variations in state corporate tax rates to instrument the subordinated debt ratio.

Ashcraft finds that for stand-alone banks, an increase in the (instrumented) ratio of subordinated debt to regulatory capital reduced the probability of bank distress before the 1990 implementation of the original Basel accord but increased it thereafter. He attributes the difference to the Basel requirement that to be included in tier 2 capital, subordinated debt could not include restrictive covenants, thereby reducing investor influence. In contrast, for banks affiliated with bank holding companies, the influence of subordinated debt in reducing distress probability persisted through the full period. He attributes this difference to the fact that bank holding companies provided a direct channel of surveillance of the affiliated banks. Ashcraft's findings provide a cautionary note to the Basel arrangements for TLAC, because the absence of restrictive covenants curbs investor control and hence makes subordinated debt a more imperfect substitute for equity.

Evanoff, Jagtiani, and Nakata (2011) use data on the publicly traded subordinated bonds of 19 large US banks and 39 bank holding companies in 1990–99 to examine the relationship between spreads and risk indicators. Their sample of about 600 representative bonds is evenly split between an "issuance" subsample, for which banks had recently issued new debt, and a "nonissuance" subsample for others. The authors find that spreads are significantly related to two measures of risk: nonperforming loans as a percent of assets (positive coefficient) and return on assets (negative coefficient). A third risk variable, the market leverage ratio (the ratio of liabilities to the market value of common stock plus the book value of preferred stock), has the correct (positive) sign but is not statistically significant. Macroeconomic variables have significant influences in the expected directions (with positive coefficients on the Treasury bill rate and unemployment and a negative coefficient for periods of economic expansion), and long-term debt has a higher spread. The authors emphasize that although both subsamples tend to obtain these same results, the significance and degree of explanation are considerably higher for the "issuance" subsample (R^2 of about 0.65 versus about 0.50). They argue that if subordinated debt were made a mandatory part of the regulatory structure, markets would be much deeper and issuance more frequent. Citing the "issuance" results as a closer representation of those conditions, they argue in support of mandatory subordinated debt requirements, and maintain that this approach should not be rejected based on the argument that in the past the signals in market data for subordinated debt spreads have been too noisy to warrant such an approach. They argue that spreads on subordinated debt can provide discipline both directly, by prompting bank management to take note of market concerns about risk, and indirectly, by informing the judgments of supervisors.

Calomiris and Herring (2013) argue that there should be a major CoCo requirement to complement the common equity requirement. Its purpose would be to provide strong incentives to bank management to carry out prompt recapitalization to deal with losses rather than waiting until it is too late and the bank has lost access to the equity market. They propose that CoCos equivalent to 10 percent of total assets be issued. Conversion would be triggered when the quasi-market value of equity ratio—the market capitalization value of equity divided by that value plus total debt (as a comprehensive measure of firm value)—falls below 4 percent, based on a 90-day moving average. The conversion rate would be set such that CoCo holders lost no value. The dilution consequences would be so severe for existing shareholders that bank management would make every effort to avoid conversion, providing discipline on risk taking ex ante and pressure to act promptly if recapitalization did become necessary.

Without providing a cost-benefit analysis, they also suggest that the common equity requirement should be set at 10 percent of total assets, but they explicitly recognize that contrary to those who invoke the Modigliani-Miller offset, "equity is costlier to raise than debt for fundamental reasons associated with both information and managerial agency problems" (p. 42). The authors maintain that interest on CoCo bonds would "continue to exploit the tax shield provided by the asymmetry of treatment between interest and dividends in the tax codes of most countries" (p. 44). However, the lack of tax deductibility in the United States has so far limited their use primarily to European banks.[3]

Their emphasis on CoCos triggered by market equity prices stems in part from their skepticism regarding supervisors' capacity to keep up with banks' ability to exploit accounting and regulatory loopholes, as well as political pressures on regulators to grant excessive forbearance. To illustrate, they cite lurid episodes from the 2008 financial crisis, including Lehman Brothers' use of disguised repos that in effect understated assets, Northern Rock's shift to internal model risk weighting, and "re-remic" resecuritization of subprime collateral debt obligations to arbitrage risk weightings of tranches. Their CoCo proposal is meant to reinforce official supervision with market discipline.

Internalizing the Too Big to Fail (TBTF) Risk Subsidy

The premise that there are major subsidies and distortions to bank behavior caused by the TBTF dynamic appears to underpin much of the public policy discussion of TLAC. The underlying proposition is that if banks are forced to maintain much larger subordinate and CoCo debt, they will behave in a less risky fashion, and creditors rather than taxpayers will be the ones to pick up the bill in the event of bank failures.

There does not seem to be much literature examining whether CEOs of large banks do in fact think and act in an especially risky fashion. In principle the issue involves the need to pursue sectoral regulation to temper otherwise bad behavior of corporate actors (such as the disguising of emissions test results in the automobile sector). In practice, in the United States at least, it was the highly leveraged investment banks (Bear Stearns, Lehman), a hedge-fund-like London unit of an insurance company (AIG), and the government-sponsored mortgage agencies (Fannie Mae and Freddie Mac) that were the core causes of the Great Recession financial crisis, not the commercial banks. Indeed, some of the largest commercial banks played stabilizing roles by absorbing large failing financial firms (JPMorgan Chase absorbed Bear Sterns, Bank of America absorbed Merrill Lynch, Wells Fargo

---

3. As of end-2015, the global outstanding issuance of CoCos was on the order of $97 billion, of which about $91 billion was by European banks and none by US banks. In the United States, CoCos with perpetual maturity (eligible for "additional tier 1" capital status under Basel III) are generally seen as ineligible for deductibility of interest because of their equity-like nature. CoCos without perpetual maturity (tier 2) might be treated as debt if conversion were sufficiently unlikely and would not reduce the value of the security significantly (von Furstenberg 2014). Calomiris and Herring (2013) implicitly recognize the US problem when they cite a proposal to allow full deduction of interest corresponding to the coupon on similar straight debt but exclude the component corresponding to compensation for conversion risk.

absorbed Wachovia; Cline 2010). Moreover, the public did not wind up losing any money on the support to the banking system from the Troubled Asset Relief Program (TARP) (Cline and Gagnon 2013). Nor would classic central banking behavior following Bagehot (1873) lead to TBTF distortions, because in a panic the central bank would provide support only to solvent institutions, large or small.[4] These considerations suggest that a dose of caution, if not skepticism, may well be warranted in approaching the literature on the TBTF implications for TLAC.

Two researchers at the Bank of England provide a useful review of approaches to estimating the TBTF subsidy, along with new estimates for the United Kingdom (Noss and Sowerbutts 2012). They identify two main approaches: "funding advantage" and "contingent claims." Within the first approach are two subcategories. "Size-based" estimates examine the differential in borrowing costs of large banks and all other banks as the measure of implicit government subsidy from TBTF. "Ratings-based" estimates use the differential between the major ratings agencies "stand-alone" and "support" ratings on banks (the "ratings uplift" for TBTF banks). The ratings approach takes account of different business models as well as judgment about the probability of official support.

The second broad approach conceptualizes public support as a put option offered to the banking system on its assets. The volatility of banking stocks is used as a basis for projecting the future volatility of banking system assets. A resulting probability distribution of asset values then provides the basis for estimating the expected shortfall of the system's asset values below what is consistent with meeting minimum capital ratios and hence the expected official sector support to the banking system. The "option price" subcategory uses current-year stock option prices for banks to estimate future asset volatility. The "historical" subcategory uses past share prices to estimate expected volatility.

The different approaches yield an extremely wide range of estimates of TBTF subsidies for the United Kingdom. The temporary steepening in the relationship of ratings to spreads boosted the estimated subsidy in the ratings uplift approach from £25 billion in 2008 to £120 (about 8 percent

---

4. Bagehot (1873, ch. II, ¶39–41; ch. VII, ¶58–59) states: "In opposition to what might be at first sight supposed, the best way for the bank or banks who have the custody of the bank reserve to deal with a drain arising from internal discredit, is to lend freely.... A panic, in a word, is a species of neuralgia, and according to the rules of science you must not starve it. The holders of the cash reserve must be ready...to lend to merchants, to minor bankers, to 'this man and that man,' whenever the security is good.... The end is to stay the panic.... And for this purpose there are two rules: First. That these loans should only be made at a very high rate of interest.... Secondly. That at this rate these advances should be made on all good banking securities, and as largely as the public ask for them. The reason is plain. The object is to stay alarm...."

of GDP) in 2009, returning to £30 billion in 2010. The options-based approach places the 2010 subsidy at £120 billion; the historical contingent claims approach places it at £20 billion. Even within the same subapproach (historical contingent claims), the estimate for 2008 soars to £350 billion under year-by-year calibration (reflecting extreme risk aversion in markets that year) but only £15 billion using longer-term through-the-cycle calibration. Rather than worrying about the implied fragility of the estimates, the authors simply conclude that "all measures point to significant transfers of resources from the government to the banking system" (p. 13).

Nguyen (2013) examines whether bank risk taking is affected by subordinated debt. As the (inverse) indicator of risk, he uses the natural logarithm of the "z-score"—that is, $z = (ROA + CAR)/\sigma_{ROA}$, where ROA is return on assets, CAR is the ratio of equity capital to assets, and σ_{ROA} is the standard deviation of the return on assets. He cites other studies showing that the logarithm of this "distance from insolvency" ratio has a strictly monotonic negative relationship with the probability of insolvency. He applies data on 727 banks in 71 countries (with nearly half of the sample located in the United States) for 2002–08, resulting in about 4,400 firm-year observations. He uses the lagged equity-to-assets ratio as the instrument for the subordinated debt ratio. In this first-stage regression there is always a negative sign, indicating that banks issue subordinated debt to raise tier 2 capital (i.e., to substitute for additional equity). In his main results, the (instrumented) ratio of subordinated debt to risk-weighted assets (or alternatively to total liabilities) shows a strong positive and highly significant impact on the (log) z ratio. These results support the general proposition that subordinated debt has a disciplining effect.

Nguyen's other results pose a major problem for enthusiasts of TLAC for large banks, however. When a dummy variable is included for TBTF banks (defined alternatively as meeting a threshold of 10, 15, or 20 percent of the country's total deposits), there is a significant negative coefficient on the interaction of the dummy and the subordinated debt ratio that is larger than the coefficient on the simple subdebt ratio in the equation (p. 138). As a consequence, the disciplining influence of subordinated debt is completely absent for the TBTF banks. Nguyen observes that this outcome is just what would be expected, implying that investors do not penalize risk taking when they expect to be bailed out. He interprets his findings as implying that subordinated debt nonetheless contributes to systemic stability by reducing the destabilization that could arise from multiple smaller banks. He therefore calls for "a package of reforms" that includes measures to "eliminate the too-big-to-fail issue" (p. 118). Unfortunately for this diagnosis, Basel III deals with TBTF precisely by encouraging the use of subordinated debt in the form of TLAC.

Marques, Correa, and Sapriza (2013) examine whether the prospect of government support causes banks to take more risk. They frame the analysis as testing two opposing hypotheses. Under the "market discipline" hypothesis, for which they cite Merton (1974) and Flannery and Sorescu (1996), government support decreases the incentive of investors and depositors to monitor or influence bank risk taking, thereby inducing greater risk. Under the "charter value" hypothesis, for which they cite Keeley (1990), government support reduces bank risk taking by increasing banks' charter values and hence reducing the gambling incentive. To measure prospective government support, the authors use the difference between the Moody's bank financial strength ratings, which exclude any external support a bank may receive from its parent or the government, and Moody's bank deposit ratings, which incorporate external support.

Marques, Correa, and Sapriza also use the z-score as the measure of risk, noting that its "distance to insolvency" property stems from the fact that when losses exceed equity, the numerator turns negative. The inverse of the z-score is the probability that losses will exceed equity capital. Using data on about 340 banks in 56 countries, they estimate the influence of (potential) government support, with a one-year lag, on the z-scores of banks in 2003–04 and 2009–10. Their results support the market discipline hypothesis rather than the charter value hypothesis. The coefficient on government support is negative in all alternative specifications (variously including bank variables, country characteristics, and instrumentation). It is significant in all specifications in the second period and most in the earlier period.

An important result is that bank size per se does not influence riskiness, which Marques, Correa, and Sapriza interpret to mean that the TBTF influence is offset by the lower volatility of returns on assets as a consequence of greater diversification. In tests examining the additional influence of regulatory stringency, they find that the term for interaction of government support with "activity restrictions" is positive and significant in the period of recent crises, although not with a large enough coefficient to offset fully the risk-inducing influence of government support. They interpret their overall findings to mean that policy measures that "increase the incentives by depositors, small shareholders, and subordinated creditors to monitor or influence banks' attitudes toward risks should decrease the moral hazard associated with government support to the financial system," including limits on the amount of support governments can pledge (p. 19).

Afonso, Santos, and Traina (2014) examine the influence of potential government support on risk taking by banks using Fitch "support rating floors" (SRF). Begun in March 2007, this Fitch rating is unique in reflecting only potential sovereign support, not other external support (such as support from a parent holding company). The authors use data for more than 200 banks in 45 countries. They find a statistically significant positive influence of the SRF on two alternative measures of (ex post realized) bank risk taking: impaired loans and net charge-offs. The significance stretches back through 11 quarters of lags (the full period of availability of the ratings), providing some reassurance that the causation is not running in the other direction (from current loss to current government support).[5] They also find that when they interact the SRF with the issuer default rating as a measure of general riskiness of the bank, the coefficient is negative and significant, indicating that banks with lower general credit ratings have a larger impact on increased risk from greater potential government support. They find that these results also hold when they limit the sample to US banks. Their data also show a clear correlation of the SRF with bank size. SRFs of A or higher had a median of $185 billion in total assets in 2012, whereas those with SRFs of BB, B, or C–CCC had median assets of $46 billion, $33 billon, and $4.2 billion, respectively. In short, the study seems to provide evidence of TBTF incentives to risk taking. Its results depend on the qualitative judgments of a rating agency, however.

Laeven, Ratnovski, and Tong (2014) examine the influence of bank size on risk taking as well as systemic risk. They emphasize that the world's largest banks experienced rapid asset expansion in the decade preceding the financial crisis, with the typical size of the top three US and top three European banks surging from about $700 billion in assets in 1999 to about $2 trillion to $3 trillion by 2008, with growing concentration of the banking sector. Their business models shifted away from loans toward market-based activities, in part in response to deregulation (the Gramm-Leach-Bliley Act in the United States, the Big Bang in the United Kingdom, and the creation of a single financial market in the European Union). Lower capitalization, more fragile funding, and increased organizational complexity accompanied this transformation.

The authors show that there is a significant negative correlation between bank size (the logarithm of assets) and the tier 1 capital ratio, the deposits-to-assets ratio, and the loans-to-assets ratio and a positive correlation with short-term funding. They contrast a benign interpretation of

---

5. One question does arise in the data they present. The median risk measures for each rating class in the support rating floor show higher risk, not lower, in the lower SRF categories. For low categories C–CCC, B, and BB, the median of the median class risk indicators is 1.81 percent for the impaired loan ratio and 0.44 percent for the net charge-off ratio. In contrast, the corresponding medians for classes BBB, A, and A–AAA are 1.38 percent and 0.06 percent, respectively (p. 49). Although the multivariate regressions seem to reverse the direction of the association of risk with potential government support, the contrary patterns in the simple summary statistics raise some doubt.

economies of scale and benefits of diversification with malign alternative explanations (TBTF subsidies, managerial empire building).

They then carry out tests using data for 370 banks with assets of $10 billion or more in 52 countries. Taking advantage of the natural experiment of the financial crisis, they use the change in bank stock prices from July 2007 to December 2008 as the indicator of bank riskiness. They regress this change on bank size, capitalization (the tier 1 capital ratio or leverage ratio), an index of funding fragility, activity (the share of loans in total assets or share of noninterest income), and complexity (measured by the number of subsidiaries). They find that larger banks are riskier than smaller ones, that lower capitalization in larger banks increases risk, and that unstable funding is associated with more bank risk. At the level of individual banks, however, neither more market-based activity nor organizational complexity increased risk. The average bank stock return was −45 percent, and the return for banks with at least $50 billion in assets was −55 percent. A five-fold increase in assets would have reduced the return another 7 percentage points, a 20 percentage point increase in reliance on funding from deposits would have increased returns by 12 percentage points, and an increase in capital ratios by 2.5 percentage points would have increased returns by 13 percentage points.

The study then examines systemic risk, measured by "SRISK." This measure calculates a bank's contribution to the deterioration of capitalization of the financial system as a whole during a crisis (Acharya, Engle, and Richardson 2012). Their estimate is based on "the dollar value of capital shortfall that a bank is expected to suffer when the US financial stock index falls by 40 percent over six months" (p. 15). This measure implicitly assumes that stock market prices accurately reflect the long-term values of assets held by the banks rather than overshooting in a panic, and thus seems likely to be overstated in a crisis period. SRISK is determined by bank stock volatility in times of distress, the covariance of the bank's stock with the market in such periods, bank leverage, and bank size.

Their list of top 10 SRISK banks places the Royal Bank of Scotland at number 1 and Bank of America at number 10. Most of the institutions on the list received government support in the crisis. Their tests show a significant influence of bank size and complexity on SRISK. When bank size is interacted with structural variables, the tests show that large banks contribute more to systemic risk when they have less capital, have fewer deposits, and engage more in market-based activities. The authors conclude that there should be more stringent capital requirements for large banks because of systemic risk, consistent with the G-SIB surcharges in Basel III. They also infer a case for CoCos and for restrictions on risky trading activities but worry that sole reliance on higher capital requirements may push risks to unregulated sectors and may impose a cost from loss of economies of scale.

Siegert and Willison (2015) provide a useful survey of studies estimating TBTF subsidies. They opine that "the existence of the TBTF problem is now widely accepted by academics, politicians and regulators across the world. . . [namely the problem from] systemic risk and moral hazard" (p. 4). This characterization is probably accurate, but it would seem to dismiss lightly such considerations as the alternative economies of scale explanation of lower funding costs of large banks and (with regard to moral hazard) the inconsistency of undue risk-taking incentive with the fact that in an insolvency shareholders are expected to be wiped out even if creditors are not. The authors do not mention the "charter value" argument at all. They do cite Davies and Tracey (2014), who note that once TBTF status is included as a control, tests no longer show economies of scale. They do not cite contrary estimates (such as those discussed below). They review event studies (the reaction of bank stock prices to the 1984 testimony of the comptroller of the currency admitting after the bailout of Continental Illinois that 11 US banks were TBTF, spreads for large banks following the Long-Term Capital Management rescue, and the opposing impact on spreads following the Bear Sterns rescue versus the Lehman Brothers collapse). Mergers provide another area for event analysis.

Among analyses of the size effect, they emphasize the findings of Acharya, Anginer, and Warburton (2014), who examine the influence of bank size on spreads after controlling for risk using the distance to default measure discussed above. Acharya, Anginer, and Warburton find that in 1990–2012, banks in the top decile of the size distribution enjoyed bond spreads 30 basis points lower than those facing other banks, and the advantage reached 100 basis points in 2009. However, by 2013 the differential had swung to a small disadvantage (8 basis points).

The survey authors cite Hindlian et al. (2013) as obtaining a similar negative TBTF effect (10 basis points) by 2013 for the six largest US banks (and a low funding advantage of only 6 basis points between 1999 and mid-2007). The negative effect by 2013 in both studies is provocative, because it suggests that the introduction of policies for resolving large banks may have sharply reduced or eliminated the previous TBTF funding advantage.

A study by the US Government Accountability Office (GAO 2014) also finds that large US banks no longer enjoy a TBTF funding advantage. It applies 42 models for the period 2006–13. All of them find that funding costs for larger bank holding companies were lower than those for smaller ones in 2008–09. However, in 2011–13 more than half of the models find that larger bank holding companies had higher bond funding costs than smaller ones, given the average level of credit risk.

Siegert and Willison (2015) also survey the ratings-based (support rating versus stand-alone rating) studies of the funding advantage of TBTF banks. They note that using this method, the International Monetary Fund (IMF 2014b) placed the advantage of being a systemically important bank at 5 basis points in the United States and 20 basis points in the euro area before the crisis. These figures rose to 30 basis points and 80 basis points, respectively, by 2010 and were still at 15 and 60 basis points, respectively, by 2013. Siegert and Willison emphasize the pattern of rising TBTF benefit in the crisis and note that the Noss-Sowerbutts (2012) estimates translate into a funding cost advantage of an extraordinary 630 basis points for the four large UK banks in 2009. They also survey estimates of the TBTF subsidy using equity price volatility but suggest that this approach may overestimate the cyclicality of default risk and hence of implicit subsidies. Regarding the type of debt, they note the findings of Araten and Turner (2012) that if federal funds, noninterest deposits, and repo financing are excluded, the TBTF funding advantage is modest (18 basis points) in comparison with ranges identified in other studies for bonds (–6 to +80 basis points), general wholesale funding (60 to 100 basis points), and deposits (17 to 80 basis points; p. 16).

Economies of Scale

Much of the TBTF literature is premised on the notion that large banks take excessive risks because of the implicit guarantee and carries an implicit policy recommendation that bank size should be held below a TBTF threshold. If, however, there were important economies of scale beyond such a threshold, there would be social as well as private losses from imposing such limits. A social benefit-cost tradeoff analysis needs to be conducted to arrive at proper policy regarding the regulation of large banks.

Wheelock and Wilson (2012) find that across the size spectrum, US banks faced increasing economies of scale in the period 1984–2006. They argue that early studies that had found an exhaustion of economies of scale once banks reach $100 million to $200 million in assets were flawed because they applied "parametric cost functions that fail basic specification tests" (p. 172). The nonparametric method they develop shows pervasive returns to scale. They identify output categories (consumer loans, business loans, real estate loans, securities, and other) and input categories (purchased funds, core deposits, and labor services). This formulation begs a question they do not address: If because of TBTF the price of purchased funds declines above some large-size threshold, is lower unit cost from an implicit subsidy being conflated with greater efficiency?

Using quarterly data for a period in which the number of US banks fell from about 14,000 to about 7,000 but average size rose fivefold in real terms, their sample has about 900,000 observations. Their technique, however, applies estimates in clusters of only about 6,000 observations each. The framework obtains "local" estimators for a "k-nearest-neighbor bandwidth" (p. 184). They find that the elasticity of costs with respect to output size is systematically only about 0.96 across nearly the full size distribution (p. 289), indicating returns to scale. This elasticity would imply that one of the largest US banks (at, say, $1.6 trillion in assets) would have unit costs that are 13 percent lower than a bank with $50 billion of assets.[6] The authors conduct a back-of-the-envelope experiment supposing the four largest US banks in 2010 (Bank of America, JPMorgan Chase, Citigroup, and Wells Fargo), with an average size of $1.9 trillion, were split into eight banks with an average size of $945 billion. They estimate that the change would raise their combined costs by $79 billion annually, an amount that would have exceeded the combined profits of the four largest banks each year for 2003–06. They conclude that the "likely resource costs of a hard limit on the size of banks are probably not trivial" (p. 195).

Hughes and Mester (2013) argue that most studies of economies of scale in banking fail to take into account bank managers' taste for risk taking. They maintain that better diversification resulting from larger scale can generate not only scale economies but also incentives to take on more risk, which can add to cost and obscure the underlying scale economies. They use the "almost ideal (AI) demand system" approach from consumer theory to estimate utility-maximizing profit and input demand functions. This approach allows for the possibility that managers trade off profit for reduced risk, incurring higher cost to reduce risk. If instead they simply maximize profit, the AI formulation reduces to the more usual translog production function often used in banking sector scale economy estimates.[7]

Their main estimates are for 842 US bank holding companies in 2007. They consider five outputs (liquid assets, securities, loans, trading assets, and off-balance-sheet activities) and six inputs (labor, physical capital, large time deposits, all other deposits, all other borrowed funds, and equity capital). They first test their managers' preferred model. They find that they

---

6. This span is approximately a cumulative fivefold doubling ($2^5 = 32 = 1,600/50$). The increase turns out to require 350 successive increments of 1 percent (which broadly tracks the rule of thumb that the number of years to double in exponential growth equals 70 years divided by the percentage growth rate ($5 = 350/70$). The corresponding ratio of cost to output at the large size would be 0.87 times this ratio for the small size: $(1.0096/1.01)^{350} = 0.87$. (This calculation is mine, not theirs.)

7. The translog production function is like the Cobb-Douglas function in that the logarithm of output is a function of the logarithms of inputs, except that it adds a quadratic term of the logarithm of each input.

can statistically reject maximization of profit alone (validating the hypothesis that managers also take account of risk in their utility function).

In their first simple test for economies of scale (the "economic cost function"), the coefficient for returns to scale (analog to the sum of output elasticities with respect to inputs) is in the range of 1.03–1.06 across the full size spectrum—about the same outcome as the nearly uniform cost elasticity of 0.96 identified by Wheelock and Wilson (2012). However, in their test using the AI-based managers' most preferred function, the scale economy coefficient reaches about 1.13 for banks under $2 billion in assets, rising with size to reach 1.34 for banks with more than $100 billion in assets. Although the authors do not quite say so, this degree of returns to scale is extraordinary. It implies that a bank with $1.6 trillion in assets would have unit costs of less than half those of a bank with $50 billion in assets.[8]

Hughes and Mester (2013) do illustrate the importance of economies of scale by showing that breaking in half each of the 17 banks with more than $100 billion in assets in 2007 would increase their aggregate costs from $410 billion to $506 billion.[9] They carry out an important test to separate out the influence of possible TBTF subsidy effects as opposed to underlying economies of scale. They do so by rerunning their estimates replacing the large banks' actual cost rates for deposits and borrowed funds with the median rates of banks with less than $100 billion in assets. They find a scale economies coefficient for banks larger than $100 billion that is almost unchanged from that in their main test, indicating that the scale economies are not a misleading artifact of TBTF subsidies. Overall, their study provides important evidence that scale economies probably do exist in banking. Their relatively circuitous and opaque method gives pause, however, as does the extreme degree of economies of scale found for banks over $100 billion in size.

Davies and Tracey (2014) examine whether estimates of economies of scale hold up even after controlling for the TBTF subsidy. They use data on about 1,400 banks in all parts of the world with assets above $50 billion in 2010. They use the ratings uplift method to estimate the price that debt would have faced in the absence of the TBTF subsidy (although they do not report the estimated relationships of interest rates to ratings category). They estimate that for 2001–10, 54 percent of all banks in the sample enjoyed a TBTF subsidy based on ratings uplift, with a relatively low proportion in the

---

8. Applying the formulation of footnote 6, the corresponding cost elasticity is $1/1.34 = 0.75$. Applying 350 increments of 1 percent to output would cut the unit cost ratio to $(1.0075/1.01)^{350} = 0.42$.

9. They do not calculate a more radical restructuring: cutting all of these banks into enough multiple spinoffs to set a $100 billion ceiling on size.

United States (23 percent), a moderate proportion in Europe (56 percent), and a high proportion in Asia-Oceania (76 percent). The mean price of debt for TBTF banks was 3.3 percent for the United States; it would have been 3.7 percent at social prices adding in the TBTF advantage. For Europe the corresponding figures are 3.8 and 4.9 percent.

The authors apply a translog cost function, with the logarithm of total cost specified as a function of logarithms of output, input prices, and control variables (such as per capita growth and nominal interest rates). Scale economies are identified as the inverse of the sum of derivatives of the logarithm of cost to the logarithm of each of the outputs. Output includes liquid assets, securities, loans, other assets, and off-balance-sheet activities; inputs include debt (including deposits), labor, and physical capital. Cost is obtained by estimating an average price for each input.

The authors first estimate a "standard model," which shows an economies of scale coefficient of 1.07 for the full sample and 1.15 for banks over $2 trillion (meaning costs rise only 0.93 percent or 0.87 percent, respectively, when output rises 1 percent). These coefficients are highly significant. They then rerun the model repricing debt at the social cost (adding back the ratings uplift advantage). When they do so, the scale coefficients are about unity for each of five size groups, and none is significantly different from unity.

A potentially important problem with the estimates is that they use a single parametric (translog) function across all observations. McAllister and McManus (1993, 390) show that "fitting a single translog cost function over a population of banks that varied widely in terms of size and output mix. . . [resulted] in a specification bias that contribute[d] substantially to the traditional conclusion of decreasing returns to scale among banks above the midpoint of the size range studied." They proposed the use of nonparametric methods instead.[10] Presumably the Davies-Tracey analysis could be repeated using nonparametric tests.

Including banks from all regions may also distort the diagnosis, despite the attempt to include controls.[11] Rather than providing definitive evidence that economies of scale are not present except for TBTF cost advantages, the study would thus seem to serve as a caution regarding the new dominant finding of returns to scale in banking.

McAllister and McManus (1993, 397) emphasize that "the most important source of financial returns to scale in banking is the fact that asset

---

10. McAllister and McManus (1993) suggest in particular kernel regression, linear spline estimation, and Fourier approximation.

11. For example, the three largest banks in the world are state-owned banks in China, which may have objectives other than profit maximization.

diversification reduces the amount of costly financial capital that an intermediary must hold in order to function." This fundamental point poses a problem of identification of causality and interpretation for the current debate on capital requirements and TBTF-induced risk taking. If larger banks with more diversification are best at dealing with risk, the fact that they take on more risk could reflect their natural comparative advantage rather than moral hazard from TBTF. Indeed, the diversification argument would tend toward the implication that larger banks need to hold less, not more, equity capital against a properly risk-weighted portfolio of assets.

A caveat to the various studies of economies of scale is that empirical work on this issue is constrained by the fact that neither the inputs nor the outputs can be expressed in straightforward physical units.[12] For example, in Wheelock and Wilson (2012), "output" comprises five categories of loans and securities and "inputs" comprise two categories of financing as well as a third input (labor). They examine scale economies along a "ray" on which the ratio of each output to the other factors remains constant. This approach is far from a test in which, for example, tons of steel are the output and capital and labor are the inputs. Nonetheless, analysis of economies of scale almost always requires some form of aggregation.[13] This strand of the literature would thus seem to warrant at least cautious attention. Ideally, case studies could provide a supplementary qualitative analysis of what efficiencies have been gained (or lost) from the fact that the largest five US banks now have an average size of 10 percent of GDP each (see figure 5.3 later in chapter), whereas the corresponding measure in 1995 was only 2.4 percent (according to 10-K data).

Panic Dynamics

The TLAC literature is surprisingly sparse regarding the susceptibility of TLAC to panics. Persaud (2014) argues that the most likely investors in CoCos would be hedge funds and other investors with short time horizons, who would be likely to run rather than hold for the longer term if a number of banks got into trouble at the same time. Regulators do not want banks to hold CoCos of other banks, because doing so would increase the likelihood of a systemic problem.

---

12. In the study group discussion of an earlier draft, one industrial organization expert emphasized this problem, noting that although it is present more generally in industry analysis, it is acute in banking.

13. For example, even in the most basic sector (agriculture), farm-level output will typically be measured by an aggregation of values across several different crops.

Persaud notes that regulators want long-term investors, such as pension funds and life insurance companies, to be the primary holders of these securities but argues that these entities are poorly designed to do so. Given the longer-term nature of their liabilities, their natural hedging advantage lies in holding diversified portfolios of instruments that offer higher returns because they are illiquid. He also observes that it is by no means clear that the outcome in crises would be more equitable if losses were imposed on pensioners holding claims on insurance companies rather than on taxpayers. As for retail investors, Persaud observes that in 2014 UK authorities suspended the sale of CoCos to them on grounds that the instruments were highly complex and inappropriate for the mass retail market. Overall, he characterizes bail-in securities as "fool's gold" that will "bring forward and spread a crisis, not snuff it out" (p. 6).

A hint of possible market panic dynamics from CoCos came in early 2016, when investors became concerned that, following unusual losses in 2015, Deutsche Bank might be forced to miss a coupon on its convertible bonds (in this case, alternative tier 1 bonds subject to contingent write-down). The yield on the bonds in question soared from 6.0 to 13.5 percent, and the bank's stock price fell 40 percent in five weeks. A leading index of CoCo bonds fell from a 2015 high of 104.6 cents to 88.8 cents on the euro in early March 2016, casting doubt on the future viability of the market for these instruments, which at that time had grown to $102 billion.[14] A new round of difficulties for Deutsche Bank arose in September 2016, when the US Department of Justice provisionally imposed a fine of $14 billion on the bank for misleading investors in sales of mortgage-backed securities. Appendix 5A examines the case of Deutsche Bank, primarily as a window into not only potential panic dynamics of TLAC but also differences between European and US banks with respect to market perceptions of the quality of asset book values.

Impact Estimates

In November 2015 an experts group chaired by the head of the Bank for International Settlements (BIS) Secretariat for the Committee on the Global Financial System submitted to the Financial Stability Board a report estimating the economic costs and benefits of TLAC implementation (Tsatsaronis et al. 2015). The study considered combinations of two alternative TLAC leverage targets (6 percent and 10 percent of the exposure

---

14. John Glover, "Deutsche Bank CoCo Holders See What Regulators Mean by Risk," Bloomberg, February 10, 2016; John Glover, "CoCo Turmoil Forces Europe to Act on Surprise Coupon Loss," Bloomberg, March 11, 2016.

measure [liabilities]) and two alternative targets for the ratio of TLAC to risk-weighted assets (16 percent and 20 percent). For 30 G-SIBs, it found that the median shortfall from the resulting TLAC targets ranged from €14 billion to €53 billion per large bank, an aggregate of €750 billion to €1.8 trillion. The report assumed that to meet the targets, banks would replace the next-most-expensive liabilities by more costly TLAC-eligible liabilities. The consequence would be to raise the average cost of TLAC and "other selected marketable liabilities" that meet some but not all criteria for TLAC eligibility by a range of 43 to 115 basis points across the four combinations of target leverage and target ratio to risk-weighted assets (p. 8). After further allowance for a 30 basis point increase in response to increased issuance of TLAC liabilities and after placing the share of G-SIBs in total bank lending at 40 percent, the study calculates that average bank lending rates would rise by 5 to 9 basis points for the two variants with 6 percent TLAC leverage and 14 to 15 basis points for the two variants with 10 percent leverage (p. 14).

To arrive at macroeconomic consequences, the study uses a central parameter from 80 macro-models involved in the Macroeconomic Assessment Group (MAG 2011) exercise: A 10 basis point rise in the economywide lending rate reduces the level of long-run GDP by 9 basis points (p. 16). This impact seems much too small. Using the aggregate production function approach of Miles, Yang, and Marcheggiano (2012) (also applied in chapter 4) and assuming a moderate capital share of one-third and a relatively high base of a 10 percent real interest rate for the cost of capital, a 10 basis point increase in the economywide lending rate would reduce long-term output by 25 basis points.[15] The study finds that the TLAC requirements would reduce long-term output in a range from about 5 basis points for low targets to 13 basis points for the high targets with high levels of G-SIB market share. If the diagnosis about understatement of output impact is correct, by implication the appropriate range would be 12 to 33 basis points. At the upper end, a permanent loss of 0.33 percent of output would have a capitalized equivalent of 13 percent of one year's GDP (discounting at 2.5 percent in real terms) ($0.33/0.025 = 13$).

The expert group's study then examined the benefits of TLAC. They find that TLAC would reduce excessive risk taking of large banks caused by the TBTF subsidy. They cite Afonso, Santos, and Traina (2014) for empir-

---

15. In the aggregate production function approach, $C = (v\alpha\sigma)/(1-\alpha)$, where C is the proportionate change in output; α is the income share of, and elasticity of output with respect to, capital; σ is the elasticity of substitution between capital and labor; and v is the proportionate change in the lending rate or unit cost of capital (see equation 4.13 in chapter 4). Setting α at 0.33 and σ at 0.5 places the ratio $(\alpha\sigma)/(1-\alpha)$ at 0.25. Defining w as the average base lending rate and Δw as the change in the lending rate, $v = \Delta w/w$. If $w = 0.10$ and $\Delta w 0.01$, $v = 0.1$ and $C = 0.025$. A 1 percentage point rise in the lending rate reduces output by 2.5 percent.

ical support of this incentive distortion (22). Their central estimate is that the disciplining effect of TLAC would reduce the likelihood of financial crisis by 26 percent (from an annual probability of 2.3 to 1.7 percent (pp. 24–25).[16] They use the BCBS (2010a) central estimate of 63 percent of one year's GDP as the cost of a financial crisis. By implication the TLAC requirement would generate gross gains of 0.38 percent of GDP annually (0.38 = 63 × (0.023 – 0.017)), although the study does not mention this implied estimate. By itself, this crisis-reducing benefit would be on the same order of magnitude as the annual cost for the high targets and high G-SIB case using the expansion suggested above (i.e., 38 basis points benefit compared with 33 basis points cost).

The authors then add other benefits from the fiscal savings of avoiding bailouts, calibrated based on the difference between the Basel III minimum 8 percent of risk-weighted assets and 20 percent of risk-weighted assets in TLAC. They estimate that the availability of the fiscal savings for alternative stimulus in the crisis would translate to a benefit of 3.8 percent of one year's GDP, reducing the total present value of damage from 63.0 to 59.2 percent. They postulate that a further benefit from avoidance of increased sovereign yields would translate into an additional gain of 1.6 percent of one year's GDP, reducing the present value of damage further to 57.6 percent. Their overall central estimate is that TLAC benefits would amount to 48 basis points of GDP (with about four-fifths of the total coming from the crisis probability reduction and one-fifth from the fiscal effects).

Evidence on US Banks in the Great Recession

The banking crisis in the Great Recession provides a natural experiment to test whether the largest banks revealed disproportionately large losses as a consequence of taking undue risks prompted by the TBTF subsidy and incentive distortion. The same dataset used in testing the Modigliani-Miller (M&M) hypothesis for US banks used in chapter 3 can be applied to examine this question. These data are from the 10-K reports filed with the Securities and Exchange Commission.

A dividing line frequently used for TBTF is $100 billion in assets. There were 16 large banks above this threshold in 2006–07. Data for the next 32 banks in order of size provide a basis for the comparator non-TBTF set of banks. These banks had assets of $5.4 billion to $95 billion (2006–07 average).

---

16. The 2.3 percent annual probability apparently takes account of the beneficial effects of meeting the Basel III standards for G-SIB equity capital but not the TLAC requirements.

Figure 5.1   Change in net income relative to assets between 2006–07 and 2008–10 for 48 large US banks and natural logarithm of asset size

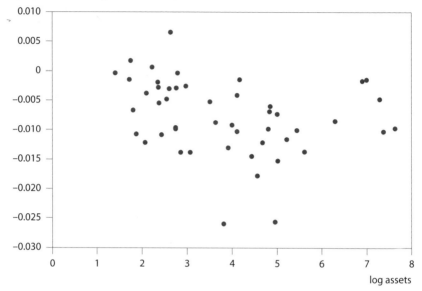

proportionate change in net income/assets

Source: Data from annual filings of Form 10-K with the Securities and Exchange Commission.

Figure 5.1 shows the change in average net income relative to assets from the precrisis base in 2006–07 to the crisis period of 2008–10, on the vertical axis, and the natural logarithm of base period assets (billions of dollars) on the horizontal axis, for these 48 medium-sized and large banks. The natural logarithm of 100 is 4.6, so the dividing line between medium-sized and TBTF banks is slightly to the right of the center in the chart.

The figure shows typical reductions in the net income-to-assets ratio of about 1 percentage point between the two periods, with reductions as large as about 2.5 percent of assets. There is no clear dichotomy between smaller reductions in net income for banks below the TBTF range (on the left side) and larger reductions for TBTF banks (on the right side).

Table 5.1 presents corresponding data averaged for the two groups and adds two other measures of bank results: charge-offs as a fraction of total assets and nonperforming assets as a fraction of total assets. The table reports the levels in each of the two periods as well as the change between the two periods. It also reports the *t*-statistic in a test for difference of means

Table 5.1   Indicators of relative impact of the Great Recession on largest banks compared with medium-sized banks in the United States (percent)

Group	Number	Average 2006–07	Average 2008–10	Change	T-statistic for difference of means
Group I					
>$100 billion assets	16				
NI/TA	16	1.14	0.17	−0.97	
NPA/TA	13	0.58	1.68	1.1	
NCO/TL	14	0.63	2.44	1.81	
Total assets	16	579.3	682.2		
Group II					
<$100 billion assets	34				
NI/TA	32	1.12	0.43	−0.68	
NPA/TA	31	0.39	1.52	1.13	
NCO/TL	34	0.46	1.72	1.26	
Total assets	34	25.8	29.4		
Group I–Group II					
NI/TA				−0.285	−1.468 (NS)
NPA/TA				−0.024	−0.076 (NS)
NCO/TL				0.548	1.637 (NS)

NI = net income; TA = total assets; NPA = nonperforming assets; NCO = net chargeoffs; TL = total loans; NS = not statistically significant at the 5 percent level

Source: Data from annual filings of Form 10-K with the Securities and Exchange Commission.

between two populations.[17] The average size of the largest 16 banks was about $580 billion in the base period, about 20 times the average size of the next 34 largest banks. Both groups had relatively similar net income relative to assets in 2006–07 (about 1.1 percent). This metric declined more for the largest banks by 2008–10 (almost 1 percentage point, compared with about two-thirds of 1 percentage point for the medium-sized banks). However, as suggested by inspection of the loose scatter in figure 5.1, the difference between the two groups with respect to the size of this decline was not statistically significant at the 5 percent level.

Two alternative measures of impact are also shown: the ratio of nonperforming assets to total assets and the ratio of net charge-offs to total liabilities. For these two measures, an increase represents a deterioration in outcome.

---

17. The test applies the assumption of equal variance for the two populations. An alternative test allowing different variations for the two populations yields similar results.

As it turns out, for nonperforming assets, the largest banks fared better than the medium-size banks. For net charge-offs, the largest banks showed worse outcomes. However, neither of the two alternative measures showed a statistically significant difference between the changes for the two groups. The absence of a significantly worse outcome for the largest banks than for the medium-size banks casts doubt on the prominence of the role of excessive risk taking induced by TBTF dynamics, because when the crisis arrived the TBTF banks performed much like the medium-size banks.

The tests in table 5.1 exclude banks that failed or were forced to be taken over in the crisis, because there are no data for their performance in the crisis period. An important question is thus whether there is a survivor bias in the analysis. The frequency of failures was slightly smaller in the large-bank group. Five institutions with more than $100 billion in assets failed (Lehman) or were forced into takeovers (Bear Stearns, Wachovia, Washington Mutual, and Countrywide). They represented 24 percent of the large-bank population $(5/(16 + 5))$. In comparison, 13 banks with assets of $5 billion to $100 billion each experienced failure, representing 28 percent of the bank population for the medium-size group $(13/(34 + 13))$.[18] Consideration of the survivor problem would thus not seem to change the finding that the large banks fared no worse in the crisis than the medium-size banks.

Share of the Largest Banks in the United States and Other Countries

It is ironic that the most intense political pressure to break up large banks because of the TBTF argument seems to be in the United States rather than in other major economies, because the size of the biggest banks relative to the size of the economy is much smaller in the United States than in most other economies.

For several decades, the United States restricted banks from opening branches outside the state of their incorporation, which restrained bank size. The McFadden Act of 1927 restricted opening branches across state lines because of concerns about financial sector concentration and difficulties in supervision. By 1990, however, most states allowed out-of-state holding companies to acquire in-state banks, although opposition from a

---

18. The largest of the failing intermediate banks was IndyMac, with $32.7 billion in assets in 2007. For the 12 other failing banks in this group (Downey, BankUnited, Guaranty, Colonial, AmTrust, WesternBank, United Commercial, California National, Corus, First Federal of California, R-G Premier, and Franklin), the median size was $12 billion (10-K reports and Federal Deposit Insurance Corporation, *Failed Banks List*, 2017, www.fdic.gov/bank/individual/failed/banklist.html).

coalition of small banks and insurance companies delayed national legislation removing the restrictions. The Riegle-Neal Interstate Banking Act of 1994 finally provided for standardized branching and acquisitions, allowing well-managed and well-capitalized banks to acquire banks in any state, subject to a ceiling of 10 percent of total US deposits or 30 percent of a single state's deposits (Medley 1994). The act took full force in 1997. The opening of interstate banking provided an opportunity for expansion by the largest banks.

Another institutional change—repeal of the Glass-Steagall Act of 1933—worked in the same direction. Glass-Steagall prohibited firms from operating simultaneously in commercial banking, investment banking, and insurance. In 1999 the Gramm-Leach-Bliley Act repealed this prohibition. With the merger of Citicorp with insurance company Travelers Group in 1998 (with a waiver from the Federal Reserve), Citigroup's assets reached about $740 billion in 1998, compared with $311 billion for Citicorp and $387 billion for Travelers in 1997.[19]

Figure 5.2 shows the combined assets of the 10 largest US banks as a percent of GDP in 1995 and then annually for 2001–15.[20] This ratio surged from 17.5 percent of GDP in 1995 to 42 percent by 2001. The combined assets of the 10 largest banks peaked at 72 percent of GDP in 2007, easing to 62 percent by 2015. Among the largest banks, real assets fell 18.9 percent at Citigroup, 12.4 percent at Bank of America, 11.5 percent at Goldman Sachs, and 1.8 percent at JPMorgan Chase between 2008 and 2015. (Real assets rose 20.9 percent at Wells Fargo, even after the more than doubling of assets in 2008, when the bank absorbed Wachovia). Like Citigroup, HSBC has substantially downsized, as both banks have curbed their ambitions to maintain a major presence in almost all countries.[21] A change in business

---

19. Mitchell Martin, "Citicorp and Travelers Plan to Merge in Record $70 billion Deal: A New No. 1: Financial Giants Unite," *New York Times*, April 7, 1998; SEC 10-K statements.

20. For the full period, the following banks (or their predecessor organizations) were among the 10 largest: JPMorgan Chase, Bank of America, Citigroup, Wells Fargo, Goldman Sachs, and Morgan Stanley. Four banks that were in the group early in the period (Wachovia, Bear Stearns, Washington Mutual, and Countrywide) were absorbed by larger banks in the financial crisis (Wells Fargo, JPMorgan Chase, JPMorgan Chase, and Bank of America, respectively), and one (Lehman) failed outright. By 2008 Bank of New York Mellon, US Bancorp, PNC, and Capital One had joined the ranks of the 10 largest institutions. The assets of the top 10 in 2015 ranged from $334 billion (Capital One) to $2.4 trillion (JPMorgan Chase). (From 10-K annual reports, deflated by the US consumer price index.)

21. Citigroup has reportedly cut the number of countries in which it is present in half, from a peak of 50, eliminating about one-fourth of its customers. HSBC has pursued a comparable scaling back, eliminating 1,600 locations in the United States (Yalman Onaran, "Citigroup, HSBC Jettison Customers as Era of Global Empire Ends," *Bloomberg*, July 26 2016). Citigroup's 10-K reports show a decline of 28.5 percent in the size of its direct staff, from 323,000 in 2008 to 231,000 in 2015.

Figure 5.2   Combined assets of 10 largest US banks as percent of GDP, 1995 and 2001–15

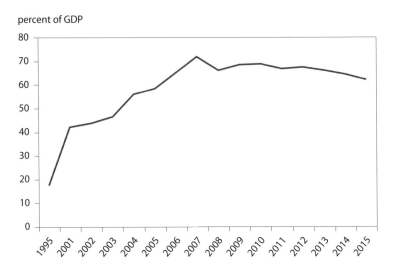

percent of GDP

Source: Calculated from annual filings of Form 10-K with the Securities and Exchange Commission.

model seems to have dominated at least the cases of Citigroup and HSBC. For the large banks more generally, it seems likely that the increased capital requirements of Basel III played a significant role in the cutbacks.

In short, the size of the large US banks relative to GDP rose sharply from the mid-1990s to a peak in 2007, easing somewhat after the Great Recession. Although within the United States this share is perceived as high, it remains modest by international standards. The combined assets of the five largest banks amounted to more than 300 percent of GDP in Switzerland and France in 2015, whereas the share in the United States was only 50 percent (figure 5.3). In both Canada and Australia—two economies that escaped the banking crises of the Great Recession—the assets of the top five banks account for about 200 percent of GDP, four times as much as in the United States. In China and Japan—two other economies that escaped the banking crises of the Great Recession—the ratio is about 125 percent of GDP. The closest one can come to the US share of the biggest banks for a major international economy is the euro area as a whole (75 percent) (figure 5.3). The implication would seem to be that if there is major danger posed by the large size of the biggest banks, this danger is substantially smaller in the United States than in other major economies.

Figure 5.3   Assets of the five largest banks as percent of GDP in selected economies, 2015

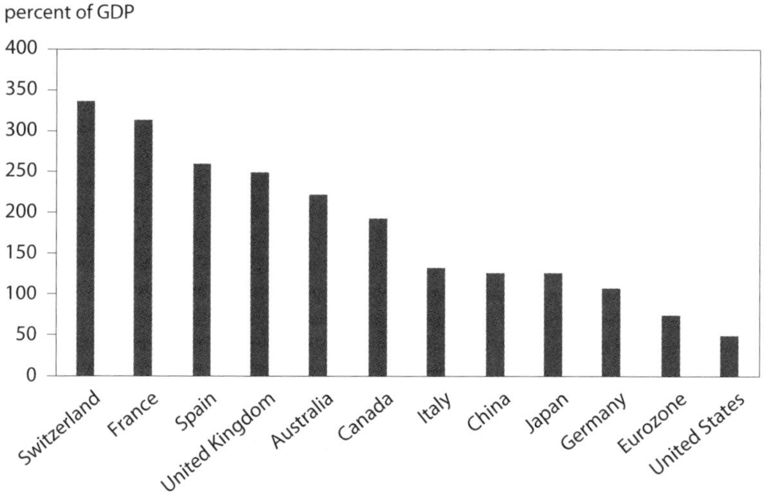

percent of GDP

Sources: www.relbanks.com; IMF (2016c).

Bank Resolution and Crisis Management

Just as the question of TBTF is inherently linked to the question of whether there are economies of scale that could make it socially inefficient to break up the large banks, TBTF and the TLAC solution are closely related to the question of whether reforms after the Great Recession addressed the challenge of what might be thought of as "immaculate bankruptcy" for the largest banks.[22] The polite term for bankruptcy in banking is "resolution"—a less alarming term that also implies a much faster workout than in normal corporate bankruptcies, as speed is critical in preventing the failure of one large bank from turning into a systemic crisis.

In the United States, the Dodd-Frank Act of 2010 sought to ensure that shareholders and creditors, rather than taxpayers, bear the burden of bank failure. To address the case of systemically important banks, its Title II provided for Orderly Liquidation Authority (OLA), in which the Federal Deposit Insurance Corporation (FDIC) takes receivership of a large financial company, including not only bank holding companies but also systemically important nonbank financial institutions. In 2013 the FDIC announced

---

22. I borrow from my colleague John Williamson's "immaculate transfer" critique of the notion of seamless corrections in countries' external imbalances thanks to spending adjustments without the need for corresponding exchange rate changes.

its Single Point of Entry (SPOE) approach to implementing OLA, whereby in effect the holding company would be placed into expedited bankruptcy while its key subsidiaries would be kept open and operating, in principle preventing a run on the subsidiaries' liabilities (see Clearing House 2013, Skeel 2014, and Kupiec and Wallison 2015).

The Dodd-Frank legislation took other actions that constrained the ability of the Federal Reserve to address a financial crisis precipitated by difficulties at large financial institutions. The legislation did not change the Federal Reserve's ability to provide emergency lending to banks through the discount window, within the classic lender-of-last-resort framework for unlimited lending against collateral to solvent banks at a penalty rate in the face of a panic (Bagehot 1873). However, it restricted the Depression-era section 13(3) of the Federal Reserve Act, which provides for emergency lending to nonbank firms in "unusual and exigent" circumstances. The new legislation requires that any such lending be within a program with "broad-based" eligibility rather than designed for single firms. Special vehicles such as Maiden Lane (set up to provide a $29 billion asset guarantee to JPMorgan Chase in exchange for its takeover of Bear Stearns) would probably not be possible now. Nor would the support of nearly $200 billion to AIG or the Federal Reserve's guarantees of about $300 billion in asset-backed securities for Citigroup and about $120 billion for Bank of America in exchange for preferred shares and warrants. The Dodd-Frank legislation also eliminates the scope for the FDIC to provide "open bank assistance," ruling out such lending as its rescue of Continental Illinois in 1984 and probably its temporary program of guarantees for new bank debt in October 2008 at the height of the crisis (see Cline 2010, 2015d). Whether Dodd-Frank increased or decreased systemic resilience to failure of large financial firms thus turns on whether the improvements from higher capital and liquidity requirements (and TLAC), together with OLA, outweigh the curtailment of lender-of-last-resort capacity.[23]

Scott (2016, 93) argues that the Dodd-Frank restrictions "have substantially curtailed the Fed's ability to be an effective lender of last resort in a future crisis and have made our financial system much less stable." He judges that the requirement for approval by the secretary of Treasury of a special program of support to nonbanks raises the risk of politicization, contributing to uncertainty. Noting that the Federal Reserve indicated in late 2015 that a program in which five or more institutions are eligible to participate would meet the test of "broad-based," he asks whether the Fed

---

23. For further discussion of the curbing of lender-of-last-resort capacity under Dodd-Frank, see Kohn (2011).

would have to wait to act until five institutions experienced a run at the same time. He emphasizes that Dodd-Frank constrains use of the discount window for Federal Reserve lending to nonbank affiliates of banks, limiting such pass-through lending to 10 percent of the capital of the bank in the group (p. 104). The effect would be extremely limiting for Goldman-Sachs and Morgan Stanley, whose depository banks constitute only a modest share of their total assets. He concludes that nonbank affiliates that previously could receive funding without limit from their associated depository institutions will now have to go to the Fed directly as nonbanks for loans under section 13(3), subject to its new restrictions. William Dudley, the president of the Federal Reserve Bank of New York, has expressed concern that the Fed currently has "very limited" ability to lend to securities groups in a crisis.[24]

Geithner (2016, 18–19) has enumerated the large lender-of-last-resort operations in the Great Recession that would no longer be possible under the constraints of Dodd-Frank. They include support for AIG and the Bear Stearns takeover (Maiden Lane), at about $90 billion each; the increased FDIC insurance ($480 billion); the Asset Guarantee Program support to Citigroup and Bank of America ($419 billion); the FDIC's Debt Guarantee Program for new senior unsecured debt ($346 billion); Treasury's guarantee of money market funds ($3.2 trillion); Troubled Asset Relief Program (TARP) investments in individual firms ($315 billion); Treasury's commitment to Fannie Mae and Freddie Mac ($188 billion); and Treasury's purchase of agency-guaranteed mortgage-backed securities ($142 billion). He argues that "a standing ability to extend broad guarantees to the core of the financial system. . . does not exist today" and that under these circumstances use of the OLA "would exacerbate rather than mitigate the crisis, intensifying the run on both individual institutions and the system as a whole."

There would seem to be substantial grounds for questioning the feasibility of a smoothly functioning resolution of one of the largest banks working through the OLA and SPOE. The approach implies the presence of relatively large assets and subordinated debt at the holding company level and neat compartmentalization of a number of moderately sized subsidiaries, so that the failure of any one of them is moderate in scale compared with the totality of the subsidiaries and bank holding company. The SPOE is premised on transferring all of the assets, short-term debt, derivatives, and senior debt of the bank holding company to a new bridge company but leaving the bank holding company's stock and unsecured long-term

---

24. Sam Fleming, "Dudley Sees Gaps in Fed's Emergency Lending Powers," *Financial Times*, May 2, 2016.

debt behind in the bank holding company.[25] The bridge entity would thus be relatively well capitalized. In contrast, the original shareholders in the bank holding company would effectively be wiped out, and the subordinated debt left behind in the bank holding company would be converted into shares in the troubled subsidiary as a form of recapitalizing it.

In principle, the real-world productive activity taking place at the troubled subsidiary (not to mention its healthy sibling subsidiaries in the bank holding company) would continue uninterrupted; the only disruption would be the reshuffling of ownership associated with the wiping out of bank holding company shareholders and creditors. The question is whether market panic from failure of one of the largest financial firms would be avoided because markets would be comfortable providing credit to its subsidiaries, even though the bank holding company was in resolution (bankrupt). Retail investors, at least, would seem likely to exit the subsidiaries immediately rather than wait around to see whether the process works.[26] To be sure, the arrangement provides for sizable FDIC funding to the bridge entity and hence to the subsidiaries.

The OLA/SPOE strategy has implications for TLAC. It implies that large bank holding companies will be required to hold substantial subordinated debt to ensure the availability of resources that can be used in the workout process just described. Some analysts are thus concerned that the strategy may lead to increased leverage and financial fragility of these banks. A practical problem is that for a number of large banks, the main banking subsidiary is almost as large as the entire bank holding company. The ideal SPOE configuration would be a number of smaller subsidiaries, each of which is unlikely to get into trouble at the same time as the others. The size of liabilities of the parent holding company is typically only about 3 to 6 percent as large as the liabilities of the subsidiary bank, so existing bank holding company debt could fall considerably short of the amount needed to be converted to equity in recapitalizing the subsidiary bank (Kupiec and Wallison 2015, 184, 192).

Overall, it is questionable that OLA and SPOE have eliminated the crisis risk associated with the collapse of a large US bank. The implication is that

---

25. Moreover, derivatives are to be subject to a 48-hour stay under new rules proposed by the Federal Reserve in May 2016 (Marc Levine, "Regulators Want to Slow Runs on Derivatives," Bloomberg, May 4, 2016). The notion that two days would suffice to carry out the necessary workouts seems optimistic.

26. For example, would depositors in Bank of America keep their accounts intact if subsidiary Merrill Lynch collapsed and holding company Bank of America went into receivership?

sufficient equity capital—and sufficiently effective supervision (including through stress tests)—are essential to help avoid putting them to the test.[27]

In the European Union, there has been a similar shift from lender-of-last-resort action to bail-in in the name of avoiding taxpayer costs. The Bank Recovery and Resolution Directive of April 2014 is even more explicit than Dodd-Frank in enforcing bail-in. When a bank is "in breach of, or is about to breach, regulatory capital requirements," restructuring can be imposed. Although "in circumstances of very extraordinary systemic stress, authorities may also provide public support instead of imposing losses in full on private creditors," the authorities can provide such support only "after the bank's shareholders and creditors bear losses equivalent to 8 percent of the bank's liabilities and would be subject to the applicable rules on State aid."[28] However, as Goodhart and Avgouleas (2014, 32) observe with regard to both the Bank Recovery and Resolution Directive and TLAC, the "market propensity to resort to herding at times of shock means that it is not realistic to believe that generalized adoption of bail-in mechanisms would not trigger contagious consequences that would have a destabilizing effect." They emphasize that whereas bail-in could be salutary for idiosyncratic bank failure, it would be counterproductive in the face of systemic collapse.

A key feature for the euro area, nonetheless, is that the European Central Bank retains broad lender-of-last-resort authority, as there has been no curtailment in its flexibility analogous to the Dodd-Frank restrictions on the Federal Reserve. In principle, in an incipient bank panic, it could make determinations of underlying bank solvency that would enable it to provide substantial liquidity support, avoiding the transit of numerous institutions into the rigid bail-in requirements of the Bank Recovery and Resolution Directive.

---

27. One industry observer judges that in part because of the curtailment of the Federal Reserve's lender-of-last-resort flexibility, and especially in view of the absence of a substantially longer stay on derivatives, "under current law, a large bank experiencing liquidity problems would be forced into bankruptcy or a Dodd-Frank resolution, events that would likely trigger a massive run on liquidity similar to that seen in 2008" (Christopher Whalen, "The Best Big-Bank Resolution Plan: Avoid Crises in the First Place," *American Banker*, May 26, 2016). He advocates adoption of the Resolution Stay Protocol proposed in 2014 by the International Swaps and Derivatives Association (ISDA), to which 18 major global banks have already voluntarily adhered. This critique implicitly raises the question of whether the presence of derivatives has somehow fundamentally undermined the adequacy of the discount window for central bank assurance of liquidity to solvent banks.

28. European Commission, *EU Bank Recovery and Resolution Directive (BRRD): Frequently Asked Questions*, Memo/14/297, 2014.

Conclusion

The proposition that TBTF incentive distortions cause excessive risk taking by large banks has dominated the TLAC policy discussion. Somehow the discussion has discarded the other side of this issue: the proposition that "charter value" poses an incentive for large banks to avoid gambling despite the TBTF incentive.

Contrary to the popular image, the evidence presented in this chapter does not provide resounding proof that TBTF and excessive risk taking by large banks dominated the US financial crisis in the Great Recession. On the disciplinary role of subordinated debt, one study (Nguyen 2013) finds that this role is present in general but absent for large TBTF banks, with the plausible interpretation that investors do not penalize risk taking when they anticipate bailout. Yet the design of TLAC assumes just the opposite: that subordinate debt will indeed discipline risk taking in TBTF banks.

Surprisingly little attention has gone to the measurement of economies of scale at the largest banks, although the issue is central to the social value of imposing penalties designed to offset TBTF distortions. The Davies-Tracey (2014) study finds no economies of scale at social prices, but it suffers from serious methodological questions (the use of a parametric function where nonparametric methods have long been seen as necessary). Moreover, when the authors of another recent study that does find large economies of scale (Wheelock and Willison 2012) rerun the tests using borrowing costs applicable to smaller banks rather than larger banks, they find little change in the scale economies identified, the opposite finding from Davies-Tracey.

The interaction between risk-taking capacity and risk-taking incentive seems especially problematic in arriving at the proper policy inference. Larger banks have greater capacity to diversify, so in principle they are likely to have a comparative advantage in undertaking activities that involve greater risk. If some risky activities have social value, as seems highly likely, greater observed risk taking will not be unambiguous evidence of incentive distortions generating external diseconomies to the system.

On the practicality of TLAC, too little attention has been given to identifying proper holders who will have long-run incentives rather than behave in a herding exodus at the first sign CoCo conversions might be triggered, causing panic dynamics to be amplified.

TLAC has been popular at the political level because it implies a promise that taxpayers will not pay for bailouts in the future. It seems to have become seen as a cheap form of quasi-equity that can play much of the role of outright equity without imposing nearly as much cost on the banks as the real thing. Both of these attractions seem illusory. As long as central banks follow Bagehot's dictum (as they basically did in the Great Recession), taxpayers do not pay for losses, because only solvent banks are supported (the US Treasury made a profit on the TARP support for banks). Subordinated debt cannot be mobilized without default-like circumstances, so it cannot prevent banking panic associated with defaults in the same way that complete avoidance of default by virtue of greater depth of equity capital can.

TLAC thus broadly seems to be at best an inadequate substitute for equity capital. Basel III sets the total target, including equity, at 18 percent of risk-weighted assets. If the appropriate true equity optimum is 13 percent, it could be argued that overproviding TLAC compensates for its imperfect ability to replace equity. Boosting common equity tier 1 capital from the Basel III requirement of 9.5 percent of risk-weighted assets (for G-SIBs) to the equivalent of an optimal level of 13 percent by adding 8.5 percent of risk-weighted assets in the form of CoCos and subordinate debt would imply that the proper regulatory exchange rate between nonequity and equity TLAC is about 50 cents on the dollar ((13 − 9.5)/8.5). Even this favorable an exchange rate, however, would seem to be on the optimistic side.

Appendix 5A

Systemic Implications of Problems at a Major European Bank

Since the financial crisis in the United States and Europe, banks on both sides of the Atlantic have been subjected to stronger supervision and regulation as well as tougher requirements on capitalization.[29] Yet recent events suggest that vulnerabilities may remain in some of the largest financial institutions, especially in Europe.

In the period from October 2015 to October 2016, equity markets severely punished the share price of Deutsche Bank, the third-largest bank in Europe.[30] Although the system did not return to the brink of a Lehman-style crisis,[31] it is useful to consider the implications of these difficulties of this global systemically important bank (G-SIB).

Areas of lingering concern about the large banks, especially in Europe, include opacity in the valuation of assets, especially for derivatives, and possible understatement of risk-weighted assets in internal risk models. Potential shocks from legal fines have been highlighted by the fine imposed by the US Department of Justice on Deutsche Bank because of the sale of questionable mortgage-backed securities before the recent crisis. Another problem has been market destabilization from selloffs of contingent debt issued to meet the new rules on total loss-absorbing capacity (TLAC) imposed by the Basel III regulatory reforms. Hovering over all of these concerns is the seeming additional evidence that Europe lags the United States in restoring bank stability.

A broad implication of Deutsche Bank's difficulties is that they provide further support for additional bank capital beyond Basel III targets established in 2010 and to be fully phased in by 2019 (BCBS 2010b). Higher equity capital provides a larger cushion against insolvency in the face of shocks. With equity providing a larger share of the TLAC target of 18 percent of risk-weighted assets under Basel III, an additional benefit would be the resulting reduction in the need for contingent (additional tier 1) capital, which has proven to be a source of market instability when investors fear write-downs on (or conversions of) such obligations. But low market

---

29. This appendix reproduces Cline (2016b).

30. If the top state-owned banks in China and Japan are excluded, Deutsche Bank is the sixth largest in the world, after Mitsubishi UFJ, HSBC, JPMorgan Chase, BNP Paribas, and Bank of America (Relbanks, *Top Banks in the World*, 2016, www.relbanks.com/worlds-top-banks/assets). It has been a supporter of the Peterson Institute for International Economics.

31. Lehman Brothers was only one-third the size of Deutsche Bank.

valuations mean that banks would need to raise additional equity over time through retained earnings rather than immediately through new issuance when share prices are depressed. This problem is currently more severe for large banks in Europe than in the United States. Banks may also need to change their basic business models and downsize their balance sheets gradually until share prices rise toward book values.

Deutsche Bank warrants special attention for systemic reasons because of its size and extensive interconnections with financial institutions through its investment and investment banking units.[32] In June 2016 the International Monetary Fund found that among G-SIBs, Deutsche Bank was "the most important net contributor to systemic risks" (IMF 2016b, 29). It is important to recognize, however, that this diagnosis did not turn on any weaknesses in the bank's balance sheet or capitalization but on its high degree of "connectedness" with other financial institutions.[33]

The proximate cause of the recent pressure on Deutsche Bank was the September 2016 announcement by the US Department of Justice of a $14 billion fine for misleading investors in the selling of risky mortgage-backed securities. Previous such fines had amounted to $16.5 billion at Bank of America in 2014 and $5 billion at Goldman Sachs in April 2016.[34] Some accounts suggest the Royal Bank of Scotland could face even higher fines for such activities.[35] Such penalties feature prominently in the category of "operational risk," for which banks need to hold capital in addition to that for credit risk on loans and market risk on traded assets marked to fair value.

At its late September 2016 low, Deutsche Bank's stock price had fallen 63 percent from its late-2015 high and 77 percent from its post–Great

---

32. Kirkegaard argues that because of the bank's size, the German government would step in if necessary to provide support and could do so under the "severe disturbance in the economy" clause of the EU Bank Recovery and Resolution Directive. He therefore maintains that "there is no real risk of a sudden collapse that might thrust the European banking system back to the acute crisis of 2012" (Jacob Kirkegaard, "What Deutsche Bank's Troubles Tell Us about the Health of Europe's Banking System," Realtime Economic Issues Watch Blog, Peterson Institute for International Economics, September 30, 2016, https://piie.com/blogs/realtime-economic-issues-watch/ what-deutsche-banks-troubles-tell-us-about-health-europes).

33. The IMF study applied the net spillover method of Diebold and Yilmaz (2014), which decomposes vector autoregression estimates from market data to discern spillover of shocks imposed by a firm on others ("to-spillover") and shocks imposed on the firm by others ("from-spillover").

34. J. Weston Phippen, "Deutsche Bank's Refusal to Settle with the DOJ," *Atlantic*, September 16, 2016.

35. Andrew MacAskill and Lawrence White, "RBS's Worst-Case Legal Bill Could Hit $27 billion," Reuters, October 10, 2016.

Recession high in early 2014.[36] The price fell about 25 percent from its level on September 9 before the announcement of the $14 billion (€12.4 billion) fine, which by itself would represent 20 percent of Deutsche Bank's shareholder equity of €62.7 billion at the end of 2015 (Deutsche Bank 2015, i). But the gap between market value and book value was much larger. On September 29 the ratio of share price to book value stood at only 0.23, compared with about 0.6 for euro area peers BNP Paribas and Banco Santander, 0.6 for Citigroup, 0.9 for Goldman Sachs, and 1.0 for JPMorgan Chase. Market capitalization of Deutsche Bank stood at only €14.1 billion. Even with the modest recovery by late October, its price-to-book ratio remained at only 0.29 (all data are from Bloomberg).

A price-to-book ratio of only 0.2 to 0.3 for a G-SIB cannot be a good sign for the financial system. In the most optimistic interpretation, such a ratio might simply represent the fickleness of stock market valuations. The pessimistic interpretation would be that the market has priced the bank's equity correctly and that the book value is out of date. If the market is wrong and book value right, it would be in shareholders' interest to systematically downsize both sides of the balance sheet and use the profits from the sale of assets at prices higher than expected by the market to repurchase shares.

Figure 5A.1 shows the path of market price-to-book value ratios for six G-SIBs over the past decade. Before the Great Recession, the ratios were in the range of about 1.5 to 2.5. Thereafter the ratios tended to be in the range of 0.5 to 1.

Anemic price-to-book ratios have not been unique to Deutsche Bank, but from late 2015 to late 2016 the bank's relative weakness on this measure became more acute. For example, from October 2015 to late October 2016 the ratio fell from about 0.8 to 0.7 for Banco Santander and Citigroup, and it did not fall for BNP Paribas. Having dropped from 0.55 to 0.29 over the same period, the ratio for Deutsche Bank declined much farther and stood markedly below those of most of its peers (all data are from Bloomberg).

From the systemic standpoint, there may be some comfort in the fact that whereas contagion from Deutsche Bank in early 2016 depressed share prices of other major banks as well, the most recent round of pressure on the bank did not further reduce the prices of other major bank stocks. In both January–February and September 2016, the decline for Deutsche Bank was prompted by the specter of losses to additional tier 1 (AT1) bonds that

---

36. Share prices were $11.48 on September 29 but rose to $14.56 by October 26. Prices are available at http://finance.yahoo.com.

Figure 5A.1   Ratio of market price to book value for selected large US and European banks, October 27, 2006 to October 26, 2016

ratio of market price to book value

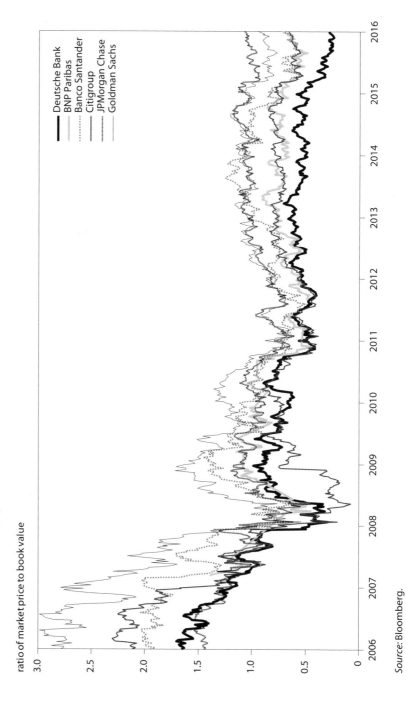

Source: Bloomberg.

count toward TLAC.[37] Thus, in early 2016, when it became a concern that the bank's net loss of €6.8 billion in 2015 might cause it to miss a coupon payment on these obligations, the price of its largest AT1 bond issue (€1.75 billion) fell from 95 cents to 70 cents. After recovering to an average of about 80 cents in March–August, the price fell to 73 cents in late September before partially recovering.[38]

Another pattern evident in figure 5A.1 is that US G-SIBs have tended to perform better than G-SIBs in Europe. Table 5A.1 confirms this pattern for 14 European and 8 US G-SIBs.[39] The average price-to-book ratio as of late October 2016 was 0.66 for the European banks but 1.04 for the US banks. More than half of the European banks had a ratio below 0.66, whereas none of the US banks did. Among the European G-SIBs, only UniCredit Group rivaled Deutsche Bank for the lowest ratio.

The outcome for European banks is poorer for two principal reasons. First, US and euro area monetary policies diverged. Recourse to negative interest rates as well as further quantitative easing likely worsened outcomes in the euro area compared with the United States. Banks cannot easily negotiate negative interest rates for depositors, a key source of their funding, and quantitative easing flattens the yield curve. Because banks are in the business of maturity transformation, the flatter yield curve erodes profits in the main business line (although there may be offsetting gains from faster growth of the economy and capital gains on long-term assets).

Second, market voting shows greater confidence that US banks have improved their capitalization and economic strength compared with European banks. In the United States, G-SIBs must hold 6 percent of total assets in capital. European banks have not been subject to a corresponding

---

37. AT1 bonds include subordinated debt that can be written down under certain circumstances (the principal form held by Deutsche Bank) and contingent convertible (CoCo) bonds that convert into equity under certain circumstances.

38. Jenny Strasburg, "Deutsche Bank Reports First Full-Year Loss Since Crisis," *Wall Street Journal*, January 28, 2016; Börse Berlin, www.boerse-berlin.com/index.php/Bonds? isin=DE000DB7XHP3. Under German Generally Accepted Accounting Principles (GAAP) accounting, in particular section 268, paragraph 8 of the German Commercial Code, certain items are blocked from being distributable under the concept of available distributable items (ADI). (The blocked items in this clause are associated with the valuation of potential tax liabilities [Küting et al. 2011].) Thus at year-end 2014, dividend potential before the amount blocked was €7.5 billion but ADI was only €2.0 billion; at end-2015 the corresponding amounts were €6.5 billion and €234 million, respectively. After an adjustment of about €800 million for certain interest expenses, the amounts available to cover AT1 interest were €2.9 billion at end-2014 and €1.1 billion at end-2015 (Deutsche Bank, *Available Distribution Items (ADI)*, www.db.com/ir/en/available-distributable-items.htm).

39. The G-SIB list also includes three Chinese and three Japanese banks (FSB 2015e). Data are not available for the privately held Groupe BPCE.

Table 5A.1   Ratio of share price to book value for global systemically important banks (G-SIBs) in Europe and the United States, October 26, 2016

European G-SIBs	Ratio	US G-SIBs	Ratio
Nordea	1.24	State Street	1.44
UBS	0.96	Wells Fargo	1.29
ING Bank	0.94	Bank of New York Mellon	1.27
HSBC	0.79	JPMorgan Chase	1.08
BNP Paribas	0.73	Goldman Sachs	0.96
Santander	0.72	Morgan Stanley	0.93
Credit Suisse	0.63	Bank of America	0.69
Standard Chartered	0.58	Citigroup	0.67
Groupe Crédit Agricole	0.54		
Barclays	0.53		
Société Générale	0.49		
RBS	0.43		
UniCredit Group	0.3		
Deutsche Bank	0.29		
Average	**0.66**		**1.04**

Source: Bloomberg.

leverage ratio, and the new European requirement soon to be introduced under Basel III is expected to be only 3 percent (EBA 2016). In the United States, the Collins Amendment to the Dodd-Frank Wall Street Reform and Consumer Protection Act requires that risk weighting of assets be no more lenient than the Basel standard model weight for the asset category. European banks have been able to rely on internal model weights even if they are lower. US banks appear to have made more progress cleansing their books of weak loans than have European banks.[40] European banks reportedly paid out nearly €200 billion in dividends in 2007–14, whereas their accumulated retained earnings remained almost unchanged during that period.[41] In contrast, for the eight US banks listed in table 5A.1, total share-

---

40. From 2009 to 2015, nonperforming loans fell from 5 to 1.5 percent of gross loans in the United States; they remained flat at 4 percent in France and rose from 4 to 6 percent in Spain and from 9 to 18 percent in Italy (IMF 2016a). In Germany nonperforming loans eased from 3.3 percent in 2009 to 2.3 percent in 2014. But Deutsche Bank "lack[s] a solid base in Germany's highly fragmented banking system" and "is mainly a global investment bank" (Martin Wolf, "Deutsche Bank Offers a Tough Lesson in Risk," *Financial Times*, October 4, 2016).

41. Boris Groendahl, "Euro Banks Splurged on Dividends Even in Crisis Years, BIS Says," Bloomberg, April 7, 2016.

holder equity rose from $738 billion at the end of 2008 to $1,044 billion in 2014 (data are from banks' annual reports).

From a systemic viewpoint, one of the worst side effects of the low market valuations of major bank stocks is that they make it extremely costly to raise capital through the issuance of new equity. If the true value of the equity is $100 per share but the current market price is only $50, then issuing new shares amounting to 10 percent of the amount outstanding will impose a value loss of 4.5 percent on existing shareholders.[42] Under these circumstances, banks are very reluctant to raise capital through new issuance. The alternative of building up capital through accumulation of retained earnings is far more attractive but also considerably slower.

Returning to Deutsche Bank, it is useful to consider the degree of capital adequacy as a possible explanation for low market valuation. At the end of 2015, total assets were €1,629 billion (Deutsche Bank 2015, 64). The €62.7 billion in shareholder equity amounted to 3.8 percent of total assets, a seemingly low level. However, under International Financial Reporting Standards (IFRS) accounting, derivatives are included in assets, whereas under US Generally Accepted Accounting Principles (GAAP) only their value after netting out is included. The market (not "notional") value of Deutsche Bank's derivatives was €515.6 billion on the asset side and €494.1 billion on the liability side, for a net of €21.5 billion. (The notional value was far larger, at €41.9 trillion [Deutsche Bank 2015, 157]). So a GAAP approach using netting would place total assets at €1,629 billion – €516 billion + €22 billion = €1,135 billion. This figure implies that the GAAP-consistent ratio of shareholder equity to assets would be 5.5 percent, a more comfortable level.

However, the sharp decline in the bank's shares implies that the market distrusts the accounts, in magnitudes that go well beyond the potential Justice Department fine. One place to look for a major gap between market valuation and book value would seem to be derivatives, which can be difficult to value (e.g., requiring internal model valuation using market inputs, level 2 assets, or, using strictly hypothesized inputs, level 3 assets). Deutsche Bank has a reputation for being especially active in derivatives. Its €42 trillion notional value of derivatives compares with $56 trillion each for Citigroup and JPMorgan Chase and $52 trillion for Goldman Sachs.[43] Using €1.14 trillion for Deutsche Bank's assets on a derivatives-netted rough GAAP-equivalent basis, the ratio of notional value of derivatives to

---

42. With N shares outstanding initially, the initial true value of equity is $100N$. The new issuance raises $50 \times 0.1N$, bringing aggregate true value to $105N$ but reducing per share value from $100 to $105/1.1 = 95.5.

43. Dakin Campbell, "Citigroup Overtakes JPMorgan as Top U.S. Derivatives Dealer," Bloomberg, June 29, 2015.

GAAP assets is 37:1. The corresponding ratios are about 23:1 for JPMorgan Chase (assets $2.4 trillion), 31:1 for Citigroup (assets $1.8 trillion), and 60:1 for Goldman Sachs (assets $860 billion). By implication, if derivatives are the problem, one might want to keep an eye on Goldman Sachs (and perhaps also Morgan Stanley, with $31 trillion notional derivatives[44] and assets of $808 billion, for a ratio of 38:1).

If derivatives were the core problem for Deutsche Bank, what degree of overoptimism in accounting would have to be present to make the recent market price trough accurate? The gap in equity between accounting and market valuation reached €62.7 billion − €14.1 billion = €48.6 billion. Considering that there are about €500 billion on both the asset and liability sides of derivatives, this figure implies about 5 percent excessive optimism in accounting valuations on both sides (abstracting from the Justice Department fine). As a rough approximation, this exercise suggests that 5 percent excessive optimism in pricing derivatives overstates net assets by about 0.12 percent of notional value (50/42,000).

If Deutsche Bank is just the tip of the iceberg for possible problems in derivatives, it could be informative to apply this parameter to other large banks. For JPMorgan Chase (with $254 billion in shareholder equity) and Citigroup (with $228 billion in shareholder equity), a corresponding 5 percent overoptimism in valuations would result in an overstatement of net assets of about $67 billion each.[45] For Goldman Sachs (with shareholder equity of $87 billion), the overstatement would amount to about $62 billion. The implied hit to equity would be about the same at Goldman Sachs (71 percent) and Deutsche Bank (75 percent) but considerably more moderate at Citigroup and JPMorgan Chase (29 and 26 percent, respectively). Of course, market valuations could be interpreted as making the judgment that at these institutions, the quality of the derivatives portfolio is considerably higher than that at Deutsche Bank.

Unlike Lehman Brothers, Deutsche Bank is solvent and has access to central bank support. Ironically, to the extent that the derivatives activity of the large US banks occurs mainly in the nondepository subsidiaries of their bank holding companies, there are relatively strict limits on what the depository subsidiary can lend to them, and liquidity support would have to go through the now-constrained Federal Reserve Article 13(3) rather than flow in the form of direct discount lending (Scott 2016).

---

44. Pam Martens and Russ Martens, "Who Is Morgan Stanley and Why Its $31 Trillion in Derivatives Should Concern You," *Wall Street on Parade*, January 21, 2016.

45. Shareholder equity figures are for September 30, 2016 (Bloomberg).

Basel III's leverage ratio is 3 percent of exposure, which includes derivatives only after netting. Using the €1,135 billion figure as the exposure basis for the leverage ratio for Deutsche Bank implies an equity capital target of €34 billion. If recent market price troughs were accurate, the implication would be that Deutsche Bank would need to raise €19.9 billion in new equity (€34 – €14.1). But regulatory decisions are not, and should not be, based on current stock market values. Even so, a potential need for Deutsche Bank to raise €20 billion in new capital if the market's recent pessimism proves right may serve as a meaningful cautionary benchmark.

Deutsche Bank has not been forced to write down its AT1 bonds, nor has it reached the point of missing a coupon payment on them. Some press reports place their total value at €4.6 billion.[46] However, this amount appears to refer only to issues in 2014. If issues in 2007–08 are included, the total rises to €10.9 billion.[47] They are subject to a write-down if certain capital thresholds are not met.[48] But even if their value were written down by half, they would provide only about one-fourth of a €20 billion hypothetical gap.

These instruments do seem to raise questions. Their coupons are in the range of 6 to 8 percent (Deutsche Bank 2016a). They are perpetuals (i.e., they have no maturity date). Considering that the current interest rate on 30-year AAA European sovereign debt stands at only 0.8 percent (ECB 2016), their risk spread even at par is extremely high. At a market price of only 70 cents on the euro, what I call the loss equivalent probability would stand at a remarkable 92 percent, meaning only an 8 percent chance of paying face value and a 92 percent chance of paying nothing at all.[49] These odds are more characteristic of high-risk gambling than long-term investing.

The illustrations above assume that Deutsche Bank's problems lie entirely in derivatives. The problems, however, may be more dispersed, perhaps

---

46. John Glover, "Deutsche Bank CoCo Holders See What Regulators Mean by Risk," Bloomberg, February 11, 2016.

47. Valuing those issued in dollars at 90.9 euro cents. Deutsche Bank (2016a) reports the total for 2014 issues at €5.0 billion and the total for 2007–08 issues at €5.9 billion.

48. On a perpetual of $1.5 billion at 7.5 percent issued in December 2014, there is a pro rata write-down on all AT1 instruments if Deutsche Bank's common equity tier 1 ratio to risk-weighted assets falls below 5.125 percent (Deutsche Bank 2014). For a list of the AT1 obligations, see Deutsche Bank (2016a).

49. For a perpetual, the loss equivalent probability is simply $s/(s + i)$, where s is the spread and i is the risk-free rate. The calculation assumes a coupon of 700 basis points and treats the 30-year AAA sovereign as the risk-free perpetual rate (see Cline and Barnes 1997, 37). At a price of 70 cents on the euro, a coupon of 700 basis points yields 1,000 basis points. With a risk-free rate of 80 basis points, the spread is 920 basis points, and the loss equivalent probability is LEP = 920/1,000.

reflecting the greater scope for mischief in the European banks' reliance on internal models in determining risk weights. It is worth considering that 78 percent of Deutsche Bank's derivatives are interest rate related (Deutsche Bank 2015, 157). On the one hand, this fact might be a source of comfort: One would think interest rate swaps would be much more plain vanilla than some other derivatives and hence much less vulnerable to mispricing. On the other hand, one might worry that the shift to a negative interest rate regime in the euro area might not help Deutsche Bank's derivatives position related to interest rates. Another 15 percent of derivatives are currency related, perhaps another source of comfort, because they are not necessarily esoteric. Of the non–Level 1 fair-value assets, by far the largest amount is Level 2 (about €700 billion on the asset side and €550 billion on the liability side), where market data inputs determine model results. The less reliable Level 3 valuations are much smaller, €32 billon on the asset side and €10 billion on the liability side (Deutsche Bank 2015, 296).

One interpretation of these decompositions would be that Deutsche Bank's problems may not be primarily in derivatives. The contrast between the low price-to-book ratio for Deutsche Bank and the near-unity ratio for even more derivatives-dependent Goldman Sachs might also be interpreted as indicating that derivatives may not be the primary source of Deutsche Bank's problem. An alternative interpretation is that because of the opacity of derivatives, there is downside risk for market perception once there is some negative shock. Contrasts with other high-derivative institutions may reflect the absence of such shocks at those institutions as much as, or more than, the inherent reliability of derivatives valuation. On balance it would seem prudent for regulators to take special care with asset valuations in derivatives, which might be playing a significant role in the Deutsche Bank case in view of the illustrative calculations.

Part of the problem seems to be a decline in franchise value as Deutsche Bank's business model is increasingly in doubt. Sarin and Summers (2016) suggest that the general malaise in market valuations of banking sector stocks likely reflects this influence. The chief executive officer of Credit Suisse recently stated that European banks are "not really investable as a sector" because of legal liability and regulatory uncertainties and "a lot of doubt" about whether the business model is viable.[50] Deutsche Bank may simply represent an unusually severe case of such doubts.

---

50. Laura Noonan, "Europe's Banks 'Not Really Investable' Says Credit Suisse's Thiam," *Financial Times*, September 28, 2016.

Deutsche Bank is not insolvent, and it would not have been even if the full $14 billion fine had been levied.[51] From its September 29 low of $11.48, the bank's share price rose 27 percent to $14.62 by the end of October, and by a cumulative 71 percent by February 1–10, 2017 (to an average of $19.6 per share).[52] In early October the bank was able to issue $4.5 billion in new senior debt, albeit at a relatively expensive spread of 290 basis points above US Treasuries.[53]

The bank's recent predicament should nonetheless help focus policy-makers' minds on the broad question of whether banking sector reform after the financial crisis is on track. The new shocks from large legal fines add to concerns about capital adequacy. Low stock market prices may fur-ther reflect doubts about asset valuations, especially for derivatives, and about risk weightings using internal models.

The overall implication of Deutsche Bank's difficulties is that addi-tional bank capital beyond Basel III targets is desirable. That implication is consistent with the finding in chapter 4 that optimal capital requirements should be 7 to 8 percent of total assets (12 to 14 percent of risk-weighted assets)—about one-third higher than the G-SIB target in Basel III.

A higher equity capital component in TLAC would also make it pos-sible to reduce the role of contingent convertible instruments in the TLAC target, a salutary shift in view of the experience of their market contagion risks. However, the predominance of equity prices below book value could mean that it would take time to phase in more ambitious equity capital targets, through accumulation of retained earnings rather than new issu-ance. Another implication is that it remains unclear whether fundamental changes will be necessary in the large banks' business models, or whether instead their equity price performance will tend to recover even without such changes as more normal monetary policies return and memories of Great Recession traumas fade. Still another implication is that shareholders would benefit from a gradual downsizing of large banks with extremely low price-to-book ratios, as long as the book valuations are correct, and that in this process it could be salutary to use the resulting profits to repurchase shares until their prices reach much closer to book value.

---

51. In late December 2016, Deutsche Bank settled with the Department of Justice for a fine half as large as the original penalty. Jan-Henrik Foerster and Yalman Onaran, "Deutsche Bank to Settle U.S. Mortgage Probe for $7.2 Billion," *Bloomberg*, December 22, 2016.

52. See www.finance.yahoo.com.

53. Neil Unmack, "With a Fine Looming, Deutsche Bank Is Still Issuing Debt," *New York Times*, October 12, 2016.

6

A Critical Evaluation of the "Too Much Finance" Literature

Chapter 2 reviews 27 studies of the costs and benefits of higher capital requirements for banks, several of which report research conducted at or for official institutions. Not a single one of these studies incorporates into its estimates a quantification of the gains that might be obtained from squeezing down the size of the financial sector by making activity more costly as a consequence of higher capital requirements. A recent strain of literature implies that such gains could be obtained, because the financial sectors are typically already too large and are inhibiting growth as a consequence. An analysis of optimal capital requirements would thus be incomplete without considering the merits and implications of this recent "too much finance" literature.

For nearly three decades, the dominant view on the role of the financial sector in economic development has been that greater financial depth facilitates faster growth. The Great Recession has shaken confidence in that view, however, because of the contributing role of high leverage and such financial innovations as collateralized subprime mortgage-backed assets and derivatives on them.[1] Important research underlying the view that financial depth fosters growth includes the seminal study by King and Levine (1993),

---

The analysis in this chapter appeared earlier in Cline (2015a, 2015e). The equations and quantitative estimates are unchanged.

1. For example, Krugman has argued that an "overgrown financial sector did more harm than good" and that "we've been devoting far too large a share of our wealth, and talent, to finance." Paul Krugman, "The Market Mystique," *New York Times*, March 26, 2009, and "Don't Cry for Wall Street," *New York Times*, April 22, 2010.

who used data for 77 countries for 1960–89 relating growth to financial depth as measured by the ratio of liquid liabilities of the financial system to GDP. They estimated that, controlling for per capita income and other influences, expected growth was 1 percentage point higher for economies at the top quartile of financial depth (average ratio of 0.6) than for economies at the bottom quartile (0.2).[2]

Recently, however, prominent studies at major international financial institutions have argued that too much finance reduces growth. Apparently working independently (neither study reports the other in its references), Cecchetti and Kharroubi (2012) for the Bank for International Settlements (BIS) and Arcand, Berkes, and Panizza (2012) for the International Monetary Fund (IMF) find that when a quadratic term is introduced into the usual regression of growth on financial depth, it has a negative coefficient. As a consequence, once financial depth exceeds an optimal level, additional financial deepening reduces rather than increases growth. Subsequent work at the IMF has proposed a Financial Development Index (Sahay et al. 2015). Finding a similar negative quadratic term relating growth to this index, the authors argue that financial development spurs growth at a low level on the index but causes slower growth once financial development exceeds an intermediate level.[3] At about the same time, researchers at the OECD provided statistical estimates showing a negative influence of financial depth on growth in OECD economies (Cournède and Denk 2015). In an environment of new doubts about finance following the Great Recession, these studies finding that there can be too much of it seem to have struck a responsive chord.

This chapter shows that these recent findings warrant considerable caution, however. For three of them, a negative quadratic term may be an artifact of spurious attribution of causality. I first show that correlation without causation could similarly lead to the conclusion that too many doctors spoil growth (for example). I then demonstrate algebraically that if the variable of interest, be it financial depth, doctors, or any other good or service that rises along with per capita income, is incorporated in a quadratic form into a regression of growth on per capita income, there will be

---

2. The other influences (all in the base year) were secondary school enrollment, government consumption/GDP, inflation, and exports plus imports relative to GDP.

3. In addition, using sectoral data for 41 countries in 1996–2011, Aizenman, Jinjarak, and Park (2015) find results that they consider mildly supportive of the nonlinear (excessive) finance hypothesis. But their quadratic term for finance is significant and negative in only 3 of 10 sectors (agriculture; public utilities; and community, social, and personal services). The quadratic term is instead significant and positive in up to 4 other sectors in the two key sets of tests (consistently for construction and for finance, insurance, and real estate). The authors do not quantify the weighted overall effects.

a necessary but spurious finding that above a certain point more of the good or service in question causes growth to decline. As for the fourth study finding a negative impact of finance even in a linear form, both technical issues and the implausibility of the logical implication that the impact of more finance would be negative even at near-zero financial depth (e.g., in poor economies) are grounds for skepticism.

Too Many Doctors? Too Many Telephones? Too Much R&D?

To illustrate the likelihood of a spurious coefficient on the quadratic term, consider three indicators that one would expect to accompany, but probably not cause, growth. Using the same countries, periods, and growth data as Cecchetti and Kharroubi (2012), regression equation (6.1) finds that growth per capita is negatively related to the logarithm of purchasing power parity (ppp) per capita income, the standard "convergence" finding. It is also positively related to a linear term on physicians per 1,000 population but negatively related to the square of this "doctors" variable. Thus:

$$g = 7.3 - 0.640 \ln y_0^* + 0.960D - 0.227D^2; \; adj. \; R^2 = 0.05, n = 290 \qquad (6.1)$$
$$(4.3)(-2.8) \qquad (+1.7) \; (-2.0)$$

In this equation, g is average real growth per capita over each of six five-year periods from 1980 to 2009, y_0^* is ppp per capita income (2005 dollars) at the beginning of each period, and D is the average number of physicians per 1,000 population in each period (see appendix 6B for data description and sources). The convergence term on the first variable is negative and significant as expected. T-statistics are shown in parentheses. The linear term on physician density is positive and significant at the 10 percent level; the quadratic term is negative and significant at the 5 percent level.

The turning point at which additional doctors per capita begin to have a negative influence on growth is at 2.12 physicians per 1,000 population. This density of doctors tends to be reached at per capita income of about $12,000.[4] In the final period observed (2005–09), Italy, Norway, and Switzerland had the highest density of doctors, at 3.9 physicians per 1,000 population. If one takes equation (6.1) literally, the consequence is that per capita growth in these economies is –0.81 percentage point lower than it

---

4. A simple regression of doctors per 1,000 population on the logarithm of ppp per capita income yields: $D = -5.37 \, (-13.2) + 0.796 \, (18.3) \ln y^*; \; adj. \; R^2 = 0.54$. (T-statistics in parentheses.)

would have been if instead they had adhered to the optimal density of 2.1 per 1,000 population.[5]

The corresponding exercise for telephones is shown in equation (6.2). This time, besides the logarithm of per capita income, the equation includes a quadratic form of fixed-line telephone subscriptions per 100 population (variable T). The coefficients are all highly significant, and as expected the quadratic term on telephones is negative. Too many fixed-line telephones reduce growth.

$$g = 19.799 - 2.279 \ln y_0^* + 0.208T - 0.00196T^2; \; adj. \; R^2 = 0.15, \; n = 290 \quad (6.2)$$
$$\;\;\;\;(7.8)\;\;\;\;\;\;(-6.9)\;\;\;\;\;\;\;\;(5.4)\;\;\;(-4.2)$$

This time the turning point beyond which additional telephone lines begin to reduce the growth rate is at 53 telephone lines per 100 population.[6] On average that telephone density is associated with a per capita income of $41,500.[7] Switzerland is slightly below this income level but substantially above optimal telephone lines (at 66), whereas the United States is at a slightly higher per capita income and lower but still above optimal fixed telephone line density (55). By implication, the risk to growth from too many phone lines is still more remote for most countries than the risk from too many doctors.

Finally, the same test using R&D technicians (100s per million population) yields the results shown in equation (6.3).

$$g = 20.07 - 2.039 \ln y_0^* + 0.164RND - 0.0020RND^2; \; adj. \; R^2 = 0.18, \; n = 132$$
$$\;\;(5.7)\;\;\;(-4.9)\;\;\;\;\;\;\;\;(3.9)\;\;\;\;\;\;\;\;(-3.9)\;(6.3)$$

Once again the coefficients are all significant and have the expected signs. The influence of additional R&D technicians on growth turns negative at 4.1 per 1,000 population.[8] This level tends to be associated with ppp per capita income of $43,000.[9] Finland and Japan substantially exceed the optimal level of R&D technicians (at 7.5 and 5.5 per 1,000 population, respectively), while the United States is slightly below it (at 3.8).

5, That is: taking the derivative of equation (6.1) with respect to D gives $dg/dD = 0.9604 - 0.4538D$. The final term shows that increasing physician density from 2.12 to 3.9 per 1,000 population changes the per capita growth rate by $(-0.4538) \times (3.9 - 2.12) = -0.81$.

6. The derivative with respect to T turns negative above this level.

7. The income level is from a regression yielding: $T = -134.37 \, (-25.1) + 17.616 \, (30.7) \ln y^*$.

8. The derivative of growth in equation (6.3) is $0.164 - 0.004 \, RND$, which turns zero at 40.65 hundred technicians per million population, or (rounding) 4.1 technicians per 1,000 population.

9. The income level is from the regression: $RND = -143.11 \, (-12.0) + 17.225 \, (14.0) \ln y^*$.

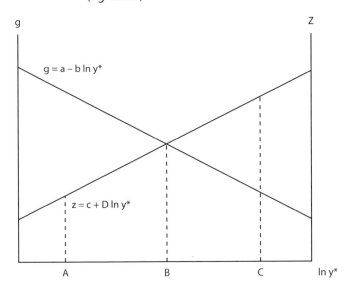

Figure 6.1 **Relationship between growth** (left axis) **and financial depth or other variable positively related to per capita income** (right axis)

g | Z

g = a − b ln y*

z = c + D ln y*

A   B   C   ln y*

Source: Author's illustration.

Demonstrating the Bias Toward Negative Quadratic Effects

To recapitulate, unless one firmly believes that too many doctors, telephones, and/or R&D technicians reduce growth, one should be suspicious of cross-country regressions showing that too much finance does so. It is possible to go further and show formally that if there is a negative relationship between growth and per capita income (as one expects from convergence) but a positive relationship between another indicator variable and per capita income (for example, doctors per capita, or financial depth), then including a quadratic form of that other variable as an explanatory variable in a growth regression will almost certainly force a negative coefficient on the quadratic term of that variable. Appendix 6A sets forth a proof of this proposition.

This inherent quadratic coefficient bias can be seen more intuitively, however, in figure 6.1. The natural logarithm of ppp per capita income is on the horizontal axis. The primary relationship of growth to per capita income is shown by the downward-sloping convergence line, *g*. Some other variable related positively to per capita income, such as financial depth or doctors per capita, is shown on the upward-sloping line *z*, against an appropriate scale on the right-hand vertical axis. Suppose the units for this other variable are chosen such that at income level B, where the two lines intersect, the value of the variable z will be the same as the growth rate g. Then if a regression of g on ln y^* is augmented by including terms z and z^2, a positive contribution from those two terms will tend to be needed in the zone AB, but a negative contribution will be needed in the zone BC where the g line lies below the z line. The only way for the contribution to shift from positive to negative will be for the coefficient on z to be positive and the coefficient on z^2 to be negative.

Too Much "Too Much Finance" to Believe?

Some of the recent "too much finance" studies arrive at estimates that indicate implausibly large negative effects for high-income countries. Thus, when the 1960–2010 equation estimated by Arcand, Berkes, and Panizza (2012) is applied to Japan, it turns out that Japan could achieve annual growth 1.6 percentage points higher if only it would reduce its ratio of private credit to GDP from 178 to 90 percent.[10] A more recent paper by several IMF staff members devises a new Financial Development Index (Sahay et al. 2015). The study then finds that at Japan's financial development (0.85) annual growth is 3 percentage points lower than it would be if the index were lower at the optimal level of 0.5 (p. 16). These estimates, especially by the IMF researchers, are too large to be credible. The latter would imply boosting annual labor productivity growth from a typical 1.7 percent per year to a remarkable 4.7 percent per year.[11] The estimates of Cecchetti and Kharroubi (2012) are less implausible in this regard. They apply private credit from banks, which stands at 105 percent of GDP for Japan (World Bank 2015b). Their optimal financial depth ratio is 94 percent. In their estimated equation, the excess finance of Japan causes a reduction in the growth rate of only 0.02 percent.[12]

It seems highly likely that the reason for the much smaller impact is that Cecchetti and Kharroubi (2012) estimate their equations for only 50 countries, whereas both the Arcand, Berkes, and Panizza (2012) and Sahay et al. (2015) studies estimate equations for about 130 countries. A central proposition of this chapter is that the supposed negative quadratic term on finance is picking up the influence of lower growth at higher per capita income. In other words, the specification of the per capita income term itself

---

10. Applying their equation (4), p. 34.

11. Japan's labor force is shrinking at 0.5 percent per year and its expected average growth is about 1.2 percent (Cline 2014b).

12. Applying their equation (1), p. 7.

is inadequate to capture convergence fully and leaves some false attribution of convergence to financial depth.[13] It is far more likely that the single per capita income variable (log of income per capita) will be overburdened and less capable of complete explanation of convergence when a large number of much smaller and poorer economies are included in the set of countries examined.[14]

The findings in the BIS and IMF studies that too much finance reduces growth should thus be viewed with considerable caution. (Appendix 6C replies to a comment from the authors of one of the IMF studies.) The reason is that there is an inherent bias toward a negative quadratic term in a regression that incorporates financial depth, or any other variable that tends to rise with per capita income, along with the usual convergence variable (logarithm of per capita income) in explaining growth. That the results may well be unreliable is demonstrated here by finding a statistically significant negative quadratic term in equations that "explain" growth by spurious influences: doctors per capita, R&D technicians per capita, and fixed telephone lines per capita. In some situations, finance can become excessive; the crises of Iceland and Ireland come to mind. But it is highly premature to adopt as a new stylized fact the recent studies' supposed thresholds beyond which more finance reduces growth.

Further Statistical Debate

A subsequent study from another international financial organization arrived at statistical findings with even more astonishing implications: For OECD countries, additional financial depth uniformly reduces growth. In the main results of two researchers at the OECD (Cournède and Denk 2015), cross-country growth equations show a strictly negative coefficient on a linear variable for financial depth (ratio of private credit to GDP) without any quadratic term. If these results were taken literally, there would be a radical policy implication: Growth would be maximized by completely eliminating credit finance. The optimal amount of credit would be zero. The authors do conduct supplementary tests that suggest the influence of finance on growth is positive at initially low levels of finance, and this enables them to state in their abstract: "...finance has been a key ingredient

---

13. This possibility is amplified in the tests of Aizenman, Jinjarak, and Park (2015), who do not include the standard convergence variable (logarithm of per capita income) in their tests.

14. The poorest country in the Cecchetti-Kharroubi dataset is India, with ppp income per capita at $5,456 in 2013 (IMF 2015c). Surprisingly, neither Arcand, Berkes, and Panizza (2012) nor Sahay et al. (2015) identify the countries they include in their tests, but with 130 countries many must be far poorer than India.

of long-term economic growth in OECD and G20 countries over the past half-century...." But they then assert that "at current levels of household and business credit further expansion slows rather than boosts growth" (p. 3). However, they seek to support this conclusion on the basis of the strictly linear negative coefficient that is estimated for the full sample, including low-financial-depth observations, and that test inescapably implies that the optimal level of finance is zero. The authors cannot reject the fully linear results when it comes to the implication of optimal zero finance but at the same time use them as the basis for asserting that at "current levels" the impact of additional finance on growth is strictly negative. The authors' (proper) insistence on a positive growth influence of finance over an initial range seriously undermines the usefulness of their main estimates.

More fundamentally, even if attention is restricted to a range of private credit above, say, 60 percent of GDP, there is a major problem regarding causality. Higher per capita income is likely to drive relatively more demand for credit as, in effect, a luxury good. If so, when combined with the long-recognized "convergence" pattern of lower growth at higher per capita incomes, the effect will be that higher credit is observed to accompany lower growth but without causality. Reduction of credit would thus not boost growth because high credit is not causing low growth; instead, the maturing of the economy is slowing growth.

It turns out, moreover, that the study's main statistical finding does not hold up to certain key changes in specification. The analysis below uses the same dataset as Cournède and Denk (2015), kindly provided by the authors, to examine this question.[15] The central findings here are that the results of that study are unreliable because, first, the tests exclude the most important variable, real per capita income at purchasing power parity comparable across countries; second, the tests apply country fixed effects and thereby throw out important information on cross-country variation; and third, incorporation of shift and slope dummy variables for lower financial depth removes the significance of the negative influence of higher financial levels on growth while tending to confirm the expected positive influence at low levels.

---

15. The Cournède-Denk results presented in table 6.1 as well as several others of their main results were successfully replicated from this database. These replications are available on request.

Table 6.1   Cournède and Denk estimates for three specifications of regressions for per capita GDP growth[a]

Variable	Annual	Annual	Five-year averages
Private credit (percent of GDP)	–0.031 (–6.2)	–0.019 (–2.1)	–0.019 (–3.2)
Investment rate		0.254 (5.0)	0.131 (2.8)
School years		0.222 (0.5)	–0.448 (–2.0)
Population growth		–0.710 (–1.9)	0.025 (0.09)
Ln (lagged national GDP per capita)			–2.029 (–1.7)
Bank crisis dummy		–1.183 (–2.5)	
Year fixed effects	No	Yes	Yes
Country trend	No	Yes	No
R-squared	0.183	0.52	0.652
Period	1961–2011	1970–2011	1961–2010
Observations	1,303	1,115	238

a. Ordinary least squares estimates for 33 OECD countries (excluding Chile due to incomplete data). *T*-statistics in parentheses. All tests have country fixed effects.
Source: Cournède and Denk (2015, 16 and 21).

The Cournède-Denk Results

Cournède and Denk use data for 33 OECD countries for the period 1961–2011 to estimate cross-country growth regressions incorporating a linear term on finance. I will focus on their results for "intermediated credit," credit to the private sector from either banks or other financial institutions.[16] Table 6.1 reports their coefficient estimates for three specifications of regressions for per capita GDP growth. In the simplest, only the credit variable is included. It has a significant negative sign.[17] In the second, once again annual data are applied, but other variables are added: the investment rate, average years of schooling, population growth rate, and a dummy variable for banking crisis. Again the credit variable has a significant negative coefficient. In the third variant, data are grouped into five-year averages. Once again the credit variable has a significantly negative impact.[18]

---

16. Namely, lines 22d and 42d in the IMF's *International Financial Statistics*. The authors alternatively use the share of the financial sector in value added, which they also find has a negative effect on growth. In contrast, they find that a third financial variable, stock market capitalization as a percent of GDP, has a positive impact on growth.

17. Table 6.1 reports *t*-statistics in parentheses. For these sample sizes, the critical thresholds for significance at the 1, 5, and 10 percent levels are respectively: t = 2.6, 2.0, and 1.65.

18. Note that in the third variant, both schooling and population growth have the wrong signs, raising questions about the reliability of that test.

The size of the negative impact of credit is extremely large. In the second and third columns, this coefficient is –0.019. This magnitude means that if credit to the private sector were reduced from 150 to 100 percent of GDP, the annual growth rate per capita would increase by 0.95 percent. If credit for such a country were eliminated altogether, then according to this linear equation the annual growth rate would rise by nearly 3 percentage points. Both the linearity (and hence optimal level of zero for credit) and the magnitude of the impact are implausible.

Nor are these results consistent with saying that, although by now the OECD has gone too far in finance, at earlier periods of lower financial depth more finance meant more growth, even though the authors seek to argue that this is the case. The absence of a quadratic term and the presence of a negative coefficient on the linear term for finance mean that additional finance reduces growth across the entire period and all OECD countries. Yet several countries had surprisingly low financial depth at the beginning of this period.

Thus, on average, Australia, Belgium, Greece, Israel, and New Zealand had private credit of only 14.5 percent of GDP in 1961–65. By 2001–05 the average for these countries had reached 83 percent of GDP. Applying the coefficient of –0.019 in the second column of 6.1, the main results reported by Cournède and Denk would imply that rising financial depth in these five countries damaged their growth performance by an average of 1.3 percent per year.[19] By this diagnosis, the five countries' GDP levels would have been 112 percent higher than their actual levels in 2001–05 if they had kept financial depth frozen at the low levels of 1961–65.[20] Such a diagnosis, however, is not credible. The basic problem is that the authors reported as their main findings results that differ from their true judgment. Instead, they should have conducted and reported tests that distinguish between economies at low versus high levels of financial depth.[21]

Even if one were to distinguish between countries starting at higher levels of finance and those starting at lower levels, the estimated magnitudes of growth impact are implausible. Consider Japan and the United States, where private credit rose from a range of 70 to 80 percent of GDP in 1961–65 to 180 to 200 percent in 2001–05. Already in 1961–65 they would have been unnecessarily sacrificing about 1.4 percent in annual growth because of excess finance, according to the equation in the third column of table 6.1;

---

19. That is: –0.019 × (83 – 14.5) = –1.3.

20. That is: $1.013^{40} = 2.12$.

21. As discussed in note 38 below, the graphical results they show on this issue do not fulfill this purpose.

by 2001–05, they would have been sacrificing 3.6 percent annual growth.[22] But if one adjusts this estimate because the negative effect really only would begin at finance of 60 percent of GDP (a threshold identified by the authors as discussed below), the resulting shift would still mean that by 2001–05 the two countries would have been sacrificing about 2.5 percent annual growth as a consequence of too much finance.[23] Such a loss would have meant that in the absence of financial deepening, their labor productivity growth by 2001–05 could have been an implausibly high 4.1 to 4.5 percent per year instead of the actual pace of 1.6 to 2.0 percent (OECD 2015a).

Another central problem with the estimates is that they do not apply the most important variable typically included in cross-country growth analysis: the logarithm of real ppp per capita income. Some tests include per capita income but it is instead for the specific country and not comparable across countries.[24] Testing cross-country growth patterns without permitting a comparable cross-country level of real per capita income is a classic instance of staging Hamlet without the Prince of Denmark.

The authors explicitly include "country fixed effects," equivalent to a dummy variable for each country, and thereby throw out potentially important cross-country information. In the tests conducted here, it turns out that this important decision is responsible for turning the influence of finance from positive to negative. Yet it is arguably inappropriate, and at best the case for including country fixed effects is ambiguous.

Reestimating the Impact of Private Credit

In reexamining the Cournède-Denk results, a crucial first question is thus whether to include country fixed effects. Classic early studies of cross-country growth typically did not include country fixed effects. Instead, they sought to obtain more variation by allowing independent variables to vary both across and within countries. These studies include King and Levine (1993) on finance; Sachs and Warner (1999) on natural resources; and Mankiw, Romer, and Weil (1992) on human capital. Although some later studies have included country fixed effects, Barro (2012) has cast doubt on doing so. He observes: "Inclusion of country fixed effects...affects the estimated coefficients of explanatory variables...variables that have little within-country time variation cannot be estimated with precision. In effect,

---

22. That is: $-0.019 \times 75 = -1.4$; $-0.019 \times 190 = -3.6$.

23. Since $-0.019 \times 60 = -1.1$, the previous calculation of growth impact (-3.6 percent) would be shifted upward over the range by $+1.1$ percentage point, thus yielding -2.5 percent.

24. Thus even the scale of the variable differs sharply with the currency across countries.

the inclusion of country fixed effects throws out much of the information in isolating the effects of X variables on growth rates"[25] (Barro 2012, 5).

The most important driver of growth in cross-country tests has traditionally been the convergence factor captured by the logarithm of ppp income per capita. This variable becomes irrelevant when country fixed effects are applied, and Cournède and Denk instead apply the (lagged) logarithm of each country's own national real per capita income. Important variation is sacrificed as a consequence.[26]

Whether to use country fixed effects is related to whether growth convergence is "absolute" or "conditional." In absolute convergence, poorer countries would tend to grow faster than richer countries, and by implication all countries would eventually tend to converge to the same real per capita income. The early cross-country growth literature applying ppp income estimates when they became available instead confronted the paradox that for 1960-90, poor countries were not growing more rapidly than rich countries, and indeed were growing more slowly (Barro 1996, Sala-i-Martín 1996). This finding led to a focus on "conditional convergence," in which each country could be converging to its own individual long-term per capita income, which could differ from those of other countries. Such variables as saving rates, human capital formation, trade openness, legal institutions, and so forth were seen as influencing long-term growth potential, and when such variables were included, the coefficient of per capita growth on the per capita income (lagged, logarithm) tended to revert to the expected negative sign rather than showing a positive sign. In this context it was a natural step to go further and apply a country fixed effect to capture still other unobservable (or "omitted variable") influences not captured in these and similar variables (Islam 1995).

It turns out, however, that beginning in the 1990s growth per capita in emerging-market and developing countries rose increasingly above that in advanced countries, such that the evidence shifted toward absolute rather than conditional convergence. Thus, per capita growth was only 1.9 percent in developing countries versus 2.4 percent in advanced countries in 1981-90 (which included Latin America's "lost decade" from the debt crisis). In successive decades, however, this comparison swung to 2.2 versus 2.0 percent, respectively, in 1989-98; 4.1 versus 2.1 percent in 1997-2006; and, in the

---

25. In particular, Barro maintains that the failure of Acemoglu et al. (2008) to find statistically significant effects on democracy from per capita GDP and education stems from their inclusion of country fixed effects.

26. Thus, for example, for the United States, average real per capita GDP in 2001-05 was 2.6 times as high as in 1961-65, a factor of 2.6. In comparison, at the period midpoint (1981-85), ppp per capita income in the United States was 4.9 times the level in Korea.

Great Recession and its aftermath, 4.1 versus 0.27 percent in 2008–14 (IMF 1999, 169; 2015b, 170). With less need to seek conditional rather than absolute convergence, the case for sacrificing variation in order to capture unobserved country-specific influences has presumably declined.

In the specific case of the Cournède-Denk estimates for the OECD, moreover, the countries included in the sample are much more homogeneous than in most cross-country tests, providing an important additional reason for excluding country fixed effects. An additional consideration is that in cross-country growth equations, country fixed effects are found in Monte Carlo experiments to exaggerate the speed of conditional convergence and thereby reduce the magnitudes and statistical significance of coefficients of explanatory variables (Hauk and Wacziarg 2009, 105).

In at least one regard, a plausible case can be made for including rather than excluding country fixed effects: The finance variable does move substantially, providing some potential basis for obtaining discrimination using within-country-only variance. Nonetheless, because the key influence of cross-country difference in real per capita income is thrown out when country fixed effects are used, and because this influence is surely the most fundamental in the cross-country growth literature, this reason alone is sufficient to prefer tests omitting country fixed effects over tests including them. The first major decision in specification of the new tests conducted here, then, is to exclude country fixed effects.

Another decision concerns the time period. The tests here end in 2007 growth, to avoid distortions from the Great Recession. Another key question is whether to use annual data or period averages. The main estimates here use five-year averages (the same approach adopted in both Cecchetti and Kharroubi 2012 and Arcand, Berkes, and Panizza 2012). The use of annual data instead will tend to introduce a bias toward a negative influence of finance on growth from cyclical patterns. Namely, in a recession, the magnitude of debt in the finance variable numerator will tend to rise from accumulation of unpaid balances, whereas the GDP denominator will tend to decline because of lower output.

Another question is whether to include investment as an explanatory variable. Because investment directly drives growth, presumably the most interesting question is whether greater financial depth benefits growth indirectly through facilitating higher investment. The tests here omit investment because otherwise there will be a tendency to understate the influence of finance working through facilitation of investment.

Table 6.2 reports the results of applying tests of per capita GDP growth on the same variable for finance as used by Cournède and Denk: the level of credit to the private sector as a percent of GDP, as well as the same variable

Table 6.2　Cline estimates for four specifications of regressions for per capita GDP growth[a]

Variable	A	B	C	D
Private credit (percent of GDP)	0.00119 (0.35)		−0.0115 (−1.6)	−0.00313 (−1.3)
Ln (private credit percent of GDP)		0.277 (1.3)		
Ln (ppp per capita income)	−2.077 (−5.9)	−2.267 (−6.4)	−3.175 (−3.3)	−1.282 (−5.2)
School years	0.191 (3.0)	0.193 (3.0)	0.019 (0.05)	0.126 (2.8)
Time period fixed effects	Yes	Yes	Yes	Yes[c]
Country fixed effects	No	No	Yes	No
R-squared	0.351	0.356	0.556	0.248
Period	1963–2007[b]	1963–2007[b]	1963–2007[b]	1961–2007
Span	5-year average	5-year average	5-year average	Annual
Observations	222	222	222	1,186

a. Ordinary least squares estimates for 33 OECD countries. Simple t-statistics in parentheses.
b. Dependent variable. Independent variable lagged two years.
c. Year fixed effects.

Source: Author's calculations.

they use for human capital (years of schooling).[27] The logarithm of ppp per capita income is taken from the Penn World Table (Feenstra, Inklaar, and Timmer 2015a, 2015b).[28]

The two preferred tests in table 6.2 are shown in columns A and B. In these tests, the independent variables are five-year (nonoverlapping) averages beginning in 1961 and the dependent variable (per capita growth) is the corresponding average for the period two years later (e.g., growth in 2003–07 regressed on 2001–05 independent variables). In column A, the finance variable turns out to have a positive coefficient, albeit not a significant one. As expected, the coefficient for the logarithm of lagged ppp per capita income is negative and highly significant.[29] The number of school years also has the correct sign and is highly significant.[30]

---

27. These two variables are drawn from the dataset provided by Cournède and Denk.

28. In four variants corresponding to table 6.2, when population growth is included it is significant only in the annual test, and its inclusion makes almost no difference in the coefficient estimates for logarithm of ppp per capita income, finance, and schooling.

29. Thus, other things being equal, at the per capita income level of the United States in 2001–05 (average natural logarithm = 10.642), per capita growth would be expected to be 2.7 percentage points lower than at the per capita income level of Mexico (average natural logarithm = 9.331). That is: −2.077 × (10.642 − 9.331) = −2.7.

30. Cross-country studies of returns to education have tended to find that the percent

For purposes of the "too much finance" debate, the key finding is that the coefficient on the financial depth variable is positive, rather than negative. Column B reports the same test but with this variable stated as the natural logarithm of private credit as a percent of GDP. This time the t-statistic on the variable is considerably higher (but still below the level needed for even a 10 percent level of significance). The estimated coefficient is again positive. The size of the coefficient indicates that as credit to the private sector doubles from 50 to 100 percent, the per capita growth rate would be expected to increase by 0.19 percentage point.[31] It would take another doubling, to 200 percent, to boost the growth rate by another 0.19 percentage point, showing diminishing returns to additional finance, but not negative returns. The higher t-statistic and (albeit only slightly) R^2 than in the linear case (column A) support this common-sense finding of diminishing returns.

In contrast, columns C and D represent "misleading" results, either because they include country fixed effects or because they use annual rather than longer-period average data. In column C, inclusion of country fixed effects turns the coefficient of the finance variable negative using the five-year average data.[32] In column D, the use of annual rather than five-year data also turns the coefficient on financial depth negative, even without country fixed effects.

It is useful to apply tests that are more in keeping with what the authors truly think: tests with specifications that allow the influence of finance on growth to diverge between countries at lower levels of finance and those at higher levels, rather than the one-size-fits-all negative linear coefficient. For this purpose, the most reasonable dividing point is a ratio of private credit to GDP of 60 percent or less. This is the threshold at which their supplementary tests show that inclusion of observations with greater financial depth begins to turn the coefficient on finance from positive to negative (Cournède and Denk 2015, 29).[33] A first approach for this purpose is simply

---

increase in wages holds relatively constant at, for example, about 10 percent, for each year of schooling added, and is actually higher at the tertiary level than at the secondary level (Montenegro and Patrinos 2013). The absolute average number of years of schooling of the adult population thus turns out to be a more appropriate specification than, for example, the percent change in number of years (which could be disproportionately larger for countries and periods with low initial average schooling levels).

31. That is: the natural logarithm of 2 is 0.6932. Multiplying by 0.277 yields 0.19 percentage point increase in the dependent variable for a doubling of the underlying finance variable (and hence an increase in its logarithm by the logarithm of 2).

32. The higher R^2 results mechanically from inclusion of the country dummies.

33. In view of their evidence of a positive relationship at lower financial depth, it is surprising that "no evidence is found of a quadratic relationship with GDP growth...." (Cournède and Denk 2015, 25).

Table 6.3   Growth results for low versus high financial depth[a]

Variable	Low (A)	High (B)	All (C)
Ln (private credit percent of GDP)	0.967 (2.4)	−0.446 (−1.0)	−0.162 (−0.3)
Ln (ppp per capita income)	−2.719 (−5.1)	−0.557 (−1.1)	−2.175 (−6.1)
School years	0.232 (2.4)	0.015 (0.2)	0.180 (2.8)
Dummy low			−3.598 (−1.4)
Dummy low x ln (pc)[b]			0.964 (1.5)
Time period fixed effects	Yes	Yes	Yes
Country fixed effects	No	No	No
R-squared	0.443	0.293	0.368
Observations	106	116	222

a. Low: credit to private sector is 60 percent of GDP or less. High: all others. Periods and lags are as in column B of table 6.2. Simple t-statistics are in parentheses.
b. ln (pc): logarithm of credit to private sector as percent of GDP.

Source: Author's calculations.

to estimate the regression equation for two separate samples: one including only country-periods with private credit less than 60 percent of GDP, and the other including all others. An alternative means of conducting this test is to include all observations, but to add a dummy variable for those cases with the finance variable less than 60 percent of GDP and allow it to interact with the finance variable.[34]

As shown in table 6.3, when these tests are conducted, and using the preferred model specification of column B in table 6.2, the results are much closer to what one would expect. The influence of additional finance is positive and statistically significant in the below-60 group (column A). The influence turns negative but is statistically insignificant in the above-60 group (column B). In the combined test, the influence of the logarithm of finance is again negative but statistically insignificant. However, the interaction term shows that this coefficient turns sizable and positive if the country-period has private credit below 60 percent of GDP, although the coefficient is not significant at the 10 percent level.[35]

When the exact variables applied by Cournède and Denk (as in table 6.1) are applied to the above 60 percent subsample using five-year averages, despite the problems with these specifications as just discussed, the nega-

---

34. That is: with $D_L = 1$ if private credit is 60 percent of GDP or less but 0 otherwise, and denoting the logarithm of private credit as a percent of GDP as $\ln(pc)$, the regression equation of column B in table 6.2 adds D_L and $D_L \times \ln(pc)$ to the set of explanatory variables.

35. The size of the coefficient becomes the sum of the first row entry in column C and the fifth row entry (−0.162 + 0.964 = 0.802).

tive linear coefficient of growth on private credit as a percent of GDP is confirmed and is highly significant. The log of lagged (national) GDP per capita has the right sign and is significant. But investment is not significant; schooling has the wrong sign and is significant; and population growth has the wrong sign. For the below-60 observations, however, private credit still has a negative sign, although the coefficient is small and insignificant. Schooling, population growth, and lagged national GDP per capita all have the wrong signs. Only investment has the right sign.[36]

Two broad patterns can be seen in these tests. First, the results for the below-60 group are extremely weak, again strongly suggesting that the use of country fixed effects and the use of lagged national rather than ppp GDP per capita income rob the explanatory role of just about all influences (including credit) except investment. Second, the poor results on the other variables raise the question of why one should trust the significant negative effect on credit in the above-60 group.

In summary, the main results reported in Cournède and Denk (2015) do not provide a solid basis for concluding that "at current levels" OECD finance is so excessive that it depresses growth, because as the authors recognize it does not apply to lower levels of finance and therefore its test statistics are not reliable. Separate tests that distinguish between low and high levels of finance find a significant positive effect at low levels but do not find a statistically significant effect at high levels. Moreover, even if the full set of data is examined without distinguishing between low and high finance observations, the sign of the finance variable switches back to positive rather than being negative if an arguably more appropriate specification is applied.[37] This specification involves (a) incorporating the traditional workhorse variable for cross-country growth regressions: logarithm of lagged ppp per capita income; (b) excluding rather than including country fixed effects; and (c) applying five-year averages rather than annual data. Their finding that more finance depresses growth is thus not robust to these three relatively basic alternatives (or, I would say, improvements).

---

36. If the same exercise is repeated but removing country fixed effects, the above-60 group again shows a significant negative coefficient on private credit, and investment has the right sign and is significant. But schooling, population growth, and the logarithm of lagged per capita GDP all have the wrong signs. Because the estimate for the most important variable, logarithm of lagged per capita GDP, is meaningless—likely reflecting the use of noncomparable national per capita GDP levels rather than ppp—the result for private credit warrants little credibility. These results and those just discussed (incorporating country fixed effects) are available on request.

37. Because the positive coefficient is not statistically significant, however, the respecification demonstrates only that the relationship of growth to finance is not significantly negative rather than that it is positive.

Finally, it should be emphasized that even if a negative linear effect were robust to estimation just for the above-60 percent of GDP private credit group, applying the logarithm of lagged ppp per capita income and omitting country fixed effects, there would still be the problem of likely reverse causation. The authors do attempt to address causality by constructing an instrumental variable for private credit, based on changes in national financial regulatory requirements. However, not only do they again apply the analysis to the full sample rather than just observations above 60 percent of GDP in private credit, but in addition they do not include lagged per capita income in their growth equations at all (neither ppp nor national), a strange test considering the primacy of this convergence variable in the cross-country growth literature.

Conclusion

Literally accepting the main results reported by Cournède and Denk (2015) would have the radical policy implication that the ideal amount of financial intermediation is no financial intermediation at all. The authors themselves instead argue that at initially lower levels of finance, additional finance benefits growth, but they do not then conduct appropriate tests that verify a shift to statistically significant negative effects of finance at higher levels.[38]

In contrast to the main results in linear specification of Cournède and Denk (2015), the quadratic specifications in Arcand, Berkes, and Panizza (2012) and Cecchetti and Kharroubi (2012) indicate a large initial range over which more finance brings higher rather than lower growth. Even those formulations yield what I suggest are unreliable turning points that advanced economies have supposedly already exceeded (Cline 2015b and appendix 6C).

That three empirical studies by teams at three international organizations nonetheless come out with the same implication that there is already too much finance in such economies as that of the United States is potentially a powerful message for policy. In particular, in the Basel Committee reforms boosting required capital for banks, a key consideration has been whether too much required capital might discourage lending and curb growth because of a resulting decline in the rate of investment. But if the too much finance results were taken literally, that outcome could be a good thing rather than a bad thing, because reducing the amount of finance rela-

---

38. Their tests reported in graphical form for successively higher thresholds of credit include all lower-credit observations at each point, and at the upper extreme return to their main reported full-sample results. As a consequence that series of tests does not constitute evidence regarding a statistically significant negative influence of additional finance within a subset of observations over a 60 percent credit threshold versus that below this threshold.

tive to GDP would (at least over the highest range) boost growth rather than reduce it. A central purpose of this chapter is to show that these studies do not have sufficiently robust findings on negative effects of finance to warrant a general policy stance welcoming rather than seeking to avoid shrinkage of finance as a consequence of higher capital regulatory requirements.

Some might argue nonetheless that the absence of a statistically significant positive effect of finance on growth in the higher ranges of financial depth means that the benefits of lesser risk of financial crisis as a consequence of even sharply higher capital requirements for financial institutions could be obtained at no cost to the economy. But cross-country growth regressions, especially with insignificant coefficients, are not a reliable basis for evaluating optimal capital requirements. Instead, a more reliable basis for investigating this issue is to use a calibrated model comparing the costs associated with higher capital requirements against the benefits they provide through reduced risk of financial crises.[39]

---

39. Economic costs from higher cost of capital and lesser capital formation associated with a shift from debt to equity will be present if the Modigliani-Miller offset (reduction in unit cost of equity capital as leverage and risk decline) is incomplete (as found in chapter 3).

Appendix 6A

Spurious Negative Quadratic Influence in Estimation Based on Related Linear Equations

This appendix demonstrates algebraically that when there is a negative relationship between a dependent variable (such as economic growth) and an exogenous variable (such as the level of per capita income), but a positive relationship between another variable (such as financial depth) and the same exogenous variable (per capita income), a regression of the dependent variable on a quadratic form of the other variable (financial depth) will tend to force a negative coefficient on the quadratic term of that variable.

Suppose the basic relationship of the dependent variable of interest, y, to the exogenous variable, x, is negative and linear, such that:

$$y = \alpha - \beta x \qquad (6A.1)$$

Suppose that a parallel variable of interest, z, instead has a positive linear relationship to the exogenous variable, such that:

$$z = \gamma + \delta x \qquad (6A.2)$$

Suppose that in a statistical test the variable y is regressed not only on x but also on a quadratic form of the parallel variable z, in an estimating equation as follows:

$$\hat{y} = \lambda + \eta x + \pi z + \theta z^2 \qquad (6A.3)$$

Substituting from equation (6A.2), we can write:

$$\hat{y} = \lambda + \eta x + \pi[\gamma + \delta x] + \theta[\gamma + \delta x]^2 \qquad (6A.4)$$

Suppose that in some sense the statistical estimation captures only half of the direct influence of x, such that the parameter η is estimated to have a value of $\eta = -0.5\beta$.

Now suppose that the statistical regression mimics the remaining half of the influence of x by incorporating the final two terms of equation (6A.4)—the contribution of the quadratic form of parallel variable z. In order for the marginal influence of x to have its full true value of $-\beta$ on the estimated dependent variable, the contribution of the marginal influence of the parallel variable will have to equal the missing amount. On this basis, it will have to be the case that:

$$\frac{d\{\pi[\gamma + \delta x]\}}{dx} + \frac{d\{\theta[\gamma + \delta x]^2\}}{dx} = -0.5\beta \qquad (6A.5)$$

Differentiating,

$$\pi\delta + 2\theta[\gamma + \delta x][\delta] = -0.5\beta \qquad (6A.6)$$

Rearranging,

$$\theta = \frac{-0.5\beta - \pi\delta}{2[\gamma + \delta x]\delta} \qquad (6A.7)$$

We know that the parameters β and δ are positive. Suppose that the exogenous variable x is such that it is also always positive (for example, the logarithm of per capita income). Suppose further that the parallel variable z is such that it is always positive even as the exogenous variable x approaches zero, such that γ is positive. Then the right-hand side of equation (6A.7) is strictly negative. As a consequence, the parameter θ on the quadratic term of the parallel variable, or z^2, is strictly negative.

In this system, then, when a regression of a variable bearing a negative linear relationship to an exogenous variable is conducted in an equation including not only that exogenous variable but also a quadratic formulation of a parallel variable that itself is a positive linear function of the exogenous variable, the result will be to estimate a positive linear coefficient and a negative quadratic coefficient on that parallel variable.[40]

The fundamental problem is that although the estimating equation (6A.3) is treated statistically as if the variable z were independent of variable x, equation (6A.2) requires that they are not independent. Correspondingly, any inference of a causal influence of z on y specified as strictly marginal (i.e., interpreted as the change in y resulting from a change in z when there is no change in x) will be spurious.

---

40. Note further that because one element in the right-hand side of equation (6A.7), x, is a variable rather than a parameter, by implication it would require varying valuation of θ to make the equation hold generally, although θ would always be negative. A reasonable assumption would be that the value of θ obtained in the statistical estimation would be that resulting from application of x at its average or median.

Appendix 6B

Description of the Data[41]

A standard specification of the growth regression used in the "too much finance" literature is adopted for chapter 6: The per capita real growth rate is related to the indicator variable such that $g = a + \ln y_0^* + bX - cX^2$, where g is per capita real growth, $\ln y_0^*$ is the natural logarithm of initial ppp per capita income, and X is the indicator variable substituted in place of the financial depth indicator.

The same countries[42] and growth indicators used in Cecchetti and Kharroubi (2012) are also used in this chapter. The cross-country growth data thus refer to per capita real growth that is constructed by using the real GDP at constant 2005 national prices (2005 dollars) and population variables available in the Penn World Table version 8.1 hosted on the University of Groningen's website. Similarly, initial ppp per capita income refers to the variable for expenditure-side real GDP at chained PPPs (2005 dollars) in the Penn World Table database.

The three variables that are substituted for a financial depth indicator as the variable of interest in the three separate panel regressions reported in this chapter are physicians (per 1,000 people), researchers in R&D (100s per million people), and fixed telephone subscriptions (per 100 people). Data for these three indicators are from the World Bank's *World Development Indicators*. As in Cecchetti and Kharroubi (2012), the regression equations for physicians and telephone subscriptions were estimated over six nonoverlapping five-year periods from 1980 to 2009, with g, the five-year average per capita real growth, regressed on the five-year average of the respective indicator variable. For the regression relating per capita real growth to the share of R&D technicians in the population, due to missing data on R&D technicians, the time period examined is 1995–2009 and the dataset comprises 44 countries (data are not available for Bangladesh, Chile, Egypt, Morocco, Nigeria, and Vietnam).

---

41. This appendix was prepared by Abir Varma.

42. The dataset is constructed from a sample of 50 countries: Argentina, Australia, Austria, Bangladesh, Belgium, Brazil, Canada, Chile, China, Colombia, Czech Republic, Denmark, Egypt, Estonia, Finland, France, Germany, Greece, Hungary, Iceland, India, Indonesia, Ireland, Italy, Japan, Korea, Luxembourg, Mexico, Morocco, Netherlands, New Zealand, Nigeria, Norway, Pakistan, Philippines, Poland, Portugal, Russia, Slovakia, Slovenia, South Africa, Spain, Sweden, Switzerland, Thailand, Turkey, United Kingdom, United States, Venezuela, and Vietnam.

Appendix 6C

Reply to Arcand, Berkes, and Panizza

In an earlier version of this chapter (Cline 2015b), I argued that statistical findings of a negative quadratic influence of finance on growth were questionable. I showed that if causation went the other way, from rising per capita income to rising financial depth, for example, because home mortgages are a luxury good, a quadratic term relating growth to finance would have a spurious negative coefficient. Arcand, Berkes, and Panizza (2015b), authors of one of the key papers in this literature, responded in an indepth (10-page) comment.

Before turning to the critiques in their comment, it is important to emphasize that even in their own study, the three authors (referred to as ABP hereafter) found virtually equal statistical performance of a formulation in which the influence of finance was logarithmic rather than quadratic. As a consequence, their own results suggest that there is little basis for stating that the influence of extra credit turns negative beyond some point rather than that this influence tapers off but remains positive. Thus, their table 1 shows in the quadratic formulation that a country with credit to the private sector at 150 percent of GDP could *increase* its growth rate by 1.57 percentage points by reducing credit back to an optimal 83 percent, but in the logarithmic formulation that reduction in credit would *reduce* the growth rate by 0.44 percentage point.[43] The R^2 in the quadratic formulation is 0.458, almost indistinguishable from the R^2 of 0.435 in the logarithmic formulation. The finance variable is significant at the 5 percent level in both formulations.

The authors do apply a statistical test to verify that their quadratic function relating growth to finance has a positive linear and negative quadratic term, yielding an inverse-U shape.[44] However, they do not apply a similar test for whether an inverse-U is significantly superior to the monotonic logarithmic form. When I apply such a test to the OECD data by adding low- and high-side dummy variables to the equation using the logarithm

---

43. The quadratic formulation has coefficients of 5.815 on PC and –3.503 on PC^2, where PC is the ratio of private credit to GDP. The logarithmic formulation has a coefficient of 0.743 on the logarithm of PC. The tests are on average per capita growth in 1970–2000 across 66 countries.

44. The test is that proposed by Sasabuchi (1980) and Lind and Mehlum (2010). It involves determining, given the covariance-covariance matrix of βx_i and $2\gamma x_i$ (respectively the linear and quadratic contributions to the derivative of growth with respect to finance, where β is the linear coefficient and γ the quadratic), whether the derivative is significantly different from zero and positive at a low level of finance but negative at a high level within the sample.

of private credit relative to GDP, the results do not provide much if any support for the inverse-U effect.[45]

If policies were aggressively pursued based on the inverse-U influence of finance on growth, punitive taxes could be required to shrink credit by more than 60 percent in economies such as the United States and the United Kingdom (where the 2010 levels reached 195 and 202 percent of GDP, respectively).[46] But a difference in explanatory power that does not show up until the second decimal place in the R^2 is too slim to warrant such policies.

Regarding the critiques of my policy brief in their recent comment, ABP (2015b) first noted that my equations demonstrated not that the quadratic term on finance was necessarily negative and spuriously so, but rather that if the linear term was positive, then the quadratic term had to be negative. But the signs could also be the reverse. That observation is true, but it is also trivial and does not constitute a meaningful critique. Inspection of my relevant equation makes it clear that the sign of the linear term does indeed have to be the opposite of the sign of the quadratic term (subject to an additional specific threshold if the linear term is negative). Namely, I showed that if half of the observed reduction in growth as per capita income rises is spuriously attributed to a quadratic influence of finance (rather than underlying convergence), then:

$$\theta = \frac{-0.5\beta - \pi\delta}{2[\gamma + \delta x]\delta} \qquad (6C.1)$$

Here, θ is the coefficient of growth on the quadratic term of finance and π is the coefficient on the linear term of finance, in a regression equation explaining growth per capita on three variables: the level (or more accurately, logarithm) of per capita income; finance (e.g., private credit as a percent of GDP); and finance squared. The other terms are per capita income (or its logarithm), x; the true parameter relating growth to per capita income, β; and the terms in a simple linear relationship showing the response of finance to per capita income (constant γ and linear coefficient δ on per capita income). With all terms in the equation except either θ or π positive,

---

45. I set the low and high dummies at $D_L = 1$ when private credit is less than 65 percent of GDP and $D_H = 1$ when it is more than 124 percent, the significance thresholds identified by Arcand, Berkes, and Panizza (2015a). Inclusion of these dummies has practically no effect on the estimates of the coefficients on either the logarithm of per capita ppp GDP or schooling, although it raises the coefficient on the logarithm of finance and turns it significant. However, the coefficient on the low-end dummy turns out to be positive and thus has the wrong sign for a strong inverse-U form, and although the high-end dummy is negative, it is not significant at even the 10 percent level.

46. Such cuts would be needed to reduce credit to 76 percent of GDP, the turning point identified in Arcand, Berkes, and Panizza (2015a). Data are from World Bank (2015a).

then if π is positive, the numerator on the right side is strictly negative and so θ on the left side must be negative. However, it is also possible that the quadratic coefficient θ will be positive, so long as not only π is negative but also $|\pi\delta| > 0.5\beta$.

But the latter condition is only a curiosity. In the large empirical literature relating growth to finance, there is to my knowledge not a single significant finding that additional finance at first reduces growth but eventually (say after finance reaches 100 percent of GDP) increases growth again, such that $\pi < 0$ while $\theta > 0$. So in the relevant application, estimating the influence of finance on growth, it is strictly the case of positive linear influence that would generate a spurious negative quadratic influence. In any event, it is unclear why ABP should be so content that any spurious influence would have to show up with an opposite sign for the quadratic term from that on the linear term. If they agree to that proposition, then they would have to recognize that their own tests preclude the result that both the linear and quadratic terms are positive, yet that is the implied alternative to their test results in which the linear is positive and the quadratic negative. If that alternative is impossible, they have set up a test that cannot be rejected, and it is not a meaningful test.

The second critique of ABP is that if the quadratic term on finance is spuriously negative because of a pattern of greater financial depth as a consequence of higher per capita income, then by the same approach I used to arrive at equation 6C.1, it would follow that in a simple linear regression of growth on per capita income and a simple (linear only) finance variable the coefficient on the latter would be negative, yet the empirical literature finds it is positive. In other words, if growth decelerates as per capita income rises, and if finance deepens as per capita income rises, then any spurious attribution would find that deeper finance reduces rather than increases growth.

But a more fruitful way to think about this issue would be to consider two types of finance: one that causes growth and the other that responds as a luxury good to rising relative demand as per capita income rises. For simplicity, the first would be business loans and the second, home mortgages and loans for consumer durables. The system I spelled out would apply to the second category of finance, not the first. Empirical results primarily capturing the first type would find a positive coefficient of growth on finance. Those primarily reflecting the second type would find a negative simple linear coefficient of growth on finance, which may explain the negative coefficients in the Cournède-Denk (2015) study. Importantly, in this interpretation, reduction of finance will not increase growth, any more than a luxury tax shifting consumption away from any other luxury good would increase overall growth.

Third, ABP take issue with my critique that their parameters indicate that implausibly large increases in growth rates could be achieved by shrinking the financial sector. I illustrated my point using the case of Japan, which (using their coefficients) could supposedly raise the growth rate by 1.6 percentage point by reducing credit to the private sector from 178 to 90 percent of GDP. They cite an alternative set of estimates, controlling for banking crises, in which reducing credit from 178 to 90 percent of GDP in Japan would boost growth by "only" 0.95 percentage point. I would consider this alternative also implausible. They go on to insist that "regressions...are not meant to, and do not, fit all points (the regression's R^2 is never one)...[so] it is singularly inappropriate to pick out a specific data point to purportedly invalidate a result." But the Japan example I gave does not involve Japan's actual residual but instead simply applies the regression line to two alternative credit levels (which the line would also predict for any other country at comparable credit levels). Nor is the large impact for Japan unrepresentative. Thus, if we take ABP's apparently preferred model (controlling for banking crises, table 11 column 4 in Arcand, Berkes, and Panizza 2015a) and apply the 2006 data for private credit relative to GDP (table 16), we obtain implausibly large estimates for the increase in growth rates that can be achieved by cutting credit back to only 90 percent of GDP for a long list of important countries.[47]

Finally, ABP run new tests finding that if I had run my regressions of growth on doctors, R&D technicians, and telephones in what they believe is the right way—including country fixed effects—the spurious but statistically significant negative quadratic terms would have disappeared in two of the three cases. I have argued above that on this issue it is more appropriate not to include country fixed effects, so my results arguably remain more relevant than their reversal of two out of three of them.

---

47. United States: 3.1 percentage points (with private credit at 195 percent of GDP in 2006); Canada, 2.5 percentage points; Denmark, 2.1; Netherlands, 1.8; Ireland, 1.7; Switzerland, 1.6; and the United Kingdom, 1.5 percentage points (private credit at 160 percent of GDP). Ironically, the same table shows Japan's private credit at only 99 percent of GDP, much lower than the 178 percent shown for 2010 in the latest World Bank (2015a) financial structure database (the number I had used), so Japan is no longer among the implausibly overstated in this exercise. ABP apparently used an earlier version of the database (Beck et al. 2010), which gave identical figures for bank credit to the private sector and total credit to the private sector from banks and other financial institutions (GFDD.D1.01 and GFDD.D1.12, respectively), whereas the most recent database places the total at 191 percent versus 99.7 percent for credit from banks alone (World Bank 2015a).

7

Conclusion and Policy Implications

The banking crisis that shocked the US economy and many other major economies in 2008–09 revealed the need for stronger banking systems. Equity capital of banks is the bulwark against bank failure, because it provides a cushion to absorb losses without defaulting on debt and provoking a panic. The postcrisis Basel III reforms accordingly call for higher bank capital as the centerpiece of strengthening the international banking system. Better supervision, including through the use of stress tests, is an important complement to higher capital.

This study examines whether the capital reform has been correctly gauged or gone either too far or not far enough. The framework of the analysis is economic optimization. Higher bank capital provides a benefit to the economy by reducing the probability of banking crises and accordingly reducing the chance of severe recessions with output loss. The cost to the economy from imposing higher capital requirements is that there is a resulting increase in the average cost of capital to banks as they shift from low-cost debt to high-cost equity capital. As banks pass along these higher costs in the form of higher lending rates—and there is some spillover to higher lending rates in nonbank finance (such as corporate bonds)—the cost of investing in physical plant and equipment increases, reducing the expansion in the stock of productive capital in the economy. The optimal amount of bank equity capital is that amount at which the marginal benefit to the economy from avoiding banking crises equals the marginal cost to the economy from lower formation of capital stock available to cooperate with labor in the production process.

Some economists have argued that banks should hold extremely high levels of equity capital because there is a theoretical reason why there would be no increase in capital cost at all. This theory is the Modigliani-Miller (1958) theorem of capital structure irrelevance, which states that the sourcing of a firm's capital as between debt and equity makes no difference whatever to the average cost of capital. The reason is that as investors perceive less risk in the firm as it deleverages from debt and moves to equity, they will provide equity at a cheaper unit cost than before. The starting point for an analysis of optimal capital requirements, then, is to test whether and to what extent the Modigliani-Miller (M&M) theorem holds for banks.

Chapter 3 conducts tests for US banks on this question. It concludes that slightly less than half of the M&M offset attains in practice. As a consequence, some cost is passed along to the economy when higher bank capital requirements are imposed, even if this cost is only about half of what would be predicted if the M&M effect were ignored altogether.

With an estimate of the M&M offset in hand, chapter 4 estimates the optimal level of equity capital. It first estimates a benefits curve, relating the value of crisis losses avoided to the level of bank capital. It then estimates a corresponding cost curve for the economy, relating output lost as higher capital requirements are imposed, based on the higher cost of capital to the economy. The cost relationship turns out to be an upward-sloping straight line. The optimal capital ratio occurs where the slope of the benefits curve equals the slope of the cost line, such that marginal benefits equal marginal costs.

The central finding is that although Basel III has made major improvements, it has not gone far enough. For the large international banks that dominate the banking aggregates, the new requirements are set at 9.5 percent of risk-weighted assets. Risk-weighted assets represent only a little more than half of total assets, because holdings such as OECD sovereign debt enjoy a zero risk weight and other assets with strong collateral (such as mortgages) also have relatively low risk weights. The Basel III target corresponds to capital of slightly more than 5 percent of total assets.

In contrast, the analysis of chapter 4 finds that the optimal capital ratio is 12 to 14 percent of risk-weighted assets (or 7 to 8 percent of total assets), with the higher end reflecting a conservative 75th percentile instead of the median outcome in the possible outcomes under differing assumptions. The Basel III capital requirements thus need to be increased by about one-third to reach optimal levels.

This study also touches on several major issues surrounding these policy questions. Chapter 5 examines total loss-absorbing capacity (TLAC), which adds other categories of finance to equity in gauging whether the bank could absorb losses. I believe that nonequity TLAC is a poor substitute for equity, because it is precisely the kind of instrument that will experience panic runs when bank stress develops (and some of it, simple subordinated debt, could not be mobilized without entering into bankruptcy resolution). The chapter also addresses the potential problem that the Dodd-Frank reform in the United States and the Banking Recovery and Resolution Directive in the European Union have gone too far in shifting from lender-of-last-resort capacity to forced bail-ins that, although designed to protect taxpayers, may exacerbate panics and do more harm than good to the economy.

Chapter 6 addresses recent research that contends that there is too much finance already in the advanced economies and that it is choking off growth. If this diagnosis were correct, a growth benefit of curbing finance through increasing capital requirements would need to be incorporated into the optimal capital calculations. Instead, the chapter finds that the too much finance diagnosis is a case of statistical illusion.

Finally, the study also provides a critical review of the literature on bank capital requirements with respect to economies of scale and the issue of too big to fail (TBTF).

Summary of Empirical Results

Size of the Modigliani-Miller Offset

The tests in chapter 3 find that for US banks, only 45 percent of the M&M offset attains in practice. As banks increase the share of their equity capital, which has a considerably higher unit cost (say, 10 percent real) than their debt finance (say, 2.5 percent real), the average cost of capital to the banks will rise, because investors will reduce the unit cost of equity capital only enough to offset 45 percent rather than 100 percent of the potential increase in average cost of capital. This finding is important, because the M&M hypothesis of capital structure irrelevance is the lynchpin of the argument of some economists that banking can be made much safer through much higher capital requirements at no resulting cost to banks or the economy.

Long-Term Costs of Banking Crises

Chapter 4 provides new estimates of the economic cost of banking crises. After taking account of the facts that on the eve of crises economies are frequently at above-potential output and productive capital not created because of the crisis would have had a finite life, it estimates the discounted total costs of a banking crisis at 64 percent of one year's GDP, almost the same as the median estimate in BCBS (2010a). Whereas some might argue that damages are far higher because of hysteresis (a permanent decline in productivity or labor force participation), it can conversely be argued that the damage estimate is overstated because several advanced economies that did not have banking crises in the Great Recession nonetheless experienced major output losses. Moreover, applying what would appear to be a more meaningful historical base period (1977–2015) significantly reduces the central expected probability of a banking crisis otherwise computed if attention is instead limited to a shorter period more heavily dominated by the Great Recession (1985–2007), as in BCBS (2010a). The analysis of chapter 4 sets the annual base probability of crisis at 2.6 percent, rather than 4.6 percent as in BCBS (2010a).

Benefits of Higher Capital Requirements

The benefit of higher bank capital requirements is the reduction in the probability of a banking crisis multiplied by the damage from such a crisis. Chapter 4 adopts the evidence in BCBS (2010a) on the response of crisis probability to the level of capital. This probability shows substantial curvature, such that after capital reaches about 7 percent of total assets, there is very little additional reduction in the probability of a crisis (see table 4.2). The calculations apply the ratio of equity capital to total assets. Based on US and euro area bank averages, risk-weighted assets (which for example apply zero weight to OECD sovereign debt) are only about 55 percent of total assets. The corresponding level at which the crisis probability curve turns nearly flat is about 13 percent for capital relative to risk-weighted assets.

Economic Cost of Higher Capital Requirements

The analysis then turns to the impact on the economy on the side of higher cost of capital. Because the M&M offset is not complete, higher capital requirements raise the average cost of capital to banks and thus the rate they charge borrowers, with a likely partial spillover to rates charged for nonbank finance as well. After considering the base average cost of capital to the economy, the proportionate increase in this cost as a consequence of higher capital requirements, and the response of capital formation in a long-term aggregate production function, chapter 4 estimates that an increase in the capital requirement by 1 percent of total assets would reduce long-term GDP by 0.15 percentage points. This figure is substantial, because it refers to the full future time path of GDP and thus occurs annually. The impact is larger than implied by typical macroeconomic models, which refer to shorter time horizons and thus do not capture the full effect of reduction in the capital stock and may include offsetting feedback effects (especially those models that build in a monetary policy response).

The Optimal Capital Ratio

The optimal ratio of capital for banks occurs where the slope of the crisis-avoidance benefits curve equals the slope of the upward-sloping line relating economic cost to the capital ratio. After considering more than 2,000 combinations of low, central, and high magnitudes for the key parameters in the model, chapter 4 finds that the median result for the optimal capital ratio is 7 percent of total assets and the 75th percentile prudential result is 8 percent. The optimal capital ratio for banks is thus 7 to 8 percent of total assets. This level corresponds to 12 to 14 percent of risk-weighted assets. In comparison, Basel III sets the requirement even for the largest banks at only 9.5 percent of risk-weighted assets. By implication, the Basel III target for capital should be increased by 25 to 45 percent. Although this increase would be substantial, it is far less than the increase needed to reach the capital requirement of 20 to 30 percent of total assets called for by Admati and Hellwig (2013)—more than three times as high as the optimal range identified in chapter 4.

Implications for Basel Targets

The optimal range of bank capital estimated in chapter 4 is the same as the median across 15 other studies reviewed in chapter 2. Those studies show a median of 13 percent as the optimal ratio of common equity tier 1 capital to risk-weighted assets (table 2.1), the midpoint of the 12–14 percent range identified in chapter 4. Even if one accepts this benchmark as the desirable target, however, two key issues of implementation arise.

Minimum or Behavioral Norm?

The first issue is whether to think of the optimal target as a minimum that banks should maintain or as an actual level that they tend to maintain in practice that exceeds a lower required minimum. At end-2014, 31 large bank holding companies in the United States representing more than 80 percent of total bank assets held common equity tier 1 capital amounting to 11.9 percent of risk-weighted assets (Federal Reserve 2015a), even though the Basel III minimum for G-SIBs is only 9.5 percent. Should one conclude that equity capital in the large US banks is already sufficient, because in practice it is already at the low end of the optimal range calculated?

How to treat the behavioral capital cushion has been a source of ambiguity in this literature. Thus, as discussed in chapter 2, a major reason why two OECD researchers (Slovik and Cournède 2011) conclude that adverse growth effects of higher capital requirements would be considerably larger than calculated by the Macroeconomic Assessment Group chaired by the

Bank for International Settlements (MAG 2010) is that they assume that banks would maintain a large cushion of about 3.5 percentage points above the Basel III target.

One way to think about the cushion is that it is a voluntary counter-cyclical component that could be expected to melt away under economic conditions less favorable than business as usual. Another way to think about this issue is to infer that the behavioral cushion implies that the system would be safe enough if the target were set at the lower end of the optimal range (12 percent of risk-weighted assets) rather than the higher end (14 percent). By implication, if the Basel III minimum for global systemically important banks (G-SIBs) were raised from 9.5 to 12 percent, large banks could be expected to hold somewhat more than 12 percent in normal years, perhaps placing them at the 14 percent higher end of the optimal range in practice. It would be difficult to argue that such a consequence would be undesirable, especially to the extent that one would expect some erosion of the cushion under more unfavorable conditions. In short, the "behavioral cushion" consideration does not fundamentally change the estimates of chapter 4, but it suggests that the lower end rather than the upper end of the optimal range might reasonably be pursued in fine-tuning Basel III.

Equity or Alternative Total Loss-Absorbing Capacity?

A closely related question is whether to count nonequity total loss-absorbing capacity—namely, contingent convertible and subordinated debt—as effectively meeting part of the capital requirement. For the reasons set forth in chapter 5, nonequity TLAC is likely to be a poor substitute for equity. Subordinated debt cannot be mobilized without going into resolution (i.e., expedited bankruptcy), but avoiding bankruptcy of the main banks should be a central policy priority, because of the risk of contagion. A stronger equity target is needed rather than reliance on a large dose of nonequity TLAC. In light of the behavioral cushion just discussed, an operational compromise would be to set the equity minimum at 12 percent of risk-weighted assets and to allow only 6 percent of the total 18 percent TLAC for large banks to comprise nonequity TLAC.

Dealing with the Risk-Weighting Problem

During the Great Recession, it became evident that measured capital adequacy could become dangerously misleading as a consequence of the risk-weighting process, including through the use of internal models—as vividly illustrated by the case of Lehman Brothers. With the average ratio of risk-weighted to total assets at about 55 percent for US and European banks (BCBS 2010a), it would seem desirable to give serious consideration to setting a minimum acceptable ratio of risk-weighted to total assets of, say, 45 percent. If a bank's ratio of risk-weighted assets to total assets fell below this threshold, for purposes of capital adequacy, its "adjusted" risk-weighted assets would simply be set at 45 percent of total assets. The overall effect of risk weighting would thus not be allowed to shrink risk-weighted assets to less than about four-fifths the amount that would be expected from the usual average.

In early 2016 the Basel Committee on Banking Supervision released a consultative document on revisions to Basel III rules that would reduce the variation in credit risk weights resulting from the application of internal risk models (BCBS 2016b). One approach the document mentioned was an "aggregate output floor" set at 60 to 90 percent of the risk weighting that would result from standardized approaches rather than internal models. In late 2016 negotiators met in Santiago, Chile to address this "Basel IV" issue of limitations on internal models.[1]

In the United States, the use of internal models for risk weighting has already been severely constrained by the Collins Amendment to the Dodd-Frank legislation, which provides that "generally applicable" risk-based capital requirements serve as a floor for banks' regulatory capital. US regulators have indicated that in implementing Basel III capital rules, capital requirements calculated under the standardized approach will be used to implement the Collins Amendment (PwC 2016). Higher floors for risk weights from internal models would thus primarily affect European and perhaps other non-US banks.[2]

A complementary way to deal with the risk-weighting problem would be to raise the Basel III leverage ratio to a more meaningful level and give it equal weight with the risk-weighted ratio in assessing capital adequacy. However, care would need to be given in setting the mapping from the ratio of capital to total assets used in this study to the Basel III leverage ratio, because the latter uses a denominator that is different from (and at least for US banks, significantly larger than) total assets. The Basel ratio is against "exposure," which includes not only assets but also securities financing

---

1. "Basel Bust-Up," *Economist*, November 26, 2016, 67.

2. The German Banking Industry Committee has warned that the Basel IV outcome could impose "much higher capital requirements" on German banks. It argues that "the Basel Committee should neither restrict nor prohibit the use of risk measurements based on internal models" ("GBIC on Basel IV Negotiations: Great Danger of German Banks Being Placed at a Considerable Disadvantage," Bankenverband press release, November 7, 2016).

transactions, security lending and borrowing, and margin lending agreements (BCBS 2014a).[3]

Large Banks versus Small Banks

The findings of this study indicate a need for higher bank capital requirements than under existing Basel III rules. However, the analysis is premised on the resulting economywide benefit from the reduced incidence of banking sector crises. Because larger banks pose the greatest systemic risks, there is a case for leaving the Basel III benchmarks unchanged for smaller banks. Smaller banks that get into trouble are much easier for regulators to place into bankruptcy, resolution, or merger, with minimal stress on the system.

Small banks constitute only a small share of banking sector assets. In the United States in 2015, for example, there were 5,309 banks (FRED 2016). Eighteen bank holding companies or banks had assets of more than $100 billion, and 3,529 banks had assets of less than $300 million (Federal Reserve 2016a). The largest banks accounted for 68 percent of total banking sector assets broadly defined;[4] the top 50 banks accounted for 74 percent of total assets. In practice, leaving the Basel III requirements at their current level for "small" banks would affect only a modest portion of the industry by asset volume (albeit a large majority by number of institutions).

Other Key Policy Issues

Lender of Last Resort

As discussed in chapter 5, in the United States the Dodd-Frank Act of 2010 weakened the lender-of-last-resort capacity of the Federal Reserve by constraining the use of section 13(3) to programs with wide eligibility (and requiring approval by the secretary of Treasury). The Fed has indicated that it would consider a program with at least five eligible institutions to meet that criterion (Scott 2016, 93). In a crisis, it would be important that the interpretation not conflate eligibility with actual inclusion, as a crisis could start with a single institution.

---

3. The ratio's treatment of derivatives tends to reduce the denominator for European banks using International Financial Reporting Standards accounting.

4. At the end of 2015, the total assets of US commercial banks were $15.5 trillion (Federal Reserve 2016a). The assets of 15 large bank holding companies in their noncommercial bank subsidiaries amounted to an additional $2.9 trillion, bringing broadly defined banking sector assets to $18.3 trillion. (Totals for banks and bank holding companies with assets of more than $100 billion are calculated from 10-K reports and Federal Deposit Insurance Corporation, *Bank Data and Statistics*, 2016, www5.fdic.gov/sdi/main.asp?formname=compare.)

An important way to restore lender-of-last-resort capacity would be to change the rules such that the nonbank subsidiaries of the large bank holding companies supervised by the Federal Reserve would be given access to the discount window that is currently limited to the depository banks within those holding companies. Without such a change, a large nonbank subsidiary could cause problems for the holding company because of the difficulty of obtaining lender-of-last-resort support through the mechanism of the now-constrained section 13(3).

At a broader level, it is important that in the aftermath of the Great Recession the principle of forceful lender-of-last-resort support of solvent financial institutions in a panic not be lost as a consequence of political backlash against the financial sector. Avoiding taxpayer losses to rescue banks is a proper objective, but by definition lender-of-last-resort lending should not lose money, because it is provided only to solvent banks. Support to the banks in the Troubled Asset Relief Program (TARP) yielded a profit for US taxpayers, not a loss. A more severe financial crisis and recession caused by reluctance to provide appropriate lender-of-last-resort support would cost the taxpayers much more, because of higher unemployment payments and lower general revenue in the more severe recession.

An important issue is the related question of lender-of-last-resort access for large nonbank institutions that are not subsidiaries of bank holding companies, which the tightening of section 13(3) could unduly constrain. The Dodd-Frank Act requires that the Federal Reserve provide supervision for systemically important financial institutions, which include not only the large US bank holding companies but also insurance companies AIG and Prudential and the US operations of Barclays, Credit Suisse, Deutsche Bank, and UBS (Federal Reserve 2016b). The simplest way to ensure lender-of-last-resort availability for these systemically important nonbanks (and foreign banks) would be to clarify that they would qualify for a program under section 13(3). An even more straightforward means to the same end would be to provide that, because such firms are under Federal Reserve supervision, they have access to the discount window in the face of a liquidity crisis.

Too Big to Fail

The call to break up the large banks has enjoyed considerable popularity in the United States.[5] A salient ongoing issue is the extent to which a too big to

---

5. Democratic presidential primary candidate Bernie Sanders urged breaking up the large banks, and both the Republican and Democratic platforms in the 2016 election called for reinstatement of the Glass-Steagall Act, which separated depository institutions from brokerage and insurance activities—a step that would substantially reduce the size of the largest bank holding companies.

fail problem exists and, if it does, whether the combination of Basel III and the post–Great Recession reforms have fixed it.

The principal response of regulatory reform to TBTF has been to impose additional capital requirements on the largest banks (an extra 2.5 percent of risk-weighted assets in required equity and an additional 9 percent in non-equity TLAC for G-SIBs). In the United States, the Dodd-Frank Act sought to end TBTF by providing for Orderly Liquidation Authority to ensure that large banks can be smoothly shut down. The Federal Deposit Insurance Corporation (FDIC) subsequently set forth the corresponding implementing mechanism, the Single Point of Entry resolution of the holding company while keeping its viable subsidiaries operating.

As discussed in chapter 5, much of the analytical framework on this issue has focused on an implicit TBTF subsidy to risk taking, which some empirical studies demonstrate. However, empirical evidence seems to be emerging that since the crisis the implicit subsidy has disappeared or even turned negative, as investors consider the additional regulatory burdens on the largest banks and (perhaps) ponder the new orderly resolution arrangements (which in the case of the European banking union include mandatory bail-ins of creditors). Moreover, data for the United States show that the largest banks did not experience proportionately larger losses than medium-sized banks in the Great Recession, which they would have done if they had systematically taken on excessive risk induced by a TBTF subsidy.

Even if the largest banks did not, or no longer, gamble with anticipated taxpayer money, dominance of the sector by a few large banks would involve an inherent potential external diseconomy in the form of the systemic spillover from the collapse of one or more of them. The central question is whether there are efficiencies from economies of scale that exceed or compensate for the spillover diseconomies of scale.

The results of research on banking economies of scale remain ambiguous. Some recent analyses show decisively important returns to scale. One study purporting to show no returns to scale when using social pricing is contradicted by another study showing the persistence of economies of scale even pricing at smaller-bank funding costs. Methodological challenges include the problem of biased estimation if a single parametric output function (such as the translog) is applied across the full size range and the problem of ambiguity in measuring what is the "output" and what are the "inputs" in the production function. Nor is there a readily accessible literature setting forth, in case studies or otherwise, analysis of key functions that can only be accomplished by large banks.

At the same time, it is taken for granted that in many other sectors (automobiles, aircraft, pharmaceuticals), large size is essential to efficiency. It is by no means evident that the prior assumption should be that in banking there are no important economies of scale. Nor is it clear that the prior assumption should be that there are no economies of scale in today's economy that warrant the relatively much larger sizes of the biggest banks in comparison to their sizes two decades ago.

In the United States, observers who worry about large bank size per se might take some comfort from the fact that in recent years the size of the largest US banks has shrunk from the peak level reached in 2007 and that their assets are considerably smaller relative to GDP than in Europe, Canada, Australia, and Japan (see chapter 5). The assets of the 10 largest US banks fell from 72 percent of GDP in 2007 to 62 percent in 2015, and the assets of the top five US banks account for 50 percent of GDP in the United States versus about 200 percent in Canada and Australia and about 125 percent in Japan and Germany (chapter 5).

The most direct implication of this study for this issue, however, is that the possible TBTF problems nevertheless underscore the importance of ensuring that bank capital is adequate to minimize the risk of financial crises. Achieving the right balance between economies of scale and negative externalities arising from large scale is best ensured by making certain that the likelihood of crises is reduced through stronger capitalization. The importance of adequate capitalization is further reinforced if one is skeptical about the plausibility of "immaculate bankruptcy" under the Orderly Liquidation Authority. It seems optimistic to presume that business as usual would continue at the major subsidiaries of a failed large bank holding company in resolution—the central premise of Single Point of Entry.

References

Acemoglu, Daron, Simon Johnson, James A. Robinson, and Pierre Yared. 2008. Income and Democracy. *American Economic Review* 98, no. 3 (September): 808–42.

Acharya, Viral, Robert Engle, and Matthew Richardson. 2012. Capital Shortfall: A New Approach to Ranking and Regulating Systemic Risks. *American Economic Review* 102, no. 3: 59–64.

Acharya, Viral, Deniz Anginer, and A. Joseph Warburton. 2014. *The End of Market Discipline? Investor Expectations of Implicit Government Guarantees*. Available at http://risk.econ.queensu.ca/wp-content/uploads/2013/10/Acharya-et-al-End-of-Market-Discipline-20141.pdf (accessed on February 24, 2017).

Admati, Anat, Peter M. DeMarzo, Martin F. Hellwig, and Paul Pfleiderer. 2011. *Fallacies, Irrelevant Facts, and Myths in the Discussion of Capital Regulation: Why Bank Equity Is Not Expensive.* Bonn: Max Planck Institute.

Admati, Anat, and Martin Hellwig. 2013. *The Bankers' New Clothes: What's Wrong with Banking and What to Do About It.* Princeton: Princeton University Press.

Afonso, Gara, João A. C. Santos, and James Traina. 2014. Do 'Too Big to Fail' Banks Take on More Risk? *Economic Policy Review* (December): 41–58. New York: Federal Reserve Bank of New York.

Aizenman, Joshua, Yothin Jinjarak, and Donghyun Park. 2015. Financial Development and Output Growth in Developing Asia and Latin America: A Comparative Sectoral Analysis. In *From Stress to Growth: Strengthening Asia's Financial Systems in a Post-Crisis World*, eds. Marcus Noland and Donghyun Park. Washington and Manila: Peterson Institute for International Economics and Asian Development Bank.

Angelini, Paolo, Laurent Clerc, Vasco Cúrdia, Leonardo Gambacorta, Andrea Gerali, Alberto Locarno, Roberto Motto, Werner Roeger, Skander Van den Heuvel, Jan Vlček. 2011. *Basel III: Long-Term Impact on Economic Performance and Fluctuations*. Staff Report no. 485 (February). New York: Federal Reserve Bank of New York.

Araten, M., and C. Turner. 2012. Understanding the Funding Cost Differences Between Globally Systemically Important Banks (G-SIBs) and non G-SIBs in the United States. *Journal of Risk Management in Financial Institutions* 6, no. 4: 387–410.

Arcand, Jean-Louis, Enrico Berkes, and Ugo Panizza. 2012. *Too Much Finance?* IMF Working Paper 12/161 (June). Washington: International Monetary Fund.

Arcand, Jean-Louis, Enrico Berkes, and Ugo Panizza. 2015a. Too Much Finance? *Journal of Economic Growth* 20, no. 2: 105–48.

Arcand, Jean-Louis, Enrico Berkes, and Ugo Panizza. 2015b. *Too Much Finance or Statistical Illusion: A Comment.* Working Paper IHEIDWP12-2015 (June). Geneva: Graduate Institute of International and Development Studies.

Ashcraft, Adam A. 2008. Does the Market Discipline Banks? New Evidence from the Regulatory Capital Mix. *Journal of Financial Intermediation* 17, no. 4: 543–61.

Bagehot, Walter. 1873. *Lombard Street: A Description of the Money Market.* Available at www.econlib.org/library/Bagehot/bagLom.html.

Barrell, R., E. P. Davis, T. Fic, D. Holland, S. Kirby, and I. Liadze. 2009. *Optimal Regulation of Bank Capital and Liquidity: How to Calibrate New International Standards.* FSA Occasional Paper 38. London: Financial Services Authority.

Barrell, R., E. P. Davis, D. Karim, and I. Liadze. 2010. *The Impact of Global Imbalances: Does the Current Account Balance Help to Predict Banking Crises in OECD Countries?* NIESR Discussion Paper 351 (April). London: National Institute of Economic and Social Research.

Barro, Robert J. 1996. *Determinants of Economic Growth: A Cross-Country Empirical Study.* NBER Working Paper 5698 (August). Cambridge, MA: National Bureau of Economic Research.

Barro, Robert J. 2012. *Convergence and Modernization Revisited.* NBER Working Paper 18295 (August). Cambridge, MA: National Bureau of Economic Research.

Bayoumi, Tamim. Forthcoming. *Unfinished Business.* New Haven: Yale University Press.

BCBS (Basel Committee on Banking Supervision). 1988. *International Convergence of Capital Measurement and Capital Standards* (July). Basel: Bank for International Settlements.

BCBS (Basel Committee on Banking Supervision). 2010a. *An Assessment of the Long-term Economic Impact of Stronger Capital and Liquidity Requirements* (August). Basel: Bank for International Settlements.

BCBS (Basel Committee on Banking Supervision). 2010b. *Basel III: A Global Regulatory Framework for More Resilient Banks and Banking Systems* (December). Basel: Bank for International Settlements.

BCBS (Basel Committee on Banking Supervision). 2013. *Basel III: The Liquidity Coverage Ratio and Liquidity Risk Monitoring Tools* (January). Basel: Bank for International Settlements.

BCBS (Basel Committee on Banking Supervision). 2014a. *Basel III Leverage Ratio Framework and Disclosure Requirements* (January). Basel: Bank for International Settlements.

BCBS (Basel Committee on Banking Supervision). 2014b. *Basel III: The Net Stable Funding Ratio* (January). Basel: Bank for International Settlements.

BCBS (Basel Committee on Banking Supervision). 2014c. *The G-SIB Assessment Methodology—Score Calculation* (November). Basel: Bank for International Settlements.

BCBS (Basel Committee on Banking Supervision). 2015. *TLAC Quantitative Impact Study Report* (November). Basel: Bank of International Settlements.

BCBS (Basel Committee on Banking Supervision). 2016a. *Literature Review on Integration of Regulatory Capital and Liquidity Instruments.* Working Paper no. 30. Basel: Bank for International Settlements, March.

BCBS (Basel Committee on Banking Supervision). 2016b. *Reducing Variation in Credit Risk-Weighted Assets—Constraints on the Use of Internal Model Approaches.* Consultative Document. Basel: Bank for International Settlements, March.

BEA (Bureau of Economic Analysis). 2016. *Table 1.12 National Income by Type of Income.* Washington.

Beck, Thorsten, Asli Demirgüc-Kunt, Ross Eric Levine, Martin Čihák, and Erik H. B. Feyen. 2010. Financial Development and Structure Dataset (November). Washington: World Bank.

Begenau, Juliane. 2015. *Capital Requirements, Risk Choice, and Liquidity Provision in a Business Cycle Model.* HBS Working Paper 15-072 (March). Cambridge: Harvard Business School

Berlin, Mitchell. 2011. Can We Explain Banks' Capital Structures? *Business Review*, Q2 2011: 1–11. Philadelphia: Federal Reserve Bank of Philadelphia

Blanchard, Olivier, Eugenio Cerutti, and Lawrence Summers. 2015. *Inflation and Activity: Two Explorations and Their Monetary Implications.* PIIE Working Paper 15-19 (November). Washington: Peterson Institute for International Economics.

BLS (Bureau of Labor Statistics). 2016. CPI Databases. Washington.

Calomiris, Charles W. 2013. Reforming Banks Without Destroying Their Productivity and Value. *Journal of Applied Corporate Finance* 25, no. 4: 14–20.

Calomiris, Charles W., and Stephen H. Haber. 2014. *Fragile by Design: The Political Origins of Banking Crises and Scarce Credit.* Princeton: Princeton University Press.

Calomiris, Charles W., and Richard J. Herring. 2013. How to Design a Contingent Convertible Debt Requirement that Helps Solve Our Too-Big-to-Fail Problem. *Journal of Applied Corporate Finance* 25, no. 2: 39–62.

Cecchetti, Stephen G. 2014. *The Jury Is In.* CEPR Policy Insight 76 (December). Washington: Center for Economic Policy Research.

Cecchetti, Stephen G., and Enisse Kharroubi. 2012. *Reassessing the Impact of Finance on Growth.* BIS Working Paper 381 (July). Basel: Bank for International Settlements.

Clearing House. 2013. *Ending "Too-Big-to-Fail": Title II of the Dodd-Frank Act and the Approach of "Single Point of Entry" Private Sector Recapitalization of a Failed Financial Company"* (January). New York.

Clerc, Laurent, Alexis Derviz, Caterina Mendicino, Stéphane Moyen, Kalin Nikolov, Livio Stracca, Javier Suarez, and Alexandros P. Vardoulakis. 2015. Capital Regulation in a Macroeconomic Model with Three Layers of Default. *International Journal of Central Banking* 11, no. 3 (June): 9–63.

Cline, William R. 1984. *International Debt: Systemic Risk and Policy Response.* Washington: Institute for International Economics.

Cline, William R. 2010. *Financial Globalization, Economic Growth, and the Crisis of 2007–09.* Washington: Peterson Institute for International Economics.

Cline, William R. 2014a. *Managing the Euro Area Debt Crisis.* Washington: Peterson Institute for International Economics.

Cline, William R. 2014b. *Sustainability of Public Debt in the United States and Japan.* PIIE Working Paper 14-9 (October). Washington: Peterson Institute for International Economics.

Cline, William R. 2015a. *Further Statistical Debate on "Too Much Finance."* PIIE Working Paper 15-16 (October). Washington: Peterson Institute for International Economics

Cline, William R. 2015b. *Quantity Theory of Money Redux? Will Inflation Be the Legacy of Quantitative Easing?* PIIE Policy Brief 15-7 (May). Washington: Peterson Institute for International Economics.

Cline, William R. 2015c. *Testing the Modigliani-Miller Theorem of Capital Structure Irrelevance for Banks.* PIIE Working Paper 15-8 (April). Washington: Peterson Institute for International Economics.

Cline, William R. 2015d. Thoughts on Systemic Risk Regulation (June). Washington: Peterson Institute for International Economics.

Cline, William R. 2015e. *Too Much Finance or Statistical Illusion?* PIIE Policy Brief 15-9 (June). Washington: Peterson Institute for International Economics.

Cline, William R. 2016a. *Benefits and Costs of Higher Capital Requirements for Banks.* PIIE Working Paper 16-6 (March). Washington: Peterson Institute for International Economics.

Cline, William R. 2016b. *Systemic Implications of Problems at a Major European Bank.* PIIE Policy Brief 16-19 (October). Washington: Peterson Institute for International Economics.

Cline, William R., and Kevin J. S. Barnes. 1997. *Spreads and Risk in Emerging Markets Lending.* IIF Research Paper no. 97-1. Washington: Institute of International Finance.

Cline, William R., and Joseph Gagnon. 2013. *Lehman Died, Bagehot Lives: Why Did the Fed and Treasury Let a Major Wall Street Bank Fail?* PIIE Policy Brief 13-21 (September). Washington: Peterson Institute for International Economics.

Cohen, Benjamin H. 2013. How Have Banks Adjusted to Higher Capital Requirements? *BIS Quarterly Review* (September): 25–41.

Cohen, Benjamin H., and Michela Scatigna. 2014. *Banks and Capital Requirements: Channels of Adjustment.* BIS Working Papers 443 (March). Basel: Bank for International Settlements.

Comptroller (Office of the Comptroller of the Currency). 2014. Regulatory Capital Rules: Regulatory Capital, Enhanced Supplementary Leverage Ratio Standards for Certain Bank Holding Companies and Their Subsidiary Insured Depository Institutions. *Federal Register* 79, no. 84 (May 1). Washington: GPO.

Cournède, Boris, and Oliver Denk. 2015. *Finance and Economic Growth in OECD and G20 Countries.* OECD Economics Department Working Paper 1223 (June). Paris: Organization for Economic Cooperation and Development.

Dagher, Jihad, Giovanni Dell'Ariccia, Luc Laeven, Lev Ratnovski, and Hui Tong. 2016. *Benefits and Costs of Bank Capital.* IMF Staff Discussion Note 16 (February). Washington: International Monetary Fund.

Damodaran, Aswath. 2007. *Valuation Approaches and Metrics: A Survey of Theory and Evidence.* Boston: Now Publishers.

Damodaran, Aswath. 2015. *S&P Earnings: 1960-Current.* New York: New York University.

Davies, Richard, and Belinda Tracey. 2014. Too Big to Be Efficient? The Impact of Implicit Subsidies on Estimates of Scale Economies for Banks. *Journal of Money, Credit, and Banking* 46, no. 1 (February): 219–53.

Davis Polk. 2014. *Supplementary Leverage Ratio (SLR)* (September). New York: Davis Polk & Wardwell LLP. Available at www.davispolk.com/dodd-frank/memoranda/bank-capital.

DeAngelo, Harry, and René Stulz. 2013. *Why High Leverage Is Optimal for Banks* (May). Los Angeles: University of Southern California, Marshall School of Business.

De Nicolò, Gianni. 2015. *Revisiting the Impact of Bank Capital Requirements on Lending and Real Activity* (June). Washington and Munich: International Monetary Fund and CESifo.

De Nicolò, Gianni, Andrea Gamba, and Marcella Lucchetta. 2014. Microprudential Regulation in a Dynamic Model of Banking. *Review of Financial Studies* 27, no. 7: 2097-139.

de-Ramon, Sebastián, Zanna Iscenko, Matthew Osborne, Michael Straughan, and Peter Andrews. 2012. *Measuring the Impact of Prudential Policy on the Macroeconomy*. Occasional Paper 42 (May). London: Financial Services Authority.

Deutsche Bank. 2014. *Fixed Income/AT1 Update.* Frankfurt. Available at www.db.com/ir/en/download/Fixed_Income_ AT1_Update_Nov_2014.pdf.

Deutsche Bank. 2015. *Annual Report 2015: Passion to Perform.* Frankfurt: Deutsche Bank Group.

Deutsche Bank. 2016a. *Capital Instruments.* Frankfurt. Available at www.db.com/ir/en/capital-instruments.htm.

Deutsche Bank. 2016b. *Available Distribution Items (ADI).* Frankfurt. Available at www.db.com/ir/en/available-distributable-items.htm.

Diebold, Francis X., and Kamil Yilmaz. 2014. On the network topology of variance decompositions: Measuring the connectedness of financial firms. *Journal of Econometrics* 182, no. 1: 119–34.

EBA (European Banking Authority). 2016. *EBA Recommends Introducing the Leverage Ratio in the EU* (August). London.

ECB (European Central Bank). 2015. *Bank Interest Rates—Loans to Corporations (New Business).* Statistical Data Warehouse. Frankfurt.

ECB (European Central Bank). 2016. *Euro Area Yield Curve* (October). Frankfurt. Available at www.ecb.europa.eu/stats/ money/yc/html/index.en.html.

Eisenberg, Larry, and Thomas H. Noe. 2001. Systemic Risk in Financial Systems. *Management Science* 47, no. 2 (February): 236–49.

Elsinger, H., A. Lehar, and M. Summer. 2006. Using Market Information for Banking System Risk Assessment. *International Journal of Central Banking* 2, no. 1: 137–66.

European Commission. 2011. *Quarterly Report on the Euro Area* 10, no. 1 (April). Brussels.

European Commission. 2014. EU Bank Recovery and Resolution Directive (BRRD): Frequently Asked Questions. Memo/14/297 (April). Brussels.

Evanoff, Douglas D., Julapa A. Jagtiani, and Taisuke Nakata. 2011. Enhancing Market Discipline in Banking: The Role of Subordinated Debt in Financial Regulatory Reform. *Journal of Economics and Business* 63, no. 1: 1–22.

Fama, Eugene F., and Kenneth R. French. 1992. The Cross-Section of Expected Stock Returns. *Journal of Finance* 67, no. 2 (June): 427–65.

Fama, Eugene F., and Kenneth R. French. 2004. The Capital Asset Pricing Model: Theory and Evidence. *Journal of Economic Perspectives* 18, no. 3 (Summer): 25–46.

FDIC (Federal Deposit Insurance Corporation). 2015. *Capital Adequacy Guidelines for Bank Holding Companies: Tier 1 Leverage Measure* (May 30). Washington.

Federal Reserve. 2013. Press Release, July 2. Washington. Available at www.federalreserve.gov/newsevents/press/bcreg/20130702a.htm.

Federal Reserve. 2014. *Financial Accounts of the United States (Z.1): Third Quarter 2014.* Washington.

Federal Reserve. 2015a. *Comprehensive Capital Analysis and Review 2015: Assessment Framework and Results* (March). Washington: Federal Reserve.

Federal Reserve. 2015b. *Consumer Credit—G.19*. Washington.

Federal Reserve. 2015c. *Selected Interest Rates—H.15*. Washington.

Federal Reserve. 2016a. *Assets and Liabilities of Commercial Banks in the U.S. – H.8*. Washington.

Federal Reserve. 2016b. *Large Institution Supervision Coordinating Committee*. Available at www.federalreserve.gov/bankinforeg/large-institution-supervision.htm.

Federal Reserve. 2016c. *Selected Interest Rates – H.15*. Washington.

Feenstra, Robert C., Robert Inklaar, and Marcel P. Timmer. 2015a. The Next Generation of the Penn World Table. *American Economic Review* 105, no. 10 (October): 3150–82.

Feenstra, Robert C., Robert Inklaar, and Marcel P. Timmer. 2015b. Penn World Table 8.1. Available at www.rug.nl/research/ggdc/data/pwt/ pwt-8.1.

Flannery, Mark J., and Sorin M. Sorescu. 1996. Evidence of Bank Market Discipline in Subordinated Debenture Yields: 1983-1991. *Journal of Finance* 51, no. 4: 1347–77.

FRED (Federal Reserve Economic Data, St. Louis Fed). 2016. *Commercial Banks in the U.S.* Available at https.fred.stlouisfed.org/series/USNUM.

FSB (Financial Stability Board). 2015a. *Historical Losses and Recapitalization Needs* (November). Basel.

FSB (Financial Stability Board). 2015b. *Implementation and Effects of the G20 Financial Regulatory Reforms* (November). Basel.

FSB (Financial Stability Board). 2015c. *Summary of Findings from the TLAC Impact Assessment Studies* (November). Basel.

FSB (Financial Stability Board). 2015d. *Total Loss-Absorbing Capacity (TLAC) Term Sheet* (November). Basel.

FSB (Financial Stability Board). 2015e. 2015 Update of List of Global Systemically Important Banks (G-SIBs) (November). Basel.

Fukao, Mitsuhiro. 2003. Financial Sector Profitability and Double-Gearing. In *Structural Impediments to Growth in Japan*, ed. Magnus Blomström, Jennifer Corbett, Fumio Hayashi, and Anil Kashyap. Chicago: University of Chicago Press.

Gambacorta, Leonardo. 2011. Do Bank Capital and Liquidity Affect Real Economic Activity in the Long Run? A VECM Analysis for the US. *Economic Notes* 40, no. 3 (November): 75–91.

Gambacorta, Leonardo, and Hyun Song Shin. 2016. *Why Bank Capital Matters for Monetary Policy*. BIS Working Papers no. 558 (April). Basel: Bank for International Settlements.

Goodhart, Charles, and Emilios Avgouleas. 2014. *A Critical Evaluation of Bail-ins as Bank Recapitalisation Mechanisms*. CEPR Discussion Paper 10065 (July). London: Centre for Economic Policy Research.

GAO (Government Accountability Office). 2014. *Large Bank Holding Companies: Expectations of Government Support*. Report GAO-14-621. Washington.

Geithner, Timothy F. 2016. Are We Safer? The Case for Strengthening the Bagehot Arsenal. Per Jacobsson Lecture, IMF–World Bank Annual Meetings, October 8. Available at www.perjacobsson.org/lectures/100816.pdf.

Goldstein, Morris. 2017. *Banking's Final Exam: Stress Testing and Bank-Capital Reform*. Washington: Peterson Institute for International Economics.

Graham, B., and D. Dodd. 1951. *Securities Analysis: Principles and Techniques*. New York: McGraw-Hill.

Haldane, A. 2010. The $100 Billion Question. *BIS Review* 40: 1–19.

Hanson, Samuel G., Anil Kashyap, and Jeremy C. Stein. 2010. *A Macroprudential Approach to Financial Regulation*. Chicago Booth Working Paper no. 10-29 (November). Chicago: University of Chicago Booth School of Business.

Hauk, William R., Jr., and Romain Wacziarg. 2009. A Monte Carlo Study of Growth Regressions. *Journal of Economic Growth* 14: 103–47.

Herring, Richard J. 2011. The Capital Conundrum. *International Journal of Central Banking* 7, no. 4: 171–87.

Hindlian, Amanda, Sandra Lawson, Jorge Murillo, Koby Sadan, Steve Strongin, and Balakrishna Subramanian. 2013. *Measuring the TBTF Effect on Bond Pricing* (May). Goldman Sachs Global Markets Institute.

Hoenig, Thomas M. 2013. Basel III Capital: A Well-Intentioned Illusion. Paper presented at the 2013 Research Conference of the International Association of Deposit Insurers, Basel, April 9.

Hughes, J., and L. Mester. 2013. Who Said Large Banks Don't Experience Scale Economies? Evidence from a Risk-Return-Driven Cost Function. *Journal of Financial Intermediation* 22, no. 4: 559–85.

IIF (Institute of International Finance). 2011. *The Cumulative Impact on the Global Economy of Changes in the Financial Regulatory Framework* (September). Washington.

IMF (International Monetary Fund). 1999. *World Economic Outlook, October*. Washington.

IMF (International Monetary Fund). 2007a. *World Economic Outlook Database, April 2007*. Washington.

IMF (International Monetary Fund). 2007b. *World Economic Outlook Database, October 2007*. Washington.

IMF (International Monetary Fund). 2008a. *Iceland: Article IV Consultation*. IMF Country Report 08/367 (December). Washington.

IMF (International Monetary Fund). 2008b. *Switzerland: Article IV Consultation*. IMF Country Report 08/170 (May). Washington.

IMF (International Monetary Fund). 2008c. *World Economic Outlook Database, April 2008*. Washington.

IMF (International Monetary Fund). 2010. *Global Financial Stability Report: Meeting New Challenges to Stability and Building a Safer System*. World Economic and Financial Surveys (April) Washington.

IMF (International Monetary Fund). 2014. *Global Financial Stability Report: Moving from Liquidity to Growth-Driven Markets*. World Economic and Financial Surveys (April). Washington.

IMF (International Monetary Fund). 2015a. *International Financial Statistics*. Washington.

IMF (International Monetary Fund). 2015b. *World Economic Outlook, April 2015*. Washington.

IMF (International Monetary Fund). 2015c. *World Economic Outlook Database, October 2015*. Washington.

IMF (International Monetary Fund). 2016a. *Financial Soundness Indicators*. Washington.

IMF (International Monetary Fund). 2016b. *Germany: Financial System Stability Assessment*. IMF Country Report no. 1/189. Washington.

IMF (International Monetary Fund). 2016c. *World Economic Outlook Database, April 2016*. Washington.

Islam, Nazrul. 1995. Growth Empirics: A Panel Data Approach. *Quarterly Journal of Economics* 110, no. 4 (November): 1127–70.

Kashyap, Anil K., Raghuram G. Rajan, and Jeremy C. Stein. 2008. Rethinking Capital Regulation. In *Maintaining Stability in a Changing Financial System*: 431–71. Kansas City: Federal Reserve Board of Kansas City.

Kashyap, Anil K., Jeremy C. Stein, and Samuel Hanson. 2010. *An Analysis of the Impact of "Substantially Heightened" Capital Requirements on Large Financial Institutions* (May). Chicago: University of Chicago, Booth School of Business.

Kato, R., S. Kobayashi, and Y. Saita. 2010. *Calibrating the Level of Capital: The Way We See It*. Bank of Japan Working Paper 10-E-6. Tokyo.

Keeley, Michael C. 1990. Deposit Insurance, Risk, and Market Power in Banking. *American Economic Review* 80, no. 5 (December): 1183–200.

King, Michael R. 2009. The Cost of Equity for Global Banks: A CAPM Perspective from 1990 to 2009. *BIS Quarterly Review* (September): 59–73.

King, Michael R. 2010. *Mapping Capital and Liquidity Requirements to Bank Lending Spreads*. BIS Working Paper no. 324 (November). Basel: Bank for International Settlements.

King, Robert G., and Ross Levine. 1993. Finance and Growth: Schumpeter Might Be Right. *Quarterly Journal of Economics* 108, no. 3 (August): 717–37.

Kohn, Donald. 2011. Will the Federal Reserve Be Able to Serve as Lender of Last Resort in the Next Financial Crisis? Paper presented at the 56th Economic Conference, Federal Reserve Bank of Boston, October 18–19.

Kotlikoff, Laurence J. 2010. *Jimmy Stewart Is Dead: Ending the World's Ongoing Financial Plague with Limited Purpose Banking*. Hoboken, NJ: John Wiley & Sons.

Kragh-Sørensen, Kasper. 2012. *Optimal Capital Adequacy Ratios for Norwegian Banks*. Staff Memo 29. Oslo: Norges Bank.

Kupiec, Paul, and Peter Wallison. 2015. Can the "Single Point of Entry" Strategy Be Used to Recapitalize a Systemically Important Failing Bank? *Journal of Financial Stability* 20: 184–97.

Küting, Karlheinz, Peter Lorson, Raphael Eichenlaub, and Marc Toebe. 2011. Die Ausschüttungssperre im Neuen Deutschen Bilanzrecht Nach §268 Abs. 8 HGB. GmbH-Rundschau, 102. Jahrgang, Heft 1, 1-10. [The Payout Block in the New German Accounting Law under Section 268 Paragraph 8, Commercial Code of Germany].

Laeven, Luc, and Fabian Valencia. 2008. *Systemic Banking Crises: A New Database*. IMF Working Paper 08/224 (November). Washington: International Monetary Fund.

Laeven, Luc, and Fabian Valencia. 2012. *Systemic Banking Crises Database: An Update*. IMF Working Paper 12/163 (June). Washington: International Monetary Fund.

Laeven, Luc, Lev Ratnovski, and Hui Tong. 2014. *Bank Size and Systemic Risk*. IMF Staff Discussion Note 14/04 (May). Washington: International Monetary Fund.

Liikanen Report. 2012. High-Level Expert Group: Reforming the Structure of the EU Banking Sector (October). Brussels: European Commission.

Lind, Jo Thori, and Halvor Mehlum. 2010. With or Without U? The Appropriate Test for a U-Shaped Relationship. *Oxford Bulletin of Economics and Statistics* 72, no. 1: 109–18.

MAG (Macroeconomic Assessment Group). 2010. *Assessing the Macroeconomic Impact of the Transition to Stronger Capital and Liquidity Requirements* (December). Basel: Bank for International Settlements.

MAG (Macroeconomic Assessment Group). 2011. *Assessment of the Macroeconomic Impact of Higher Loss Absorbency for Global Systemically Important Banks.* Basel: Bank for International Settlements. Available at www.bis.org/publ/bcbs202.htm.

Malkiel, Burton G. 2015. *A Random Walk Down Wall Street.* New York: W. W. Norton.

Mankiw, N. Gregory, David Romer, and David N. Weil. 1992. A Contribution to the Empirics of Economic Growth. *Quarterly Journal of Economics* 107, no. 2 (May): 407–37.

Marques, Luis Brandão, Ricardo Correa, and Horacio Sapriza. 2013. *International Evidence on Government Support and Risk Taking in the Banking Sector.* IMF Working Paper 13/94 (May). Washington: International Monetary Fund.

McAllister, Patrick H., and Douglas McManus. 1993. Resolving the Scale Efficiency Puzzle in Banking. *Journal of Banking and Finance* 17: 389–405.

Medley, Bill. 1994. *Riegle-Neal Interstate Banking and Branching Efficiency Act of 1994.* Washington: Federal Reserve. Available at www.federalreservehistory.org/Events/DetailView/50.

Mendicino, Caterina, Kalin Nikolov, Javier Suarez, and Dominik Supera. 2015. Welfare Analysis of Implementable Macroprudential Policy Rules: Heterogeneity and Trade-offs. European Central Bank, Frankfurt. Mimeo (August).

Merler, Silvia, and Nicolas Véron. 2015. Moving Away from Banks: Comparing Challenges in China and the European Union. In *China's Economic Transformation: Lessons, Impact, and the Path Forward.* PIIE Briefing 15-3 (September). Washington: Peterson Institute for International Economics.

Merton, Robert C. 1974. On the Pricing of Corporate Debt: The Risk Structure of Interest Rates. *Journal of Finance* 29, no. 2: 449–70.

Miles, David, Jing Yang, and Gilberto Marcheggiano. 2012. Optimal Bank Capital. *Economic Journal* 123, no. 567 (March): 1–37.

Miller, Merton H. 1995. Do the M&M Propositions Apply to Banks? *Journal of Banking and Finance* 19, no. 3-4: 483–89.

Minneapolis Plan. 2016. *The Minneapolis Plan to End Too Big to Fail* (November). Minneapolis: Federal Reserve Bank of Minneapolis.

Modigliani, Franco, and Merton H. Miller. 1958. The Cost of Capital, Corporation Finance and the Theory of Investment. *American Economic Review* 48, no. 3 (June): 261–97.

Montenegro, Claudio E., and Harry Anthony Patrinos. 2013. *Returns to Schooling Around the World.* Background Paper for the World Development Report 2013. Washington: World Bank.

Neumann, Uwe, and Philip Turner. 2005. The Regulation of Banks in Emerging Markets. In *Regulation of Financial Intermediaries in Emerging Markets*, ed. T. T. Ram Mohan, Rupa Rege Nitsure, and Mathew Joseph. New Delhi: Response Books.

Nguyen, Tu. 2013. The Disciplinary Effect of Subordinated Debt on Bank Risk Taking. *Journal of Empirical Finance* 23: 117–41.

Noss, Joseph, and Rhiannon Sowerbutts. 2012. *The Implicit Subsidy of Banks*. Financial Stability Paper 15 (May). London: Bank of England.

OECD (Organization for Economic Cooperation and Development). 2015a. *Growth in GDP Per Capita, Productivity and ULC*. Paris. Available at http://stats.oecd.org/Index.aspx?DataSetCode=PDB_GR.

OECD (Organization for Economic Cooperation and Development). 2015b. *Population*. Paris. Available at https://data.oecd.org/pop/population.htm#indicator-chart.

OECD (Organization for Economic Cooperation and Development). 2015c. *Working Age Population*. Paris. Available at https://data.oecd.org/pop/working-age-population.htm#indicator-chart.

Persaud, Avinash D. 2014. *Why Bail-In Securities Are Fool's Gold*. PIIE Policy Brief 14-23 (November). Washington: Peterson Institute for International Economics.

PwC (PricewaterhouseCoopers). 2016. Five key points from Basel's proposed restrictions on internal models for credit risk. *First Take*, April 1. Available at www.pwcregulatory.com.

Rajan, Raghuram G., and Luigi Zingales. 1995. What Do We Know about Capital Structure: Some Evidence from International Data. *Journal of Finance* 50, no. 5 (December): 1421–60.

Reinhart, Carmen M., and Kenneth S. Rogoff. 2008. *Banking Crises: An Equal Opportunity Menace*. NBER Working Paper 14587 (December). Cambridge, MA: National Bureau of Economic Research.

Roger, S., and J. Vlček. 2011. *Macroeconomic Costs of Higher Bank Capital and Liquidity Requirements*. IMF Working Paper 11/103. Washington: International Monetary Fund.

Sachs, Jeffrey D., and Andrew Warner. 1999. The Big Push, Natural Resource Booms and Growth. *Journal of Development Economics* 59, no. 1: 43–76.

Sahay, Ratna, Martin Čihák, Papa N'Diaye, Adolfo Barajas, Ran Bi, Diana Ayala, Yuan Gao, Annette Kyobe, Lam Nguyen, Christian Saborowski, Katsiaryna Svirydzenka, and Seyed Reza Yousefi. 2015. *Rethinking Financial Deepening: Stability and Growth in Emerging Markets*. IMF Staff Discussion Note 15/08 (May). Washington: International Monetary Fund.

Sala-i-Martín, Xavier. 1996. The Classical Approach to Convergence Analysis. *Economic Journal* 10, no. 437 (July): 1019–36.

Sarin, Natasha, and Lawrence H. Summers. 2016. Have Big Banks Gotten Safer? Brookings Papers on Economic Activity, Conference Draft, September 15–16. Washington: Brookings Institution.

Sasabuchi, S. 1980. A Test of a Multivariate Normal Mean with Composite Hypotheses Determined by Linear Inequalities. *Biometrika* 67: 429–39.

Schanz, Jochen, David Aikman, Paul Collazos, Marc Farag, David Gregory, and Sujit Kapadia. 2011. The Long-Term Economic Impact of Higher Capital Levels. In *Macroprudential Regulation and Policy*, BIS Paper no. 60 (December): 73–81. Basel: Bank for International Settlements.

Scott, Hal S. 2016. *Connectedness and Contagion: Protecting the Financial System from Panics*. Cambridge, MA: MIT Press.

Siegert, Caspar, and Matthew Willison. 2015. *Estimating the Extent of the 'Too Big to Fail' Problem—A Review of Existing Approaches.* Financial Stability Paper 32 (February). London: Bank of England.

Sironi, Andrea. 2003. Testing for Market Discipline in the European Banking Industry: Evidence from Subordinated Debt Issues. *Journal of Money, Credit, and Banking* 35, no. 3: 443–72.

Skeel, David A., Jr. 2014. *Single Point of Entry and the Bankruptcy Alternative.* Faculty Scholarship Paper 949 (February). Philadelphia: University of Pennsylvania School of Law. Available at http://scholarship.law.upenn.edu/faculty_scholarship/949.

Slovik, Patrick, and Boris Cournède. 2011. *Macroeconomic Impact of Basel III.* OECD Economics Department Working Paper 844. Paris: Organization for Economic Cooperation and Development. Available at www.oecd-ilibrary.org/economics/macroeconomic-impact-of-basel-iii_5kghwnhkkjs8-en.

Tahyar, Margaret E. 2010. *Collins Amendment Sets Minimum Capital Requirements* (July). Cambridge, MA: Harvard Law School Forum on Corporate Governance. Available at https://corpgov.law.harvard.edu/2010/07/08/collins-amendment-sets-minimum-capital-requirements.

Tsatsaronis, Kostas, et al. 2015. *Assessing the Economic Costs and Benefits of TLAC Implementation.* Report to the Financial Stability Board (November). Basel: Bank for International Settlements.

Van den Heuvel, S. J. 2008. The Welfare Costs of Bank Capital Requirements. *Journal of Monetary Economics* 55: 298–320.

Von Furstenberg, George M. 2014. *Contingent Convertibles [CoCos]: A Potent Instrument for Financial Reform.* Singapore: World Scientific Publishing.

Webber, Lewis, and Matthew Willison. 2011. *Systemic Capital Requirements.* Working Paper 436. London: Bank of England.

Wheelock, D. C., and P. W. Wilson. 2012. Do Large Banks Have Lower Costs? New Estimate of Return to Scale for US Banks. *Journal of Money, Credit, and Banking* 44, no. 1: 171–99.

World Bank. 2015a. *Global Financial Development Database.* Washington. Available at http://data.worldbank.org/data-catalog/global-financial-development.

World Bank. 2015b. *World Development Indicators.* Washington. Available at http://databank.worldbank.org/data/views/variableSelection/selectvariables.aspx?source=world-development-indicators.

Yan, Meilan, Maximilian J. B. Hall, and Paul Turner. 2011. *A Cost-Benefit Analysis of Basel III: Some Evidence from the UK.* Working Paper 2011-05. Loughborough, UK: Department of Economics, Loughborough University.

Yang, Jing, and Kostas Tsatsaronis. 2012. Bank Stock Returns, Leverage and the Business Cycle. *BIS Quarterly Review* (March): 45–59.

Index

stocks, price of, 61
stress tests, 1, 18–19
studies, quantitative findings of, 4
Stulz, René, 56
subordinated debt, 1, 118, 133–34
    Basel accord on, 2
    disciplinary role of, 135–36
    mandatory requirements, 136
    as part of capital requirement, 210
    and risk of panic dynamics, 19, 163
    risk taking of banks and, 139
    TLAC and, 9–10
Summers, Lawrence H., 174
Sweden
    financial crisis, 91
    output loss estimates from banking
        crises, 92t
Switzerland
    combined assets of large banks as
        percent of GDP, 156
    doctors' density, 179
    output loss estimates from banking
        crises, 92t
    telephones, 180
Synovus Financial, 65n
systemic risks, Deutsche Bank contribution
    to, 166
systemically important financial
    institutions (SIFIs), 53

tangible common equity, 19
    optimal level, 4
    relative to total assets, 14
taxes, punitive to shrink credit, 202
taxpayers
    avoiding losses to rescue banks, 213
    and future bailouts, 133, 162
Taylor rule, 128
telephones, density, per capita income and,
    180
10-year Treasury bond rate, 89n
tier 1 capital, 62, 163
tier 2 capital, 2n
    subordinated debt to raise, 139
time period, for cross-country tests, 189
TLAC. See total loss-absorbing capacity
    (TLAC)
Tong, Hui, 123, 141–42
too big to fail (TBTF), 10, 118, 213–15

incentive distortions, 3
    and risk taking, 162
internalizing risk subsidy, 137–44
Minneapolis Plan to end, evaluation,
    123–31
questionable link to surcharge, 130
response of regulatory reform, 214
studies estimating subsidies, 143
and subordinated debt, Basel III on, 139
"too much finance" studies, 191
    literature survey, 177
    plausibility, 182–84
    as statistical illusion, 207
total assets
    nonperforming assets and charge-offs as
        fraction of, 152
    risk-weighted assets vs., 12–16, 23
total loss-absorbing capacity (TLAC), 1,
    9–11, 118, 133, 205, 210
    benefits, 150–51
    impact estimates, 149–51
    literature survey, 134–51
    panic dynamics and, 148–49
    shortfalls from target, 46n
    target, 19
total tier 1 capital, 53n
Tracey, Belinda, 10, 146–47, 162
Traina, James, 10, 140–41
transient analyses, 21
transient estimates, 41–47
translog cost function, 147
translog production function, 145, 145n
Travelers Group, Citigroup merger with,
    155
Treasury inflation-protected (TIP) five-year
    bonds, 62
Troubled Asset Relief Program (TARP), 138,
    159, 213
Tsatsaronis, Kostas, 69, 80
Turner, C., 144
Turner, Paul, 34

UBS, 213
UniCredit Group, 169
UnionBanCal, 65n
unit cost of equity capital, 7, 65–66, 108
    base value, 25n
    cost to economy, 131
    relationship to debt to equity ratio, 85f

Other Publications from the
PETERSON INSTITUTE FOR INTERNATIONAL ECONOMICS

POLICY ANALYSES IN INTERNATIONAL ECONOMICS SERIES

* = out of print

51 **Competition Policies for the Global Economy** Edward M. Graham and J. David Richardson
November 1997 ISBN 0-88132-249-0

52 **Improving Trade Policy Reviews in the World Trade Organization** Donald Keesing
April 1998 ISBN 0-88132-251-2

53 **Agricultural Trade Policy: Completing the Reform** Timothy Josling
April 1998 ISBN 0-88132-256-3

54 **Real Exchange Rates for the Year 2000** Simon Wren Lewis and Rebecca Driver
April 1998 ISBN 0-88132-253-9

55 **The Asian Financial Crisis: Causes, Cures, and Systemic Implications** Morris Goldstein
June 1998 ISBN 0-88132-261-X

56 **Global Economic Effects of the Asian Currency Devaluations** Marcus Noland, LiGang Liu, Sherman Robinson, and Zhi Wang
July 1998 ISBN 0-88132-260-1

57 **The Exchange Stabilization Fund: Slush Money or War Chest?** C. Randall Henning
May 1999 ISBN 0-88132-271-7

58 **The New Politics of American Trade: Trade, Labor, and the Environment** I. M. Destler and Peter J. Balint
October 1999 ISBN 0-88132-269-5

59 **Congressional Trade Votes: From NAFTA Approval to Fast Track Defeat** Robert E. Baldwin and Christopher S. Magee
February 2000 ISBN 0-88132-267-9

60 **Exchange Rate Regimes for Emerging Markets: Reviving the Intermediate Option** John Williamson
September 2000 ISBN 0-88132-293-8

61 **NAFTA and the Environment: Seven Years Later** Gary Clyde Hufbauer, Daniel Esty, Diana Orejas, Luis Rubio, and Jeffrey J. Schott
October 2000 ISBN 0-88132-299-7

62 **Free Trade between Korea and the United States?** Inbom Choi and Jeffrey J. Schott
April 2001 ISBN 0-88132-311-X

63 **New Regional Trading Arrangements in the Asia Pacific?** Robert Scollay and John P. Gilbert
May 2001 ISBN 0-88132-302-0

64 **Parental Supervision: The New Paradigm for Foreign Direct Investment and Development** Theodore H. Moran
August 2001 ISBN 0-88132-313-6

65 **The Benefits of Price Convergence: Speculative Calculations** Gary Clyde Hufbauer, Erika Wada, and Tony Warren
December 2001 ISBN 0-88132-333-0

66 **Managed Floating Plus** Morris Goldstein
March 2002 ISBN 0-88132-336-5

67 **Argentina and the Fund: From Triumph to Tragedy*** Michael Mussa
July 2002 ISBN 0-88132-339-X

68 **East Asian Financial Cooperation** C. Randall Henning
September 2002 ISBN 0-88132-338-1

69 **Reforming OPIC for the 21st Century** Theodore H. Moran
May 2003 ISBN 0-88132-342-X

70 **Awakening Monster: The Alien Tort Statute of 1789** Gary Clyde Hufbauer and Nicholas Mitrokostas
July 2003 ISBN 0-88132-366-7

71 **Korea after Kim Jong-il** Marcus Noland
January 2004 ISBN 0-88132-373-X

72 **Roots of Competitiveness: China's Evolving Agriculture Interests** Daniel H. Rosen, Scott Rozelle, and Jikun Huang
July 2004 ISBN 0-88132-376-4

73 **Prospects for a US-Taiwan FTA** Nicholas R. Lardy and Daniel H. Rosen
December 2004 ISBN 0-88132-367-5

74 **Anchoring Reform with a US-Egypt Free Trade Agreement** Ahmed Galal and Robert Z. Lawrence
April 2005 ISBN 0-88132-368-3

75 **Curbing the Boom-Bust Cycle: Stabilizing Capital Flows to Emerging Markets** John Williamson
July 2005 ISBN 0-88132-330-6

76 **The Shape of a Swiss-US Free Trade Agreement** Gary Clyde Hufbauer and Richard E. Baldwin
February 2006 ISBN 978-0-88132-385-6

77 **A Strategy for IMF Reform** Edwin M. Truman
February 2006 ISBN 978-0-88132-398-6

78 **US-China Trade Disputes: Rising Tide, Rising Stakes** Gary Clyde Hufbauer, Yee Wong, and Ketki Sheth
August 2006 ISBN 978-0-88132-394-8

79 **Trade Relations Between Colombia and the United States** Jeffrey J. Schott, ed.
August 2006 ISBN 978-0-88132-389-4

80 **Sustaining Reform with a US-Pakistan Free Trade Agreement** Gary Clyde Hufbauer and Shahid Javed Burki
November 2006 ISBN 978-0-88132-395-5

81 **A US–Middle East Trade Agreement: A Circle of Opportunity?** Robert Z. Lawrence
November 2006 ISBN 978-0-88132-396-2

82 **Reference Rates and the International Monetary System** John Williamson
January 2007 ISBN 978-0-88132-401-3

83 **Toward a US-Indonesia Free Trade Agreement** Gary Clyde Hufbauer and Sjamsu Rahardja
June 2007 ISBN 978-0-88132-402-0

84 **The Accelerating Decline in America's High-Skilled Workforce** Jacob F. Kirkegaard
December 2007 ISBN 978-0-88132-413-6

85 **Blue-Collar Blues: Is Trade to Blame for Rising US Income Inequality?** Robert Z. Lawrence
January 2008 ISBN 978-0-88132-414-3

86 **Maghreb Regional and Global Integration: A Dream to Be Fulfilled** Gary Clyde Hufbauer and Claire Brunel, eds.
October 2008 ISBN 978-0-88132-426-6

BOOKS

Trade Liberalization and International
Institutions*   Jeffrey J. Schott
September 1994   ISBN 978-0-88132-3
Reciprocity and Retaliation in U.S. Trade Policy*
Thomas O. Bayard and Kimberly Ann Elliott
September 1994   ISBN 0-88132-084-6
The Uruguay Round: An Assessment*
Jeffrey J. Schott, assisted by Johanna Buurman
November 1994   ISBN 0-88132-206-7
Measuring the Costs of Protection in Japan*
Yoko Sazanami, Shujiro Urata, and Hiroki Kawai
January 1995   ISBN 0-88132-211-3
Foreign Direct Investment in the United States,
3d ed.   Edward M. Graham and Paul R. Krugman
January 1995   ISBN 0-88132-204-0
The Political Economy of Korea-United States
Cooperation* C. Fred Bergsten and Il SaKong, eds.
February 1995 ISBN 0-88132-213-X
International Debt Reexamined* William R. Cline
February 1995   ISBN 0-88132-083-8
American Trade Politics, 3d ed.   I. M. Destler
April 1995   ISBN 0-88132-215-6
Managing Official Export Credits: The Quest for
a Global Regime*   John E. Ray
July 1995   ISBN 0-88132-207-5
Asia Pacific Fusion: Japan's Role in APEC
Yoichi Funabashi
October 1995   ISBN 0-88132-224-5
Korea-United States Cooperation in the New
World Order* C. Fred Bergsten and Il SaKong, eds.
February 1996   ISBN 0-88132-226-1
Why Exports Really Matter!* ISBN 0-88132-221-0
Why Exports Matter More!* ISBN 0-88132-229-6
J. David Richardson and Karin Rindal
July 1995; February 1996
Global Corporations and National Governments
Edward M. Graham
May 1996   ISBN 0-88132-111-7
Global Economic Leadership and the Group of
Seven   C. Fred Bergsten and C. Randall Henning
May 1996   ISBN 0-88132-218-0
The Trading System after the Uruguay Round*
John Whalley and Colleen Hamilton
July 1996   ISBN 0-88132-131-1
Private Capital Flows to Emerging Markets after
the Mexican Crisis*   Guillermo A. Calvo,
Morris Goldstein, and Eduard Hochreiter
September 1996   ISBN 0-88132-232-6
The Crawling Band as an Exchange Rate Regime:
Lessons from Chile, Colombia, and Israel
John Williamson
September 1996   ISBN 0-88132-231-8
Flying High: Liberalizing Civil Aviation in the
Asia Pacific*   Gary Clyde Hufbauer and
Christopher Findlay
November 1996   ISBN 0-88132-227-X
Measuring the Costs of Visible Protection in
Korea*   Namdoo Kim
November 1996   ISBN 0-88132-236-9
The World Trading System: Challenges Ahead
Jeffrey J. Schott
December 1996   ISBN 0-88132-235-0
Has Globalization Gone Too Far?   Dani Rodrik
March 1997   ISBN paper 0-88132-241-5

Korea-United States Economic Relationship*
C. Fred Bergsten and Il SaKong, eds.
March 1997   ISBN 0-88132-240-7
Summitry in the Americas: A Progress Report*
Richard E. Feinberg
April 1997   ISBN 0-88132-242-3
Corruption and the Global Economy
Kimberly Ann Elliott
June 1997   ISBN 0-88132-233-4
Regional Trading Blocs in the World Economic
System   Jeffrey A. Frankel
October 1997   ISBN 0-88132-202-4
Sustaining the Asia Pacific Miracle:
Environmental Protection and Economic
Integration   Andre Dua and Daniel C. Esty
October 1997   ISBN 0-88132-250-4
Trade and Income Distribution
William R. Cline
November 1997   ISBN 0-88132-216-4
Global Competition Policy   Edward M. Graham
and J. David Richardson
December 1997   ISBN 0-88132-166-4
Unfinished Business: Telecommunications after
the Uruguay Round   Gary Clyde Hufbauer and
Erika Wada
December 1997   ISBN 0-88132-257-1
Financial Services Liberalization in the WTO
Wendy Dobson and Pierre Jacquet
June 1998   ISBN 0-88132-254-7
Restoring Japan's Economic Growth
Adam S. Posen
September 1998   ISBN 0-88132-262-8
Measuring the Costs of Protection in China
Zhang Shuguang, Zhang Yansheng, and Wan
Zhongxin
November 1998   ISBN 0-88132-247-4
Foreign Direct Investment and Development:
The New Policy Agenda for Developing
Countries and Economies in Transition
Theodore H. Moran
December 1998   ISBN 0-88132-258-X
Behind the Open Door: Foreign Enterprises
in the Chinese Marketplace   Daniel H. Rosen
January 1999   ISBN 0-88132-263-6
Toward A New International Financial
Architecture: A Practical Post-Asia Agenda
Barry Eichengreen
February 1999   ISBN 0-88132-270-9
Is the U.S. Trade Deficit Sustainable?
Catherine L. Mann
September 1999   ISBN 0-88132-265-2
Safeguarding Prosperity in a Global Financial
System: The Future International Financial
Architecture, Independent Task Force Report
Sponsored by the Council on Foreign Relations
Morris Goldstein, Project Director
October 1999   ISBN 0-88132-287-3
Avoiding the Apocalypse: The Future of the Two
Koreas   Marcus Noland
June 2000   ISBN 0-88132-278-4
Assessing Financial Vulnerability: An Early
Warning System for Emerging Markets
Morris Goldstein, Graciela Kaminsky, and Carmen
Reinhart
June 2000   ISBN 0-88132-237-7

Global Electronic Commerce: A Policy Primer
Catherine L. Mann, Sue E. Eckert, and Sarah Cleeland Knight
July 2000   ISBN 0-88132-274-1
The WTO after Seattle   Jeffrey J. Schott, ed.
July 2000   ISBN 0-88132-290-3
Intellectual Property Rights in the Global Economy   Keith E. Maskus
August 2000   ISBN 0-88132-282-2
The Political Economy of the Asian Financial Crisis   Stephan Haggard
August 2000   ISBN 0-88132-283-0
Transforming Foreign Aid: United States Assistance in the 21st Century*   Carol Lancaster
August 2000   ISBN 0-88132-291-1
Fighting the Wrong Enemy: Antiglobal Activists and Multinational Enterprises
Edward M. Graham
September 2000   ISBN 0-88132-272-5
Globalization and the Perceptions of American Workers Kenneth Scheve and Matthew J. Slaughter
March 2001   ISBN 0-88132-295-4
World Capital Markets: Challenge to the G-10
Wendy Dobson and Gary Clyde Hufbauer, assisted by Hyun Koo Cho
May 2001   ISBN 0-88132-301-2
Prospects for Free Trade in the Americas
Jeffrey J. Schott
August 2001   ISBN 0-88132-275-X
Toward a North American Community: Lessons from the Old World for the New Robert A. Pastor
August 2001   ISBN 0-88132-328-4
Measuring the Costs of Protection in Europe: European Commercial Policy in the 2000s
Patrick A. Messerlin
September 2001   ISBN 0-88132-273-3
Job Loss from Imports: Measuring the Costs
Lori G. Kletzer
September 2001   ISBN 0-88132-296-2
No More Bashing: Building a New Japan–United States Economic Relationship   C. Fred Bergsten, Takatoshi Ito, and Marcus Noland
October 2001   ISBN 0-88132-286-5
Why Global Commitment Really Matters!
Howard Lewis III and J. David Richardson
October 2001   ISBN 0-88132-298-9
Leadership Selection in the Major Multilaterals
Miles Kahler
November 2001   ISBN 0-88132-335-7
The International Financial Architecture: What's New? What's Missing?   Peter B. Kenen
November 2001   ISBN 0-88132-297-0
Delivering on Debt Relief: From IMF Gold to a New Aid Architecture   John Williamson and Nancy Birdsall, with Brian Deese
April 2002   ISBN 0-88132-331-4
Imagine There's No Country: Poverty, Inequality, and Growth in the Era of Globalization   Surjit S. Bhalla
September 2002   ISBN 0-88132-348-9
Reforming Korea's Industrial Conglomerates
Edward M. Graham
January 2003   ISBN 0-88132-337-3

Industrial Policy in an Era of Globalization: Lessons from Asia   Marcus Noland and Howard Pack
March 2003   ISBN 0-88132-350-0
Reintegrating India with the World Economy
T. N. Srinivasan and Suresh D. Tendulkar
March 2003   ISBN 0-88132-280-6
After the Washington Consensus: Restarting Growth and Reform in Latin America
Pedro-Pablo Kuczynski and John Williamson, eds.
March 2003   ISBN 0-88132-347-0
The Decline of US Labor Unions and the Role of Trade   Robert E. Baldwin
June 2003   ISBN 0-88132-341-1
Can Labor Standards Improve under Globalization?   Kimberly Ann Elliott and Richard B. Freeman
June 2003   ISBN 0-88132-332-2
Crimes and Punishments? Retaliation under the WTO   Robert Z. Lawrence
October 2003   ISBN 0-88132-359-4
Inflation Targeting in the World Economy
Edwin M. Truman
October 2003   ISBN 0-88132-345-4
Foreign Direct Investment and Tax Competition
John H. Mutti
November 2003   ISBN 0-88132-352-7
Has Globalization Gone Far Enough? The Costs of Fragmented Markets   Scott C. Bradford and Robert Z. Lawrence
February 2004   ISBN 0-88132-349-7
Food Regulation and Trade: Toward a Safe and Open Global System Tim Josling, Donna Roberts, and David Orden
March 2004   ISBN 0-88132-346-2
Controlling Currency Mismatches in Emerging Markets   Morris Goldstein and Philip Turner
April 2004   ISBN 0-88132-360-8
Free Trade Agreements: US Strategies and Priorities   Jeffrey J. Schott, ed.
April 2004   ISBN 0-88132-361-6
Trade Policy and Global Poverty
William R. Cline
June 2004   ISBN 0-88132-365-9
Bailouts or Bail-ins? Responding to Financial Crises in Emerging Economies   Nouriel Roubini and Brad Setser
August 2004   ISBN 0-88132-371-3
Transforming the European Economy
Martin Neil Baily and Jacob Funk Kirkegaard
September 2004   ISBN 0-88132-343-8
Getting Aid To Work: Politics, Policies and Incentives For Poor Countries*
Nicolas Van De Walle
Septbember 2004   ISBN 0-88132-379-9
Chasing Dirty Money: The Fight Against Money Laundering   Peter Reuter and Edwin M. Truman
November 2004   ISBN 0-88132-370-5
The United States and the World Economy: Foreign Economic Policy for the Next Decade
C. Fred Bergsten
January 2005   ISBN 0-88132-380-2

Does Foreign Direct Investment Promote Development? Theodore H. Moran, Edward M. Graham, and Magnus Blomström, eds.
April 2005 ISBN 0-88132-381-0
American Trade Politics, 4th ed. I. M. Destler
June 2005 ISBN 0-88132-382-9
Shell Global Scenarios to 2025: The Future Business Environment: Trends, Trade-offs and Choices*
June 2005 ISBN 0-88132-383-7
Why Does Immigration Divide America? Public Finance and Political Opposition to Open Borders Gordon H. Hanson
August 2005 ISBN 0-88132-400-0
Reforming the US Corporate Tax
Gary Clyde Hufbauer and Paul L. E. Grieco
September 2005 ISBN 0-88132-384-5
The United States as a Debtor Nation
William R. Cline
September 2005 ISBN 0-88132-399-3
NAFTA Revisited: Achievements and Challenges
Gary Clyde Hufbauer and Jeffrey J. Schott, assisted by Paul L. E. Grieco and Yee Wong
October 2005 ISBN 0-88132-334-9
US National Security and Foreign Direct Investment Edward M. Graham and David M. Marchick
May 2006 ISBN 978-0-88132-391-7
Accelerating the Globalization of America: The Role for Information Technology
Catherine L. Mann, assisted by Jacob Funk Kirkegaard
June 2006 ISBN 978-0-88132-390-0
Delivering on Doha: Farm Trade and the Poor
Kimberly Ann Elliott
July 2006 ISBN 978-0-88132-392-4
Case Studies in US Trade Negotiation, Vol. 1: Making the Rules Charan Devereaux, Robert Z. Lawrence, and Michael Watkins
September 2006 ISBN 978-0-88132-362-7
Case Studies in US Trade Negotiation, Vol. 2: Resolving Disputes Charan Devereaux, Robert Z. Lawrence, and Michael Watkins
September 2006 ISBN 978-0-88132-363-2
C. Fred Bergsten and the World Economy
Michael Mussa, ed.
December 2006 ISBN 978-0-88132-397-9
Working Papers, Volume I Peterson Institute
December 2006 ISBN 978-0-88132-388-7
The Arab Economies in a Changing World
Marcus Noland and Howard Pack
April 2007 ISBN 978-0-88132-393-1
Working Papers, Volume II Peterson Institute
April 2007 ISBN 978-0-88132-404-4
Global Warming and Agriculture: Impact Estimates by Country William R. Cline
July 2007 ISBN 978-0-88132-403-7
US Taxation of Foreign Income
Gary Clyde Hufbauer and Ariel Assa
October 2007 ISBN 978-0-88132-405-1
Russia's Capitalist Revolution: Why Market Reform Succeeded and Democracy Failed
Anders Åslund
October 2007 ISBN 978-0-88132-409-9

Economic Sanctions Reconsidered, 3d ed.
Gary Clyde Hufbauer, Jeffrey J. Schott, Kimberly Ann Elliott, and Barbara Oegg
November 2007
ISBN hardcover 978-0-88132-407-5
ISBN hardcover/CD-ROM 978-0-88132-408-2
Debating China's Exchange Rate Policy
Morris Goldstein and Nicholas R. Lardy, eds.
April 2008 ISBN 978-0-88132-415-0
Leveling the Carbon Playing Field: International Competition and US Climate Policy Design
Trevor Houser, Rob Bradley, Britt Childs, Jacob Werksman, and Robert Heilmayr
May 2008 ISBN 978-0-88132-420-4
Accountability and Oversight of US Exchange Rate Policy C. Randall Henning
June 2008 ISBN 978-0-88132-419-8
Challenges of Globalization: Imbalances and Growth Anders Åslund and Marek Dabrowski, eds.
July 2008 ISBN 978-0-88132-418-1
China's Rise: Challenges and Opportunities
C. Fred Bergsten, Charles Freeman, Nicholas R. Lardy, and Derek J. Mitchell
September 2008 ISBN 978-0-88132-417-4
Banking on Basel: The Future of International Financial Regulation Daniel K. Tarullo
September 2008 ISBN 978-0-88132-423-5
US Pension Reform: Lessons from Other Countries Martin Neil Baily and Jacob Funk Kirkegaard
February 2009 ISBN 978-0-88132-425-9
How Ukraine Became a Market Economy and Democracy Anders Åslund
March 2009 ISBN 978-0-88132-427-3
Global Warming and the World Trading System
Gary Clyde Hufbauer, Steve Charnovitz, and Jisun Kim
March 2009 ISBN 978-0-88132-428-0
The Russia Balance Sheet Anders Åslund and Andrew Kuchins
March 2009 ISBN 978-0-88132-424-2
The Euro at Ten: The Next Global Currency?
Jean Pisani-Ferry and Adam S. Posen, eds.
July 2009 ISBN 978-0-88132-430-3
Financial Globalization, Economic Growth, and the Crisis of 2007–09 William R. Cline
May 2010 ISBN 978-0-88132-499-0
Russia after the Global Economic Crisis
Anders Åslund, Sergei Guriev, and Andrew Kuchins, eds.
June 2010 ISBN 978-0-88132-497-6
Sovereign Wealth Funds: Threat or Salvation?
Edwin M. Truman
September 2010 ISBN 978-0-88132-498-3
The Last Shall Be the First: The East European Financial Crisis, 2008–10 Anders Åslund
October 2010 ISBN 978-0-88132-521-8
Witness to Transformation: Refugee Insights into North Korea Stephan Haggard and Marcus Noland
January 2011 ISBN 978-0-88132-438-9

Foreign Direct Investment and Development: Launching a Second Generation of Policy Research, Avoiding the Mistakes of the First, Reevaluating Policies for Developed and Developing Countries   Theodore H. Moran
April 2011   ISBN 978-0-88132-600-0

How Latvia Came through the Financial Crisis
Anders Åslund and Valdis Dombrovskis
May 2011   ISBN 978-0-88132-602-4

Global Trade in Services: Fear, Facts, and Offshoring   J. Bradford Jensen
August 2011   ISBN 978-0-88132-601-7

NAFTA and Climate Change   Meera Fickling and Jeffrey J. Schott
September 2011   ISBN 978-0-88132-436-5

Eclipse: Living in the Shadow of China's Economic Dominance   Arvind Subramanian
September 2011   ISBN 978-0-88132-606-2

Flexible Exchange Rates for a Stable World Economy   Joseph E. Gagnon with Marc Hinterschweiger
September 2011   ISBN 978-0-88132-627-7

The Arab Economies in a Changing World, 2d ed.   Marcus Noland and Howard Pack
November 2011   ISBN 978-0-88132-628-4

Sustaining China's Economic Growth After the Global Financial Crisis   Nicholas R. Lardy
January 2012   ISBN 978-0-88132-626-0

Who Needs to Open the Capital Account?
Olivier Jeanne, Arvind Subramanian, and John Williamson
April 2012   ISBN 978-0-88132-511-9

Devaluing to Prosperity: Misaligned Currencies and Their Growth Consequences   Surjit S. Bhalla
August 2012   ISBN 978-0-88132-623-9

Private Rights and Public Problems: The Global Economics of Intellectual Property in the 21st Century   Keith E. Maskus
September 2012   ISBN 978-0-88132-507-2

Global Economics in Extraordinary Times: Essays in Honor of John Williamson
C. Fred Bergsten and C. Randall Henning, eds.
November 2012   ISBN 978-0-88132-662-8

Rising Tide: Is Growth in Emerging Economies Good for the United States?   Lawrence Edwards and Robert Z. Lawrence
February 2013   ISBN 978-0-88132-500-3

Responding to Financial Crisis: Lessons from Asia Then, the United States and Europe Now
Changyong Rhee and Adam S. Posen, eds
October 2013   ISBN 978-0-88132-674-1

Fueling Up: The Economic Implications of America's Oil and Gas Boom   Trevor Houser and Shashank Mohan
January 2014   ISBN 978-0-88132-656-7

How Latin America Weathered the Global Financial Crisis   José De Gregorio
January 2014   ISBN 978-0-88132-678-9

Confronting the Curse: The Economics and Geopolitics of Natural Resource Governance
Cullen S. Hendrix and Marcus Noland
May 2014   ISBN 978-0-88132-676-5

Inside the Euro Crisis: An Eyewitness Account
Simeon Djankov
June 2014   ISBN 978-0-88132-685-7

Managing the Euro Area Debt Crisis
William R. Cline
June 2014   ISBN 978-0-88132-687-1

Markets over Mao: The Rise of Private Business in China   Nicholas R. Lardy
September 2014   ISBN 978-0-88132-693-2

Bridging the Pacific: Toward Free Trade and Investment between China and the United States
C. Fred Bergsten, Gary Clyde Hufbauer, and Sean Miner. Assisted by Tyler Moran
October 2014   ISBN 978-0-88132-691-8

The Great Rebirth: Lessons from the Victory of Capitalism over Communism
Anders Åslund and Simeon Djankov, eds.
November 2014   ISBN 978-0-88132-697-0

Ukraine: What Went Wrong and How to Fix It
Anders Åslund
April 2015   ISBN 978-0-88132-701-4

From Stress to Growth: Strengthening Asia's Financial Systems in a Post-Crisis World
Marcus Noland; Donghyun Park, eds.
October 2015   ISBN 978-0-88132-699-4

The Great Tradeoff: Confronting Moral Conflicts in the Era of Globalization
Steven R. Weisman
January 2016   ISBN 978-0-88132-695-6

Rich People, Poor Countries: The Rise of Emerging-Market Tycoons and their Mega Firms   Caroline Freund, assisted by Sarah Oliver
January 2016   ISBN 978-0-88132-703-8

International Monetary Cooperation: Lessons from the Plaza Accord After Thirty Years
C. Fred Bergsten and Russell A. Green, eds.
April 2016   ISBN 978-0-88132-711-3

SPECIAL REPORTS

1   Promoting World Recovery: A Statement on Global Economic Strategy*   by Twenty-six Economists from Fourteen Countries
     December 1982   ISBN 0-88132-013-7

2   Prospects for Adjustment in Argentina, Brazil, and Mexico: Responding to the Debt Crisis*   John Williamson, ed.
     June 1983   ISBN 0-88132-016-1

3   Inflation and Indexation: Argentina, Brazil, and Israel*   John Williamson, ed.
     March 1985   ISBN 0-88132-037-4

4   Global Economic Imbalances*
     C. Fred Bergsten, ed.
     March 1986   ISBN 0-88132-042-0

5   African Debt and Financing*   Carol Lancaster and John Williamson, eds.
     May 1986   ISBN 0-88132-044-7

6   Resolving the Global Economic Crisis: After Wall Street*   by Thirty-three Economists from Thirteen Countries
     December 1987   ISBN 0-88132-070-6

7   World Economic Problems*
     Kimberly Ann Elliott and John Williamson, eds.
     April 1988   ISBN 0-88132-055-2

Sales Representatives

In Asia, North America, and South America
Perseus Distribution
210 American Drive
Jackson, TN 38301
orderentry@perseusbooks.com

Tel. (800) 343-4499
Fax (800) 351-5073
Email: cup_book@columbia.edu

Secure online ordering is available on the CUP website at: www.cup.columbia.edu

In Africa, Europe, the Middle East, South Africa, South Asias, and the United States
Columbia University Press
c/o Wiley European Distribution Centre
New Era Estate
Oldlands Way, Bognor Regis
West Sussex PO22 9NQ

Tel. (1243) 843-291
Fax (1243) 843-296
Email: customer@wiley.com

(Delivery via Wiley Distribution Services Ltd., or you may collect your order by prior arrangement)

United States and Canada Sales and Publicity Representatives
Brad Hebel, Director of Sales and Marketing
61 West 62nd Street
New York, NY 10023

Tel. (212) 459-0600, ext. 7130
Fax (212) 459-3678
Email: bh2106@columbia.edu

Columbia University Sales Consortium Manager and Souther US
Catherine Hobbs

Tel. (804) 690-8529
Fax (434) 589-3411
Email: catherinehobbs@earthlink.net

Northeast US and Eastern Canada
Conor Broughan

Tel. (917) 826-7676
Email: cb2476@columbia.edu

Midwest US and Central Canada
Kevin Kurtz

Tel. (773) 316-1116
Fax (773) 489-2941
Email: kkurtz5@earthlink.net

Western US and Western Canada
William Gawronski

Tel. (310) 488-9059
Fax (310) 832-4717
Email: wgawronski@earthlink.net

United Kingdom and Europe
The University Press Group Ltd.
Lois Edwards
LEC 1, New Era Estate
Oldlands Way, Bognor Regis
PO22 9NQ England

Tel. 44 (1243) 842-165
Fax 44 (1243) 842-167
Email: lois@upguk.com

Ben Mitchell
U.K. Sales Manager
62 Fairford House
Kennington Lane
London SE11 4HR England

Tel. (44) 776-691-3593
Email: ben.mitchell.upg@gmail.com

Andrew Brewer
Managing Director
57 Cobnar Road
Sheffield S8 8QA England

Tel. (44) 114-274-0129
Mobile (44) 796-703-1856
Email: andrew.brewer@virgin.net

Middle East and Africa
Andrew Brewer
Managing Director
57 Cobnar Road
Sheffield S8 8QA England

Tel. (44) 114-274-0129
Mobile (44) 796-703-1856
Email: andrew.brewer@virgin.net

Asia
Brad Hebel
61 West 62nd Street
New York, NY 10023

Tel. (212) 459-0600, ext. 7130
Fax (212) 459-3678
Email: bh2106@columbia.edu